Jewish Philosophy and Western Culture

12·19

'More than just an introduction to contemporary Jewish philosophy, this important book offers a critique of the embedded assumptions of contemporary post-Christian Western culture. By focusing on the suppressed or denied heritage of Jewish and Islamic philosophy that helped shape Western society, it offers possibilities for recovering broader dimensions beyond a narrow rationalism and materialism. For those impatient with recent one-dimensional dismissals of religion, and surprised by their popularity, it offers a timely reminder of the sources of these views in the Enlightenment, but also the wider humane dimensions of the religious quest that still need to be considered. By recognising the contribution of gender and post-colonial studies it reminds us that philosophy, "the love of wisdom", is still concerned with the whole human being and the complexity of personal and social relationships.'
Jonathan Magonet, formerly Principal of Leo Baeck College, London, and Vice-President of the Movement for Reform Judaism

'*Jewish Philosophy and Western Culture* makes a spirited and highly readable plea for "Jerusalem" over "Athens" – that is, for recovering the moral and spiritual virtues of ancient Judaism within a European and Western intellectual culture that still has a preference for Enlightenment rationalism. Victor Seidler revisits the major Jewish philosophers of the last century as invaluable sources of wisdom for Western philosophers and social theorists in the new century. He calls upon the latter to reclaim body and heart as being inseparable from "mind."'
Peter Ochs, Edgar Bronfman Professor of Modern Judaic Studies, University of Virginia

JEWISH PHILOSOPHY AND WESTERN CULTURE

A Modern Introduction

VICTOR J. SEIDLER

I.B. TAURIS

LONDON · NEW YORK

Published in 2007 by I.B.Tauris & Co Ltd
6 Salem Road, London W2 4BU
175 Fifth Avenue, New York NY 10010
www.ibtauris.com

In the United States of America and Canada distributed by
Palgrave Macmillan, a division of St. Martin's Press, 175 Fifth Avenue,
New York NY 10010

ISBN: (PB) 978 1 84511 281 3
ISBN: (HB) 978 1 84511 280 6

A full CIP record for this book is available from the British Library
A full CIP record is available from the Library of Congress

Library of Congress Catalog Card Number: available

Designed and Typeset by 4word Ltd, Bristol, UK
Printed and bound in Great Britain by T.J. International Ltd, Padstow, Cornwall

Dedication

For Daniel Jeleniewski, who died on
13 January 1950 in New York City

and

For each member of the Jeleniewski,
Ickowitz, Placek, Rosenbaum, Singer and Seidler
families who were murdered in Europe
between 1940 and 1945

'If what we do now is to make no difference in the end, then all the seriousness of life is done away with. Your religious ideas have always seemed to me more Greek than Biblical. Whereas my thoughts are one hundred percent Hebraic.'

Drury: 'Yes I do feel that when, say Plato talks about the gods, it lacks that sense of awe which you feel throughout the Bible – from Genesis to Revelation. "But who may abide the day of his coming, and who shall stand when he appeareth?"'

Wittgenstein: (standing still and looking at me very intently) 'I think you have just said something very important. Much more important than you realize."'

'Conversations with Drury'
in *Ludwig Wittgenstein: Personal Recollections*
edited by Rush Rhees (Oxford: Blackwell, 1981)

'It is not the truth which any one possesses, or thinks he does, but rather the pains he has taken to get to the bottom of the truth, that makes a man's worth. For it is not in having the truth but in searching for it that those powers increase in him in which alone lies his ever growing perfection. The possession makes one placid, lazy, proud.'

Lessing, *Theologische Streitschriften*, 'Eine Duplik' (1978)

'In western civilization a Jew is constantly judged by the wrong measures which don't fit. That the Greek thinkers were not philosophers in the western sense, nor in the western sense scientists either…many people see this. But it is the same with the Jews. For us the words of our language seek like absolute measures or standards, and we misjudge them again and again. There are now overrated, now underrated….'

Wittgenstein, *Vermischte Bermerkungen* p.37 (written 1931)

Table of Contents

Preface and Acknowledgements

My father, Daniel Jeleniewski, was the only member of his family living outside the country when the German armies marched into Poland in 1940. He was also the only person to survive the Holocaust. No one else was left. None of my uncles, aunts or cousins were to escape alive. My father was my link to Jewish orthodoxy. Some of my earliest memories are of going with him to the local Adath synagogue in Brent Street, Hendon, not far from our home, and hiding behind his prayer shawl (*tallit*), a place of warm refuge. This did not last long, however, because he was to die in New York in January, 1950 when I was just five.

He remained my connection to orthodoxy but it was a connection that became virtual and in some ways hidden. Each year, on the anniversary of his death, myself and my brothers would return to the Adath synagogue to attend morning prayers and recite the Prayer for the Dead. I am not sure whether my father was a Holocaust 'survivor' because he was *also* a victim who could not live with the news of the destruction and murder of his family. His heart could not stand the strain.

As a child, I somehow felt as if it were up to me to keep his memory alive, especially when my mother remarried and we eventually changed our names. It was as if no visible traces of Jeleniewski were left and that somehow, through his death, a connection was made to all the deaths of the Holocaust.

I am not sure that it is possible to 'come to terms' with the enormity of the Holocaust and it has taken me almost a lifetime to realise that I still often stay on the margins of the horror out of a fear that if I were to get any closer I, too, would be caught up in the fires and would not be able to survive. Children of survivors and refugees find their differ-ent ways of coping with these histories, but for years the post-war world seemed to be largely indifferent to what had happened to European Jewry in the Holocaust. It might seem strange thing to claim this now that the events of the Holocaust have become so familiar in different ways. As children growing up in the 1950s and 1960s, the Holocaust was something we felt at some level that we could not really talk about without feeling unsafe.

In this way I have always lived with the tension between Jewish philosophies and 'Western cultures' and there have been different rela-tionships of concealment, shame and sharing. As I was growing up in the Jewish refugee community of north-west London, I knew that my parents had come from elsewhere, even if I was unsure where Vienna or Warsaw really were. Their foreign accents remained a source of shame since they seemed to undermine my attempts to 'fit in' and so become invisible and like everyone else, as I experienced the 'shadows of the Shoah'.

But if it was different in those years before mass migrations to acknowledge experiences of dislocation, migration and diasporas we knew that we carried, often uneasily, different inheritances that could prove difficult to bring into dialogue with each other. Often it was eas-ier to feel *split* and so to perform different aspects of identity in different spaces without really imagining or hoping that these different aspects *could* somehow be brought into conversation with each other. As chil-dren we often felt we needed to fulfil some of the unrealised dreams of our parents whose careers had often been cruelly interrupted. This meant finding ways to 'get on' in the world while at the same time some-how feeling pride in a Jewishness that was so easily shamed.

Somehow my unresolved relationship with my dead father kept me in some kind of creative relationship to Judaism though for years I would seek to escape an inheritance that seemed to have relatively little mean-ings in the worlds I was moving in. I had been affected by my readings of Martin Buber as a child, both with his telling of *Hasidic Tales* as well as with some of his philosophical writings about relationship. I felt a sense of connection with the ways he was thinking and wherever I trav-elled I would have a copy of his small collection of Hasidic sayings, *Ten Rungs of the Ladder* with me. I was also drawn to reading Freud as a teenager and it was through a sense of the unconscious that I could make sense of some of the things I felt I could never really share with others. It was as if my relationship with my father had been internalised and it was through him that I remained connected to Judaism but also indirectly to the terrors of the Holocaust. Within Buber there is an often an uneasy relationship between the abstractness of some of his language and the lived experiences shared through the Hasidic masters. Possibly this tension is inescapable but it seems to reflect an important tension between Athens and Jerusalem.

It was through being introduced to the philosophical writings of the later Wittgenstein as an undergraduate at Oxford in the early 1960s where I also learnt from Isaiah Berlin and Herbert Hart, and found echoes of Wittgenstein's insistence on returning abstract language to its contexts of use in everyday life that I felt a certain resonance with the Hasidic writings. There was a certain distrust of abstract language that could so easily become disconnected and assume a life of its own. There was a need to question a Greek/Platonic tradition of forms if they left you feeling constantly inadequate because your experience somehow never lived up to the ideals. Of course this has proved a powerful sense of motivation within a Protestant culture but there are also ways that it can prove undermining to a sense of fulfilment since you can be constantly haunted by a sense that whatever you achieve, you could always have done more. Judaism offered a vision of original *blessings* that seemed potentially more helpful than a vision of original sin that had shaped a dominant Christian inheritance within Western cultures.

At some level as I hope to explain this is also something that Wittgenstein recognised in Freud as he appreciated that Freud was also attempting to *ground* people's experience in the events of their everyday lives that they might otherwise attempt to escape from. Freud was suspicious of the idealisation of parental figures, as if they could be radically split into a good parent who could be idealised and an evil parent who was responsible for all our suffering. Rather Freud recognised that it *takes time* for people to come to terms with their emotional inheritances and that if trust between parents and child has been broken it will take time to repair something that cannot be healed through a matter of will alone. In their questionings of the ways we so easily rationalise and intellectualise our experience as a means of escape and the time it takes to recover a sense of the meaning of what we are saying, they are sharing aspects of a Jewish inheritance. This is something that Wittgenstein comes to acknowledge when he thinks about his later work as 'Hebraic'.

It is also why I have sought to introduce examples, sometimes personal and sometimes drawn from the experience of imagined others, to ground some of the philosophical discussion. These examples are not merely illustrative but hopefully they help to *show* what is at stake in the more theoretical discussions. It grows out of a sympathy with the methods of 'ordinary language philosophy' whilst also recognising that these insights could be well applied to concerns more often framed through continental philosophies. It also attempts to show *how* Jewish philosophical methods are already tacitly at work within 'modern philosophy' and social theories in ways that we might not otherwise be able to recognise.

If this text feels different from what you might expect from an introduction to Jewish philosophy this is partly because it refuses a usual historical approach that would tell the narrative of different contribution to a self-contained 'Jewish philosophy' as if it is a story that can simply be told on its own terms. Rather I have sought to introduce Jewish philosophy through its complex relationships with 'Western cultures' and so through the crucial relationship between Athens and Jerusalem. But at the same time I have attempt to open up an important dialogue with Islam that has been significant at almost every stage of the development of this dialogue between Jewish Philosophy and 'Western culture'.

This has meant recognising how at different stages of the argument we have had to make problematic both the categories of 'Jewish philosophy' and 'Western Cultures'. Of course this remains an impossible task and some figures of central importance like Maimonides and Nachmanides would assume much greater significance in a different account. This would be a different way of telling a different story but one of no less significance. It is a narrative I would be interested in writing one day. Through focussing upon a tension between Athens and Jerusalem a figure like Philo becomes more significant than others would expect. But within the larger framework that ambitiously takes us from Biblical times to Auschwitz I needed to find a different way of presenting what a post-Holocaust introduction calls for.

The feeling for writing on these themes has been around for a long time, partly stimulated by conversations with Isaiah Berlin who encouraged me to explore tensions between Athens and Jerusalem, but it was the invitation by Jonathan Magonet to teach a course on Jewish Philosophy to the first year rabbinic students at Leo Baeck College, London in Autumn 2003 that proved vital. The support of Michael Shire and other teaching staff while I was teaching there created an intellectually stimulating setting different from what I knew that included at the time Albert Friedlander who shared his memories of Leo Baeck with me and Lionel Blue who taught about prayer as well as such revered teachers of blessed memory as Louis Jacobs and John Rayner. I learnt much from conversations with Sheila Shulman who was also teaching philosophy there and over many years with dear friends Larry Blum, Paul Morrison, Tony Seidler and Howard Cooper. An earlier inspiration was provided by an invitation from David Hartman to Jerusalem where I learnt about issues of authority with Hilary Putnam, Michael Sandel, Charles Taylor and Michael Walzer amongst others.The group of rabbinic students I had at the Leo Baeck College were also lively and reflective and they provided a context in which we could also think across the boundaries of the 'secular' and the 'spiritual' that proved immensely rewarding.

In different ways their inspiration helped me shape some of the language to explore the complex relationships between Jewish Philosophies and Western cultures. For some it might have been easier to learn about different philosophers in their own language and context and it was challenging to take time to relate some of these philosophical concerns with issues to do with identity, culture and spirituality in the present. In order to teach well I felt I needed to teach and learn differently and this meant grounding some of the concerns in the present at the same time as being aware of how different the concerns of the past could be.

Educated within the terms of Western culture it is often easier to approach Jewish philosophies in an externalised and historical way as if they can no longer speak into the present. Often it is through gradually recognising *how* our thinking, feeling and relationships to bodies, emotions and sexualities are *already* shaped within a Greek tradition that we can begin a process of grasping what the insights of an embodied Jewish philosophical tradition so long disdained and treated with contempt can offer in the present. But it is also that we were thinking and learning *after Auschwitz* and that we were coming together 'as Jews' and as people interested in Judaism in some way to explore *how* tensions between Athens and Jerusalem resonated differently for us after Auschwitz. I was also concerned to write about the relationships between Jewish philosophies and Western cultures in ways that went beyond the terms of 'inter-faith' discussion and did not accept these categories but probed their meanings in a globalised and postcolonial world.

These different journeys both towards and away from Judaism at different times are partly shared in the writings but it has been a shared journey particularly with my partner Anna who has constantly insisted on the gendered experience of Judaism and on how different it is for a woman to find her place within a still largely patriarchal tradition, especially within orthodoxy. Anna's insight and compassion and our family life that sustained Daniel and Lily into adulthood has been a constant source of challenge and inspiration. Issues of gender and sexuality remain vital and they are introduced as concerns in this text in ways that might be unfamiliar in more standard introductions to Jewish philosophy that tend to echo the patriarchal terms of the tradition.

But it has also been as a family learning to establish practices and traditions we felt good about passing on and the inspiration of people who supported us on the way. The mixed community that gathered around the North London Progressive Synagogue in Amhurst Park, Hackney was supportive through the Bar and Batmitzvah's of Daniel and Lily. Marsha Plumb was an inspiration as a Rabbi and she could communicate what mattered in the tradition in ways that touched different generations. But it was also the community that gathered that was alive to issues of gender, race and sexualities and the difficult questions they posed for the tradition. More recently returning to Hendon Reform Synagogue with Steven Katz, following his late father Arthur Katz as rabbi, reconnected me to a childhood source of Judaism.

But this is a text that moves across the diverse denominations of Judaism and it seeks its inspiration across different traditions. I find myself still seeking out different communities and moving between them in ways that Judaism happily allows. Often it is the inspiration of individual teachers and the joy that can be expressed through song and melody that draws me. I can feel 'at home' in different ways in an orthodox grouping like Yakar where Jeremy Rosen was very encouraging as I can in my own reform and orthodox communities. They have different things to offer, as I have learnt from Tony Bayfield and Jonathan Sachs, and it is in the recognition of multiplicity and an awareness that there are different paths and also different needs that we have at different times, as Rabbi Lionel Blue is so clear about, that is part of the richness of a Jewish tradition. This is a richness and diversity so beautifully expressed in the study anthologies of the prayer books of the Movement for Reform Judaism prepared by Jonathan Magonet. I found so much valuable material exemplifying my argument that Jewish sources offer a different voice that is illuminating of the present.

These themes have also been shaped through my years of teaching social theory and philosophy in the Department of Sociology, Goldsmiths, University of London. Generations of students have encouraged me to make connections across differences that could also help validate the experience of such a vital multicultural student body that is such a joy for anyone teaching at Goldsmiths. As I have explored these different inheritances and made space for dialogue across diverse cultural and spiritual traditions I have also had to test the limits of traditions of secular rationalism. Many people have listened to my attempts to make visible what is so often silenced and rendered invisible within prevailing traditions in philosophy and social theory.

The Philosophy and Human Values Group at Goldsmiths was vital at a particularly significant moment. There were numerous important discussions with Howard Caygill, Sally Alexander, Andrew Benjamin and Josh Cohen that took me beyond the boundaries of my own department where I also enjoyed discussions over the years with amongst others, Sally Inman, Susan Steadman Jones, David Lazar, Dave Walsh, Paul Gilroy, Fran Tonkiss, Vikki Bell, Caroline Ramazanoglu, Ros Gill, David Hirsh, Brian Alleyne, Kate Nash, Nikolas Rose, Chetan Bhatt, Celia Lury, Nirmal Puwar and Marsha Rosengarten.

The group I set up with Joanna Ryan on Embodied Psyches/Life Politics has also provided a rich source of insight and dialogue to which many people have contributed. Some of the issues framed here were also shared more recently with friends like Larry Blum, Zygmunt Bauman, Steven Lukes, Alan Montefiore, Anna Ickowitz, David Heyd, Paul Morrison, John Simopoulos, Stanley Cavell, Anthony Stone, Joana Ryan, Judy Smith, Richard Sennett, Craig Calhoun, Hilmar and Carol Schonauer, the late Dennis Scott, Angelica Strixner, David Robson, David Boadella, Asta and Hans Fink, Tony Seidler and Richard Morrison. An invitation by Terry Cooper and Jenner Roth and the Spectrum Staff group I worked with to give three days of presentations to the postgraduate workshop conference at Spectrum in January 2005 proved to be an inspiring setting in which I could give shape to some related concerns. The teaching and learning with Bob and Anni Moore and the spiritual community that gathered through the 1980s and 90s in Ringkobing, Denmark allowed so many of us to grow in our own authority while appreciating the depths of lived experience that can speak across diverse secular and spiritual traditions.

But if there is a tendency for Jewish traditions to close in on themselves in the shadows of the Holocaust it is a tradition that needs to again learn how to be open and aware of the diversity of influences that it has always carried in its relationship with Western cultures. For it has always been aware that it crosses the boundaries of 'East' and 'West' and in these troubled times after 9/11 it is possibly as a bridge that can help to open up a different kind of conversation between Islam and 'the West' that Jewish philosophies have an important contribution still to make. But it will only be once trust can be re-established through finding a just and lasting peace settlement between Israel and the Palestinians that Jerusalem can again hope to become a light to the nations.

2007

1

Introduction:
Jewish Philosophy and
Western Culture

Imagining 'Western Culture'

The ways we have learned, within an Enlightenment vision of modernity, to think of a distinction between 'East' and 'West' is often tacitly influenced by the historical distinction drawn between the Eastern and Western churches. This immediately raises the question of whether Christianity can be thought of as a 'Western' religion, especially if its Jewish sources are understood and the 'Jewishness' of Jesus historically is fully acknowledged when it is so often radically denied. What sense does it make to think of 'Christian Europe' or even of the West as 'Christian'? These are not simply issues of definition that cause us to rethink the ways in which histories of 'the West' have been written; they are issues that are very much *alive* in the present, ways in which 'Europe' in the shadow of the Holocaust could be conceptualised. It is a matter of the division between Athens and Jerusalem, their historical and cultural relationships with Islam and the ways in which these have shaped the formation of academic disciplines in the West. An awareness of these complexities helps to call into question a particular narrative that views Athens as the singular 'birthplace' of what we have learned to think of as 'Western culture'. As soon as we introduce the relationship of Jewish philosophy to Western culture we are directly confronted with these complexities.

Our image of 'Western Culture' matters because it encourages a particular narrative concerning the relationship of Christianity to Greek philosophy and Roman power that, according to Martin Bernal's pioneering *Black Athena*, strives to disavow Semitic and African influences, as well as influences from the Indian cultures of the East in the shaping of Greek civilisation and culture. It was through these exclusions and denials that the 'whiteness' of Europe was to be imagined, and the vital contributions of Jewish and Islamic philosophies and cultures across both humanities and sciences were to be denied and largely forgotten in the dominant cultural narratives that were largely to shape disciplinary fields in nineteenth-century Germany and Britain.[1] Within rationalist visions of modernity shaped through a radical distinction between 'reason' and 'faith', this also led to the exclusion of Jewish and Islamic philosophies as 'religious' and thus *unable* to contribute to philosophy and social theory within modernity.

Can these narratives, that have become almost 'second nature' and still define a taken-for-granted superiority of the West over its colonised others, be sustained in a changing post-modern and post-colonial world? As Freud recognised, it is partially through the denial of minor differences that the source of intense global conflict can be found, and this becomes even clearer when it is realised that the post-9/11 changing landscapes of fear and terror originate almost exclusively in the Middle East, particularly in ongoing conflicts between Israel and Palestine. This remains an issue of current concern with implications for Middle Eastern politics, for Israel has often intellectually constructed itself as part of 'the West' in ways that threaten to set it apart from the rest of the Middle East and so make it harder to create the conditions for peace, social justice and community.[2]

In part, this helps reinforce the notion of a 'Judeo-Christian' tradition – or however we learn to think of it – that can be identified as 'Western' in contrast to Islam that is definable as an Eastern Other. Not only can this work to deny the historical relationships between the Islamic and Jewish philosophies and the vital part that Islam has played in the preservation of a Greek philosophical tradition for Europe, but the very construction of a 'Judeo-Christian' tradition has made it difficult to think creatively about the diverse provocations of Jewish philosophy in Western culture.[3] We learn to forget the immense contribution of Islamic and Jewish philosophers, especially in Spain during the *Convivencia* period, to the rediscovery of Greek philosophy, science and culture that would otherwise have been lost. It is the philosophies and learning of Judaism and Islam that prepared the cultural conditions which were to make the Renaissance in Europe possible, the construction of 'the West' having been critically inspired by the philosophy, science and democracy of Ancient Greece.

The concept of 'Western culture' is also related to 'modernity', certain claims to 'modernity' and a tacit sense of having advanced 'beyond religion', thus breaking with tradition. It is through modernity that 'the West' has supposedly made a historical transition between nature and culture, and helped to shape a critical vision of 'progress' that was to be framed through the Scientific Revolution and rational Enlightenment of the seventeenth century. This allowed 'the West' to come to be identified with the dominant European powers to take its 'modernity' for granted in ways that served to *legitimate* European cultural expansion through empires and colonial domination.

Western culture came to be considered 'superior' because it was 'modern' and because it defined the terms which the colonised Others would have to follow in their turn *if* they wanted to make their own transition from nature to culture, from tradition to 'modernity'. To be 'Eastern' came to be identified within the Western psyche with being 'traditional', and so trapped within the cycles of nature and religious tradition. This was often disdained and identified as 'backward' or 'uncivilised' within a tradition of Enlightenment rationalism that would claim history, freedom, reason and progress as uniquely its own.

Colonised Others came to be identified with 'backwardness' and thus as somehow 'lacking' the conditions that could make progress possible. To be somehow locked into the conditions of 'backwardness' meant that 'non-European' countries were supposedly *unable* to free themselves without somehow accepting a form of colonial dependency. Only subordination to 'the West' would allow eventually the 'uncivilised natives' to make the necessary transition from nature to culture, from dependency to forms of self-rule.[4]

At some level, as I gradually came to realise, the ways in which we learn to think about the historical evolution of states is still tacitly connected to a Darwinian theory that has been construed to legitimise a hierarchy of races, with white Europeans being firmly placed at the pinnacle. This attitude was also fuelled by a dominant Christian tradition in the West that has historically construed a particular notion of the 'Judeo-Christian' tradition. This becomes established in the Western imagination as a kind of 'historical block' that has seemed to offer protection to a weakened Judaism of the Diaspora, historically sustained by the power of the Church which regarded the Jews as potential witnesses to the Second Coming of Christ. It also implies that Judaism had to be *superseded* for, even if Jews would want to think of this as an equal relationship between two independent but historically related civilisations, the historical formation of this construction is largely set within the terms of a dominant, hegemonic Christianity. Not only has this concept often worked to *deny* the 'Jewishness' of Jesus, it has considered as provocation the recognition of Christianity as having its origins in Jewish traditions. This has affected the ways in which Christianities have sought to imagine themselves in pre-modern and modern histories, but it also works to homogenise and, in some sense, *fix* Judaism within a dominant Christian narrative.

Of course, there are different ways of presenting this construction and different histories within Catholic and Protestant traditions. In part, they also show themselves in different histories in relation to the Holocaust and the less-than-wholehearted resistance of the Churches to the Nazi policies for the extermination of European Jewry. It can also echo an early Catholic tradition. However, that would seek to 'protect' Judaism and 'take it under its wing', for if Jews had to suffer for the crimes of their ancestors they also had to be preserved as a necessary witness to the Second Coming. This would place Jews in a specific position within a dominant Christian symbolism. Even though there has been a radical re-thinking through the Second Vatican Council that sought to portray Judaism as an older sibling that had its own Covenant, there were still older theological assumptions at work in the positioning of Jews within a dominant Christian imaginary that has still to come to terms with the Holocaust.[5]

In some ways, the notion of a 'Judeo-Christian' tradition has been recreated within the shadow of the Shoah to offer some kind of belated protection – as a kind of linking together which should make such terror impossible again. It is a protection that many Jews, traumatised by the events of the war and by an unspoken sense that the world did not really seem *to care* what happened to them, have been prepared to accept, so often did European countries fail to come to the rescue of their Jewish citizens. Jews found themselves bereft of the protection that legal and political rights should have given them. Their fellow Europeans, with a few right-eous exceptions, were indifferent to the fate of the Jews and the world seemed ready to abandon them to their fate. As Jewish philosophy had been largely superseded, it supposedly had nothing more to contribute to modern Western culture, and if the Nazis had had their way, Jewish communities would by now have ceased to exist and only be identified through the museums that were being specially prepared to receive their artefacts.

At some level, a tacit recognition seems to persist that – despite everything that has happened – Christianity has refused to accept the fact that Christianity and Judaism exist as discrete and distinct traditions. There is a Christian attempt to perpetuate the myth that they exist as distinct civilisations that have been joined together through painful histories of power, humiliation and terror. Intellectual traditions can still be at a loss as to *how* to present and teach these histories in the present. This reflects difficulties within notions of modernity tacitly wedded to ideas of progress of how to acknowledge ways, as Walter Benjamin recognised, in which the past *is* present in the present. At the same time as there have been welcome periods of peaceful co-existence and creative learning across the boundaries of different religious and secular traditions, there have been corresponding times of expulsion, contempt, denigration and genocide.

It is vital to recognise the inter-relations between the different Abrahamic traditions and the ways in which they have often existed in creative tension, at least in the good times when they have been able to appreciate *how* they can learn from each other for their own growth and spiritual vitality. Too often, there has been a desire for Christianity to appropriate Judaism, for at some level it still exists *as* a way of justifying the Christian story. This has also sometimes happened in feminist and gay theologies that have sought to attribute patriarchal and homophobic assumptions to an 'old' Jewish tradition that somehow still works to undermine the potential 'purity' of a 'new', non-patriarchal Christianity. So it is that, in different ways, Judaism with its faults is necessary to make Christianity possible. In this sense, the Jew makes the Christian *possible*, for often it is only through defining himself/herself in relation to 'the Jew' that Christians can traditionally come to define themselves. There is thus a constant – if unspoken and unrecognised momentum – to bring Judaism together through a particular relationship of parts, somehow coming to constitute a 'whole', unified civilisation.

This attempted harmonisation is often implicitly connected to the project of a 'Christian Europe' which historically has ended so catastrophically in the Holocaust for European Jewry. So when we ask the question 'Is Europe Christian?', we are not simply asking about the clearly diverse religious communities that now inhabit the European geographical zone, but we are questioning an important historical self-concept of Europe that lives on as a crucial cultural image in the ways the story of Europe is told. An echo of these narratives survives in the present, as has been shown in the discussions around a potential constitution for Europe and the place of Christianity within it. This often relates to the unspoken heritage of the Holocaust as taking place in the civilised heart of Europe and the place of the various forms of Christianity in making it possible.

At some level, an awareness of Jewish philosophies as being able to speak relevantly to the present of 'Western cultures' *is* a challenge to the way in which history is still communicated and taught across Europe. It also challenges the construction of *cultural memories* that are echoed in the present; for instance, in ways of misreading the Crusades, so that, for example, the murder of Jews in the Rhineland and of Jews and Muslims on the way to Jerusalem becomes an 'incidental event' because the dominant narrative still has to be about defending 'European Christendom' against the attacks of the 'infidel'. At some level, Jewish communities are defined as Other and when they are not expelled, as they were from Britain, they become internally colonised as they are forced to live in ghettoes and thus in spaces to which they are confined.

This narrative construct of a 'Judeo-Christian tradition' also helps to *separate* Judaism from Islam, and it makes it more difficult to open up a dialogue between different spiritual, religious and secular traditions and thus trace the complex inter-relationships. At the same time as they regret a broken dialogue with Islam, Jewish communities can feel threatened if they lose whatever privileges they have gained from their 'special', unique relationship to Christianity. Feeling fragile and insecure after the Holocaust, it is easy for Judaism to feel that it has to seek the protection of whichever power is ready to offer support. This has had tragic consequences in the Middle East for relationships between Israelis and Palestinians, since Israel is too closely identified with the global power of the United States. Through rethinking its relationship with 'the West' through an exploration of relationships between Jewish philosophies and Western cultures, Judaism could also be helped to rethink its relationship with Islam.

The Crusades and 'The West'

To a considerable extent, the Crusades still mark the ways in which we perceive 'the West' and thus Western culture and civilisation. The events of 9/11 and the ways in which the Crusades were invoked on different sides *show* how both the power and wounds of historical memory help to shape the present. In popular discourse, we still regard the Crusades as a 'virtuous' project, as in the term 'crusading journalist' – a journalist whose work is to be admired. We still teach our children to admire 'Richard the Lionheart', who played a crucial role in the massacre and expulsion of Jews from England. In the narratives of the Crusades, at least as they continue to resonate within the contemporary imagination, he is a figure of 'good' against which the Jew, and later the Turk, were constructed as figures of 'evil', even as embodiments of evil. It was not only that Jews and Moslems were deemed to be Other, they were perceived as *threats* to Christian rule and so often to the very existence of a 'civilised', i.e. Christian, world.[6]

So Europe learned to think about 'new' Crusades of which there is a strong echo in the reassertion of a Christian Spain that had to win back territory from Moslem control. Spain as a 'Catholic state' had to be liberated from the 'infidels' if its 'purity' was to be restored, and so with the Reconquista and the consolidation of the nation-state, the notion that different civilisations could somehow live together in peace was undermined. The 800 years of Muslim rule in Andalusia were to be treated as an aberration, and to this day, Spain has difficulties in coming to terms with its complex history because it finds it hard to renounce a Catholic vision of a singular truth to honour the richness of dialogues across religious differences within the Convivencia. So it was that the West was to be defined *against* Islam as Christianity came also to be defined *against* Judaism, and this prepared the ground for the Expulsion of the Jews from Spain in 1492 and of the Muslims soon after.[7]

This produced a collective act of forgetting, crucially of the fact that it was through Arabic and Jewish scholarship that the West was to rediscover the Greco-Roman culture that was to be a vital element in redefining modern Western culture in relation to the classical world. So it was that the West was fed a different history of its cultural origins, one that would make Judaism and Islam somehow invisible in respect of their contributions to Western culture. The Jewish sources of Christianity could also be ignored as Christianity could be recast in its relationship with Greece. Simone Weil was committed to this project which was a form of anti-Judaism, a process of 'purification' through which Christianity was to be 'purified' of its Jewish sources and so learn to think of itself as 'Greek', particularly through Plato. Jerusalem could more easily be *forgotten* as a source of Western imagination and Jewish philosophies would be relegated solely to religious discourses alone.[8]

There was no longer a need for the West to focus its understanding of itself in a dialogue between Athens *and* Jerusalem, and thus appreciate the importance of a dialogue between Jewish philosophies and Western cultures.

Rather, as Martin Bernal explored in *Black Athena*, there is an abiding racialisation that would treat Jews as 'Semitic' and thereby as 'non-white'. In this reorganisation, Judaism was identified with Islam, the Jew and the Moslem being identified as 'non-white' and thus as 'non-European', while Europe was defined as white Christian Europe to which 'others' could not really expect to belong. What was crucial in the splitting of Jesus from Judaism was that it prepared the ground for the reclaiming of Jesus as 'white', and the recasting of Christian Europe with 'whiteness' as a marker of 'purity' and thus of virtue and goodness. Athens was to be *split* from its Egyptian and Phœnician sources, allowing it to become a marker of white superiority in relation to 'non-white' and 'non-European' and thereby the uncivilised 'others'.

The Crusades helped to redefine the boundaries of 'Christian Europe', but they also served to imagine the West in fundamentally oppositional terms between the West and 'the rest'. Much later, in the eighteenth and nineteenth centuries, we see a strengthening of the identification between Greece – Europe – Whiteness. In this context those who 'became Christian' became in some ways 'honorary' whites, since Christianity came very much to be identified with 'Whiteness'. It was by virtue of the construction of a 'Judeo-Christian' tradition that Jewish people could be given *access* to 'whiteness'. This was part of a play of inclusions and exclusions with Islam being defined as radically Other, especially when the story is told of 'how close they came' with the siege and subsequent battle of Vienna. They help to mark a boundary as they are excluded from the boundaries of 'Christian' Europe. If they are allowed to enter it could only be as 'visitors', for it was not a space in which they could 'belong' while Jews could somehow be included in the story of a 'Christian Europe' as long as they were prepared to maintain their silence.

In some versions of the Crusades, it could be said that Jerusalem was being taken from the 'infidels' in order to be returned to the Jews, thus consolidating an alliance that would create a 'Judeo-Christian' civilisation. But this narrative involves *forgetting* how often Jews were targets for the Crusaders, how they were brutally murdered on the way to Jerusalem and how they were even massacred in the Holy City. But how then could Jews 'belong' to a Europe defined as 'Christian Europe'? Their belonging was bound to be ambivalent and they remained objects of attack in times of trouble when anger could be deflected upon them. As an example, there is the story of the Jewish community in Gerona, Catalonia. The community flourished as a place of Kabbalistic learning where it existed in close proximity to the cathedral, but when times got tough the community was attacked and it declined long before the Expulsion of the Jews from Spain. Jews could be tolerated as a minority once they had been marked out so that Christians always knew who they were dealing with. Since they could *not* be *trusted* they had to be 'made visible' through being obliged to wear particular clothing.[9]

If they could be forced to do what Christians were not allowed to do – lending money as usury – so they could be 'useful' while still being despised. There was a Christian teaching of *contempt* which meant the Jews were to be despised so they could not really be 'loved as neighbours' nor really be allowed to be 'friends'. Rather, Jews were not to be treated as individuals, especially in pre-modern Europe, but were to be deemed examples of the archetypal 'Jew'. They were to be categorised, regulated and controlled within a Christian world, for within a Catholic tradition it was out of the 'wrongs' of Judaism that the 'truths' of Christianity were supposed to emerge. There was an assumption that with the coming of Jesus and the refusal of the Jews to accept him as the Messiah they had been waiting for, Judaism had somehow spiritually died. It could not grow and develop because it had *outlived* its 'historical purpose', and Judaism's covenant with God had been supplanted, or rather fossilised, for it could only 'exist' in the way it could be imagined within Christian symbolism.

Superseding Judaism

Within dominant Christian narratives, Judaism could only be 'realised' within Christianity. This was its historical mission, once Jesus had appeared as the 'Son of God', even though this was a title he never claimed for himself, as Leo Baeck explores it, preferring to regard himself as the 'son of man'. This meant that within the dominant Christian discourses that framed 'Western Culture' Judaism had outlived its purpose, and the only function that Jews could have was as a *reminder* of their refusal to accept the divinity of Jesus and their supposed part in his death. This is something that had led to the divine punishment of exile marked in their destiny to wander the world. The expulsion from Jerusalem and the destruction of the Temple by the Romans were a divine punishment, as well as a continual reminder that Jews no longer had a part to play in God's purpose and in the divine order of things.[10]

Thus it was that the provocation offered by Judaism to the Christian concept of Western culture could be displaced, as Jews served exclusively as a 'reminder' of what had to be transcended. An ethic of envy and revenge had to give way to an ethic of love and forgiveness which meant that Judaism was not allowed to recognise itself in the Jewish bible's ethic of 'love thy neighbour'. Rather the ethic of brotherly love was to be *appropriated* within a Christian narrative that did not need to *listen* to what the Jews had to say for themselves about their own traditions of love and justice because whatever there was of value had already been *superseded* within Christianity. Later, within modernity, this established a sense in which the Hegelian dialectic was established in fundamentally Christian terms. It was part of a process of superseding that was given secular and historical form within Hegel's phenomenology. It also involved a *spiritualisation* of history as I shall explore, since the meaning of history did not lie in the quality of individual lives but in the ideas that were somehow to be expressed through these lives – the Spirit/Geist that was to be given form.

So it was that Judaism could be forgotten as it had been in some way 'assimilated' into the dominant Christian discourses of the West. It could be left alone supposedly to wither and die as it would prove incapable of renewing its own traditions and so speaking into the conditions of modernity. There were moments, such as in the famous disputations in Spain, when Jewish thought was called upon to give an account of itself, but it was generally assumed that whatever it had to offer had already been subsumed and taken to a higher level in Christianity. Within modernity, Judaism was to exist as 'religion' alone and though Judaism was to be called upon to prove its rationality, it was not really allowed to engage critically with the dominant philosophical traditions of an Enlightenment rationalism. It could be classified, along with Islam, as a religious 'other'.

Judaism having been accorded this position, it was Jews, somehow separated from Judaism, that were the 'Other' for they had outlived their historical mission. They only existed as witnesses to the Second Coming and it was only for this reason that they were owed the protection of the Church. In time they would be converted to Christianity; this was the only future they could hope to have. Judaism could *not* be allowed to grow or develop for it was merely a foretaste of what was already known. Nothing new could come into the world through Judaism and that was why no purpose was served by opening up a dialogue between Jewish philosophies and Western cultures. For a time, at least, the self-confidence of European rationalist traditions and their disembodied concepts of philosophical knowledge were deaf to the provocations of Jewish thought. Within the rationalist distinction that insisted that religion was a matter of 'faith' while philosophy was a concern with 'reason', an ethics of love could be safely reserved for Christianity.

As I tried to explore in *The Moral Limits Of Modernity: Love, Inequality And Oppression*, there was no space for a recognition of love within a rationalist modernity.[11] For Kant, love came to be presented as a 'rational feeling' because, within a secularised Christian tradition, it could only be 'pure' if it were disembodied and thus disconnected from human flesh and untouched by sexuality – this being a source of sin. The status of love became a central concern in the shaping of the traditions of Christian antisemitism, for Judaism allegedly only knew law and commandment whereas Jesus alone talked of 'love' and 'mercy'. This was an appropriation that refused to hear what the 'Jewishness' of Jesus had learned about the importance of love.

The central prayer of Judaism, the *Shema,* says 'you should love your God with all your heart and with all your soul and with all your strength'. It was through framing Judaism as 'carnal Israel', so separating sexuality from love that a radical split with Judaism came to be produced and Jews could be blamed for the murder of Christ and therefore held in contempt. Judaism was to be identified with bodies and so with the flesh and sexuality and thus with the 'sins of the flesh'. Jewish spirituality was deemed to be defective because it remained embodied and so tied and connected with the flesh, and so could not 'rise above' the earthly and material conditions of life. The idea that spirituality could also reside in the sanctification of everyday life and embodied love went unappreciated.

History teaches, however, that it was not Judaism that approved of burning people alive for disagreeing with the doctrines of the Church which remained largely silent when Jews were being burned in the crematoria of Nazi death camps. At the time of the Inquisition it was the Catholic Church that justified torture, execution and life-long suffering on earth in the name of a God of Mercy and Love, and it still justifies eternal suffering in Hell in the name of that same God. Contemporary Catholics stand in a direct tradition that burned and tortured in God's name for centuries. So do many Protestants. Of course, Judaism was also ready to punish religious and other forms of impurity and shaped its own patriarchal traditions, such as that of regarding women as impure at a particular moment in the menstrual cycle. It also shaped homophobic traditions with which it is still struggling to come to terms. Yet it would be mistaken somehow to blame Judaism for the patriarchal and homophobic inheritance within Christianity. The sects of Christianity do not need to 'purify' themselves of their Jewish sources but need to engage critically with *their own* histories and disembodied traditions of spirituality if they are to become more committed to equating ideals of gender and sexual equality with spirituality.

Western cultures still carry the influence of their Christian inheritance even if they have broken with it intellectually. Once Christianity began to recruit converts among the gentiles, the Jews would be weakened. It was they who had murdered Christ and persecuted his followers, as was clearly shown in the New Testament and the writings of the Church Fathers. This was the shaping of a tradition of contempt that meant that, in the Christian imaginary, Jews came to be identified with the

Devil and the anti-Christ. They were not to be trusted and there was nothing that could be learned from them. As St John Chrysostom, whose Greek nickname means the 'Golden Mouth' for his eloquence in the service of the Christian faith, makes clear, there was to be no dialogue: 'How dare Christians have the slightest intercourse with Jews, those most miserable of all men. They are lustful, rapacious, greedy, perfidious bandits – pests of the universe! Indeed, an entire day would not suffice to tell of their rapine, their avarice, their deception of the poor, their thievery, and their huckstering. Are they not inveterate murderers, destroyers, men possessed by the devil? Jews are impure and impious, and their synagogue is a house of prostitution, a lair of beasts, a place of shame and ridicule, the domicile of the devil, as is also the soul of the Jew'.[12]

If the references to vermin carry a particular sense of horror now that we know about the Nazi films that represented Jews as vermin – as rats who multiplied as they moved over the body politic – St John Chrysostom's sermons also contain a narrative of 'degeneration' that was to prove so influential in discourses around race and white European supremacy in the nineteenth century, thus shaping traditions of scientific racism that, in turn, engendered the 'common sense' racism that was so integral in sustaining European colonialisms. St John Chrysostom asks a question that was to find an echo in European traditions of antisemitism that prepared the ground for the Holocaust: 'Why are Jews degenerate? Because of their hateful assassination of Christ. This supreme crime lies at the root of their degradation and woes. The rejection and dispersion of the Jews was the work of God, not of emperors. It was done by the wrath of God and because of His absolute abandonment of the Jews. Thus, the Jew will live under the yoke of slavery without end. God hates the Jews, and on Judgement Day He will say to those who sympathise with them. "Depart from Me, for you have had intercourse with My murderers!" Flee then, from their assemblies, fly from their houses, and, far from venerating the synagogue, hold it in hatred and aversion' (quoted in *Flesh Inferno*, p.16.)

Even if this is an extreme view that some modern Christian apologists try to excuse by saying that such invective was customary in those days and that it was directed against Christians returning to Judaism, rather than against Jews, it was the influence of such language in *shaping* the cultural imaginary of the West and it echoes with a particular intensity the language and representations of Nazism. It remained a resource of Christian antisemitism that could be drawn upon at will and also helped to shape a long-standing contempt that often made a creative dialogue between Jewish philosophies and Western cultures impossible.

In the nineteenth century, after the Jewish Emancipation, when Jews were no longer restricted to living in ghettoes, Heinrich Heine could remark 'The baptismal certificate is the entry ticket to European culture'. In June 1825, one month before he received a doctorate in Jurisprudence, Heine was baptised and received into the Lutheran Church. As Bluma Goldstein notes: 'Religion does not seem to have been a motivating factor. Heine may have harboured religious sentiments, but he certainly expressed throughout his life a deep antagonism to organised religion, to which he referred as "positive religions"' (p.25).[13]

For Heine, as Goldstein explains, 'Hellenism had promised an almost unbelievable unity of the sensual and the spiritual, of a fulfilled individuality and utopian society. "Hellenistic cheerfulness, love of beauty and blossoming vivacity" proffered sensuous gratification and laid the foundations for a society in which "the divinity of man reveals itself also in his physical appearance"'(p.28). She explains that 1848 was the critical year in Heine's life when he broke with Athens, representing a significant shift in value that mediated the different interpretations of Moses. In the Afterward to *Romanzero* (1851), Heine recalls a day in May 1848, the last before debilitating illness confined him to bed, when he dragged himself with great difficulty to the Louvre to bid farewell to the goddess of beauty. He claims that he collapsed before the statue of the Venus de Milo and cried so violently that stone would have been aroused to pity: 'The goddess even looked down upon me with compassion, yet at the same time so hopelessly as if to say, "Don't you see that I have no arms and therefore cannot help?"' (*Samtliche Schriften*, vol. 6/1, 184 quoted on p.27).

This was a moment of transformation when Heine felt he had to turn away from Hellenism, since in 1848 Heine, as a sick man, needed assistance in everyday life as well as help for Europe, then in the throes of a revolutionary struggle that this political poet applauded. As Goldstein recognises: 'But now, in the Louvre, Heine confronted the glorious spirit of ancient Greece in a fragmented statue of a goddess and recognised its lifelessness and inefficacy, its impotence in the face of a person being consumed by a mortal ailment and a society struggling for transformation'. As he recognises: 'This poor dreamy being is interwoven and grown together with the world...will-less and powerless' (vol. 6/1, 182). He turns instead to a God with a will, to 'an old superstition, to a personal God', who could lend a helping hand. 'In order to have a will', he observed, 'one must be a person, and in order to manifest it, one must have one's elbow free' (vol. 6/1, 182–3). Although terminally ill, Heine was not seeking a transcendential God to save his soul or guarantee immortality but an active deity, able to attend to worldly needs and endeavours.

The separation of matter and spirit in Christianity that also framed the separation from Judaism as 'Carnal Israel', as explored by Daniel Boyarin, was, in Heine's view, responsible for the lingering malaise of Western civilisation. Referring to the primacy of the spirit and the evil of matter that has framed the *disdain* for worldly things that have had such a disastrous ecological consequence for the relationship between human beings and the natural world, Heine noted in 1834 'This world view, the actual idea of Christianity, has disseminated with unbelievable speed throughout the entire Roman Empire....lasted throughout the entire Middle Ages, and we moderns still feel cramps and weakness in our limbs'. As Goldstein recognises: 'Contradiction, however, is not limited to Heine's admiration for a highly abstract and spiritual conception of love that he finds in Jesus; Christian spirituality is also called into question because of its destructive powers. Speaking of the crucifixion, Heine realizes that the "white marble Greek gods were splashed with this blood and fell from inner horror, and could never again recover!"'(vol. 4, 44).

The discussion of Moses in the *Confessions* follows Heine's rejection of German philosophy, especially Hegel's, because of the impotence of its idealism and its egotism. In a letter written in 1850, Heine shows that the distinction between Hegel and Moses is important for him as he acknowledges that he has not undergone any change in his religious sentiments but that his ideas about religion have been through a 'February Revolution': 'I have, namely, to elucidate the matter in word, given up the Hegelian god or rather godlessness and in its stead have again placed a real, personal god, which is outside of nature and the human mind....For me Hegel has very much declined, and old Moses is flourishing'. His new conception of Moses does not mark a return to religion but is part of his attempt to bring Jews and Judaism into the realm of social thought and Western culture.

Though he significantly re-evaluated his conception of Moses and the Torah, the narrative of his discourse about the relationship between Jews and Germans remains relatively unchanged. Heine detected an elective affinity between these two ethical peoples who shared 'the most courageous hatred of Rome, a personal sense of freedom, ethics'. As Goldstein notes: 'It is surprising that nowhere before the *Confessions* does Heine connect Moses with the religion founded on law that had such a profound influence on the Western world'.

In the *Confessions*, as Goldstein recognises, the Jews are no longer 'presented as culturally moribund, shards from the past that can be overlooked, an idea that must be overcome. They are alive and vital in their ghettoes, they have preserved their Bible and therewith the ethics of justice and liberation and, hidden behind the walls, their biblical scholars tutor Europe's most progressive thinkers, the Protestant reformers' (p.37). As Heine says: 'Indeed to the Jews, to whom the world owes its God, it also owes His word, the Bible' (vol. 6/1, 483–5). It was through the isolation afforded by the ghetto that the Jewish people were also preserved as a nation by keeping alive and active 'the great realm of the spirit, the realm of religious feeling, of love of neighbour, of purity and of true ethics (*Sittlichkeit*), which cannot be taught by dogmatic conceptual formulations, but by image and example, as they are contained in the beautiful, holy, educational book for small and large children, in the Bible' (vol. 6/1, 485).

Heine comes to see the inadequacy of Hegelian philosophy in the face of the concrete ethic of loving one's neighbour, justice, freedom of thought and liberation which he comes to identify with Moses and the Torah. But his approach to the Bible and Moses is largely secular and he does not regard the role of a transcendent God with any seriousness, though this could also be because issues of belief are much less significant in Judaism. According to Goldstein, 'he does take the Bible and Moses very seriously; for Heine, they seem necessary for the cultural, social and political foundations of modern life. They are also vital to the understanding of his own values'. As he says of Hegel, 'The cobweb-like Berliner dialectics can not lure a dog out of a hole in the oven, it can kill no cat, much less a god' (vol. 6/1, 478).

Of Jews, he writes: 'I now see that the Greeks were merely beautiful youths; the Jews, however, were always men, powerful, unyielding men, not only then, but until the present day, despite eighteen hundred years of persecution and misery. So powerful have they become that cultured and revolutionary Western Europeans are seen coming into the ghetto to unearth texts that may contribute to the reformation of Western society' (vol. 6/1, 481). In his waning years, according to Goldstein, 'Heine seems to be extending an invitation to enter the ghetto, be it segregated territory, Bible, or sickroom, where suffering may still fuel the struggle for justice, freedom of thought, and a liberated life' (p.39).

Between Athens and Jerusalem

Heine questions an ideal that still prevails in some Christian circles that since Judaism had been superseded and has been realised within the project of Christianity there was nothing that could be learned from Jews that was not *already* known. Thus it was that Jews could be talked about in their presence as if they were not even there, but were some relic of the past. Some years ago I experienced such a sense of non-being while attending a United Nations-sponsored interfaith conference in Valetta, Malta on 6–8 May 1999, convened to consider 'Human Rights and Our Responsibilities towards Future Generations'. There was a logic to the order of presentations but it took me awhile to appreciate it. The papers that presented a Jewish viewpoint were presented first, then came the Islamic scholars, followed by the Christians, which in this setting meant Catholicism represented by the Vatican. It was these latter papers that I found most disturbing, for they assumed possession of a singular *truth* and the existence of one true path, that of Christianity, that others might have been able to glimpse – or prepare for – from their traditions but which they could not properly articulate or express.

This was a strange and uncomfortable moment for me as I had not really experienced being talked about in my presence in such a way. I realised that I was being somehow seen as a representative or voice of Judaism even though this was supposedly an academic conference. It was as if Judaism could be talked *about* because whatever was of 'value' had already been superseded by Christian doctrine. So it was that the Jewish participants, for most of whom it was very unfamiliar to be treated this way, did not have to be *listened* to or addressed directly because we had already been historically *spoken for*. There was nothing 'new' that we could say and nothing that we could really contribute to the conversation that was not already *known*. Somehow we could only *repeat* or *echo* what had already been said before because for this Catholic tradition it was as if Judaism existed – could only exist – as 'outside' of history, stuck in some kind of historicised present.

This conference was taking place 40 years after the end of the Second World War and the Holocaust, and even if there were many official, theological expressions of regret, it seemed as if little had changed. There was no way of recognising *how* Judaism could contribute something *new* to the consideration of the millennium or how it could help to unsettle relations of power and privilege that had sedimented within the West and which very much needed to be reconsidered in a post-modern era. It seemed as if there was still little space for a creative dialogue between Jewish and non-Jewish philosophies that could speak effectively into the present.

In crucial ways, Judaism subverts the notions of being superseded that, as Walter Benjamin recognised, have been written into Western notions of freedom and progress. At some level, Benjamin was tacitly invoking Judaism in his critical response to both a liberal tradition and orthodox Marxist traditions that in different ways both fostered an identification between reason, history and progress. If reason no longer exists in a critical relationship with history, but rather is imminent within a historical project, for Benjamin, it is Judaism that marks a challenge to an Enlightenment vision of modernity for it *refuses* to be superseded. It refuses to die the death that has been prepared for it and insists that it is very much alive within modernity and able to speak to the present.[14]

In this way, as I hope to show, it demands that the West learns to reconsider a self-image that it has long taken for granted. But, as both Wittgenstein and Freud understood in different ways, this often means questioning the idealisation and spiritualisation fostered through a Platonic Greek tradition that saw the forms as 'real' and everyday experience as somehow always falling short and thus lacking the conditions of fulfilment. In their different ways, Wittgenstein and Freud sought to question the escapes into abstractions and insisted upon the *grounding* of ideals experienced in personal life and the grounding of language in contexts of use in everyday life. In their different ways, their practice of psycho-analysis and philosophical investigation tacitly speak from Hebraic sources that insist on the *quality* of everyday life and experience.[15]

Within Catholic tradition, at least as represented in the conference, it was as if Judaism had spoken once and for all time. It had nothing to say which could illuminate the present but it could only *repeat* what had been said in the past. Consequently, it was difficult for the Judeo-Christian to exist as a coming together of different traditions with their own integrities and dignity of difference. Rather it was to create a 'block', with a clear sense of ordering that would help to provide a space/position for Jews within 'Christian' Europe. If this seemed to give Jews a secure position within the West, it was tacitly through having to accept that Judaism has been superseded. Judaism was to be given a form of protection, but the doctrine of contempt survived and this protection was proved to be illusory when it came to preparing the ground for the Holocaust.

Judaism and Modernity

In its own way, this was to serve to separate Judaism from Islam and make it harder to explore what these different traditions shared, as well as their relationships with Christianity. For it was Islam that was to be cast as the 'other'. Somehow Jews were to find a place within Christian Europe that was to be denied to Islam, securely positioned as it was beyond the gates of Europe and the West. It was Jews who were alone to be offered rights subsequently as 'free and equal' citizens within secular European states. Christianity was gradually to give way to secular terms of the self-concept of Europe, but it was to remain tacitly coded in its relationship with 'whiteness' within the project of colonisation that was to frame a new relationship with Islam as a colonised Other. In this context, Jews as citizens were to be 'tolerated' as honorary 'whites'.

As 'free and equal' citizens, Jews were to be accepted as long as they were ready to forsake their Jewishness as part of their public identity. Jews were no longer to be recognised as a *people* who had been expelled from their land by the Romans with an aspiration towards a state of their own. Rather Zionism was often deemed to be a *threat* to a secular rationalism which had imagined the 'disappearance' of the Jews as a religious group, withering away in the face of the progress of science. Even if citizenship of Western European states seemed to present a 'solution' to the 'Jewish Question' for those who refused to accept that Jews could be citizens 'like everyone else' – Levinas frames the project of modernity as being that 'others' can become like 'the same' – there were emerging traditions of antisemitism and scientific racism. Conversion, as Heine realised, was not the solution that it often seemed to be. An uneasy assimilation that often left Jews to see themselves through the eyes of the dominant culture could produce its own forms of Jewish Self-Hatred, something that Sander Gillman has explored.[16]

Many Jews were to welcome the Enlightenment and its vision of human equality as a realisation of a prophetic dream. They were often more than willing to pay the price. Moses Mendelssohn was a central figure in the Berlin Enlightenment who worked hard to show the rationality of Judaism and so prove that its beliefs could be accepted by any 'rational agent'. Jews were to welcome the legal and political rights they were guaranteed as citizens and the freedoms they received to live where they wanted and as they pleased. For the most part, they were ready to make Jewishness a matter of individual religious belief alone and to accept that within the public realm of citizenship they existed as rational selves 'like everyone else'. In Germany, in particular, there were also movements for the reform of Judaism itself so that it could be brought more into line with modernity. Thus it was that Jews were to be 'tolerated' as a legitimate minority within civil society, and for their part they would accept the division between public and private spheres and accept that religion was a private matter that need not affect participation within the public realm. In Germany, Jews were to be Germans 'like everyone else', who were no longer talked about as Jews or Hebrews but as people who happened to be of the 'Mosaic faith'.[17]

If this meant that they were to be *invisibilised* as Jews this was nothing to regret because the freedom that was being offered was so much more important. Jews had the freedom to assimilate into the dominant culture and they learned to identify with German culture in Germany and with French culture in France. The fact that people might share a religious tradition was to become less significant within modernity than their citizenship of a nation-state. If Jews ceased to believe in their religion then they *ceased* to be Jews, at least in their own eyes. They might recall the traditions of their ancestors but these might have nothing to do with them. They were no longer Jews because they did not share any religious beliefs.

But these histories are complex, even more so in the shadows of the Shoah. In *Works of Love*, Gillian Rose has shared what she learned when she visited Julius Carlebach, a professor at the University of Sussex whose family had lived for generations in Hamburg before the Holocaust. She recalls: 'Julius sat at the head of the table in a dining-room which was a museum and mausoleum of the Carlebach family's distinguished and dreadful history....Julius's father, Joseph Carlebach, the famous Rabbi of Hamburg, accompanied his congregation to their death outside Riga, with his wife and the four youngest of their nine children' (p.19).[18]

The square in Hamburg where his synagogue had stood has recently been renamed *Carlebach Platz*. In his acceptance speech in Hamburg, when Julius received the honour on behalf of his family, as Rose retells it, 'he pointed out to his audience that they were assembled in the same school hall where he had stood, a fifteen-year-old schoolboy, when the Gestapo came and told the children that they had four weeks to leave Germany. "You could hear people collapse internally", Julius commented on his adult audience. What happened to those children?' (p.20).

'At dinner, Julius explained "An orthodox Jew doesn't have to worry about whether he believes in God or not, as long as he observes the law". Subsequently, I became familiar with the notoriously inscrutable Midrash: "Would that they would forsake Me, but obey my Torah".' Reflecting back on that evening, Rose recalls: 'It was the occasion of my initiation into the anti-supernatural character of Judaism: into how *non-belief in God* defines Judaism and how change in that compass registers the varieties of Jewish modernity. The more liberal Judaism becomes, the less the orientation by Halachah, the law, and the greater the emphasis on individual faith in God' (p.19).

Reflecting on her own movement towards Judaism, Rose recalls how 'My disastrous Judaism of fathers and family transmogrified into a personal, Protestant inwardness and independence. Yet, as with the varieties of historical Protestantism, progenitor of modernity, the independence gained from the protest against illegitimate traditional authority comes at the cost of the incessant anxiety of autonomy. Chronically best with inner turmoil, the individual may nevertheless become roguishly adept at directing and managing the world to her own ends. Little did I realise then how often I would make the return journey from Protestantism to Judaism' (p.35–6).

Rose also recognises the difference, given that she had not really been brought up religiously in any sense, that 'These return journeys between Protestantism and Judaism deny any idea of "ethnic identity". My Protestantism has been imbibed with the vapours of the culture; my learning helps me to describe it. My Judaism is cerebral and consciously learned; it permits me to develop a perspective on quandaries which would otherwise remain amorphous and alien'. I find Rose's reflections helpful because they recognise how most people growing up as Jews within Western culture *remain shaped* by Christian religious traditions that still mould their subjectivities within secular cultures. It can take time to appreciate what Jewish philosophies have to offer and how they can help shape a different feeling for life in 'Western culture'.

Within an Enlightenment dream of modernity, history only played an incidental role. For Kant, history – like culture – was a form of unfreedom and determination which people had to 'rise above' – and so split or separate from if they were to claim their freedom *as* autonomous individuals. People were to learn to recognise each other as 'rational selves' and this was what people were to 'see' when they came face-to-face. They were to see individuals with particular preferences and tastes, and it was *as* individuals that they were to find themselves assessed and judged. Within the dream of modernity, Jews did not have to 'recognise' themselves *as* Jews and no-one could supposedly force them to assume this identity. If it were a 'religious' identity that had no significance for them in the present they were free to make this choice about their lives and supposedly this would have few consequences. In this sense, Jewishness could be renounced or *erased* within a tradition of secular rationalism which discounted its significance in relation to individual identities. Presumably, differences would wither away as people learned to recognise themselves and others as 'fellow' human beings and so as individuals in their own right.

Within an Enlightenment rationalism that still largely shapes 'modern philosophy' in its ongoing dialogue with Western culture, unless people choose to give history weight and significance, it has none. Rather people learn to 'put history beside them' as something that might have shaped their parents' lives but has little consequence for them. Thus it was that many Jews became secular Jews or just secular, as they often refused any identification with Judaism considering it had little consequence in the present. As religions were framed as a matter of individual belief and practice so it became *easy* to erase/discount/disavow a Jewish identity, even though this is very much a Christological reading that defines religion as a matter of belief rather than practice. Such a disavowal proves more difficult for people of colour since there is often a suspicion that they are trying to portray themselves as 'white' and so refusing to identify with their own history and culture.

As Jews learn to come to terms with the Shoah they may feel a similar unease. They may also feel that the emergence of Nazism had shattered, once and for all, the promises and dreams of an Enlightenment rationalism. It meant that history had assumed a different kind of *weight* and thus an unconscious, symbolic presence which could not be easily disavowed. Even if Jews felt uneasy about their Jewishnesss they could feel that, in some ways at least, they had to 'come to terms' with the events of the Shoah as people of African descent might feel they need to come to terms with slavery. They might think of Jewishness as part of a cultural identity towards which they feel nostalgic but they might not so easily ignore it. Within a post-modern recognition of differences young Jews have often learned from people of colour about the importance of history and culture and are often concerned to redefine their Jewishness. Often they are less likely to discount it though this does not mean they feel identification with the Jewish religion or that it is likely to affect their choice of partners. Often, when young people with children have to face what they want to pass on to their children, questions of belief re-emerge and people in contemporary Western societies find themselves thinking anew about questions of religious belief.

Post-Holocaust Jewish Identities

Often it is through children that people recognise that if they do nothing to sustain their Jewish identities they unwittingly grow up with Christian beliefs – even if presented in secular forms. They recognise *how* modernity within secularised Western cultures is tacitly framed through a secularised Christianity. They realise that modernity was a much more ambivalent project than they have been led to believe and that Christianity still has a very powerful hold within the dominant culture. Paradoxically, it has often been through feminist and Black scholarship and politics that younger Jews have come to re-assess their Jewishness. They have learned to identify ways they have been silently *shamed* in their own eyes through liberal tolerance and ways they had come to see their own experience as Jews through the disdainful eyes of a dominant secularised Christian tradition.

The disavowal of identities became possible within a modernity that felt threatened by a sense of difference. If differences existed, they were transitory and would disappear as people recognised each other as 'free and equal' human beings. Post-modernism has helped identify differences which modernity would have easily passed over. But while Judaism was disavowed in this way, Islam was often presented as 'outside' modernity, as somehow existing beyond the pale and untouched by modernity. At some level, Islam was positioned as a threat to modernity. Islam often chose to hold on to its self-conception as a way of life, something that Judaism also felt but often had to compromise. With the breakdown of the Soviet Union in the late 1980s and the disappearance of Communism as an external threat to the West, Islam has been cast as a threat that no longer exists 'outside' the borders of the West, but has become a threat within. Supposedly, especially since 9/11, it exists as a threat to the very project of modernity through its allegiance to 'fundamentalism'.

The identification of Islam with fundamentalism has made it difficult to open up a dialogue with Judaism and to explore the significance of Jewish and Islamic philosophies within Western cultures. It has also made it difficult to explore the rediscovery of religions within a post-modern world. In part, this rediscovery is linked to a spirituality that is partly informed by changing relationships with nature and a desire to question the disenchantment of nature that has typified modernity within Western culture since the Scientific Revolution of the seventeenth century. The relationship between culture and nature, between the 'human' and the 'animal', is in the process of a postmodern re-assessment.

As the relationship between modernity and the nation-state is also called into question, people begin to conceive of new transnational and transcultural identities as well as new visions of citizenship which no longer involve an 'assimilation' into a dominant culture. Rather than thinking about 'minorities' who need to be tolerated by a dominant majority, we are rethinking tolerance in ways that allow a respect for difference and which can foster a celebration of differences within re-imagined communities as I explore in *Urban Fears & Global Terrors* (London, Routledge, 2007). These have become urgent concerns in the wake of the Al-Qaida attacks in New York, Bali, Madrid and London.

It becomes pressing to imagine how different cultural and faith communities within multicultures can learn to live together as they also learn to shape a shared cultural inheritance and respect for each others' language and traditions.

As Jews growing up in the 1950s we were experiencing a very different world, one in which we learned to minimise signs of difference. We were ready to hold our peace – refusing to draw attention to ourselves in the hope that we would be 'accepted' by others – we very much wanted to be liked and accepted. We were often wary of admitting our Jewishness, since we feared this might give others reasons to reject us. This moment has passed as people no longer feel a need to assimilate, even if they are questioning traditional models of multiculturalism and attempting to conceive of new forms of belonging together within a *critical multiculturalism* within nation states. Whilst wanting differences to be respected even when this means challenging patriarchal and homophobic traditions within religions, people are often seeking simultaneously to explore everyday multicultures and what is shared within 'common cultures' as well as celebrate what different groups can offer for future hope.[19]

This also means opening up a radically different kind of *dialogue* between diverse philosophical and spiritual traditions and specifically between Jewish philosophies and Western culture. Within a post-modern sensibility there are different economies of identity and difference. People refuse to be fixed and pigeonholed and insist on being able to define themselves as moving between diverse categories. There is a search for resources that can help people to *validate* their own experience rather than judge themselves externally as failing to live up to some Platonic ideal. This is part of what Wittgenstein and Freud offer, producing, in their different ways, a critique of idealisation and an honouring of the quality of everyday life and experience. 'I do not have to be like you' to feel that I am entitled to exist, rather I can feel pride in my difference, in my ethnic background, religion, gender and sexuality. This is part of an exploration of differences that have long been suppressed within a modernity that was in subtle and powerful ways intolerant of differences.

At the same time and also within 'Western culture', the breakdown of the Soviet Union and the revolutions of 1989 have borne witness to the re-emergence of nationalism and the difficulties of people learning to live with each other when old histories and ethnic nationalisms have come back into focus. People have often sought to live in ethnically homogenous states, as the tragic events that followed the break up of the former Yugoslavia so clearly demonstrated. In part, this shows the difficulty of suppressing painful history and denying significant differences. It is very much what happened in Communist times when people were encouraged to think of themselves not as Slovenians, Serbs or Croats, but as 'Yugoslavs' who were defined through a broader national identity. These new identities proved difficult to sustain, however, and we need to learn the lessons if we are to imagine *how* different communities are to live peacefully together in the new Europe. Again, reflections on Jewish experience and philosophy can be helpful in engaging with these aspects of Western culture.

As young Jews explore their Jewishness, they can learn to appreciate the challenge Moses Hess put to Marx, when he claimed that Jewishness would not just wither and die away.[20] As a post-modern culture promises people new forms of recognition and self-acceptance, this can help people explore their own 'voices'. Rather than feel that history can be side-stepped, that we can, in Kant's terms, 'rise above them', people are exploring new ways of giving them *due* weight and discovering freedom through 'working through' their diverse inheritances. This often means liberal notions of tolerance need to be rethought since traditionally they have unwittingly sought to erase or silence cultural difference. At the conference in Malta, I was struck by a Turkish woman who grew up in secular Turkey saying that she had somehow learned more about Christianity than she had about Islam. This was a predicament I could recognise, having unknowingly learned more about Christianity through growing up in post-war England than I knew about Judaism.

In part, this has to do with processes of minimising differences and seeking the 'common ground' that is so often established through the dominant culture. In post-war Britain, wanting to be 'like everyone else' was already tacitly framed within the terms of secularised Protestant tradition.

Post-modernism can be welcomed to the extent that it assists in the recognition of the integrity of diverse cultural and spiritual traditions. Rather than minimising differences, we can learn to envisage a 'common ground' in post-humanist ways that respects individuals not simply as rational selves but as *embodied* subjects with their own emotional, cultural and spiritual lives. Helping to ground such an awareness is a contribution that an embodied Jewish philosophy can make to post-modern Western cultures. In its own way, this involves questioning a tradition of secular rationalism. Such a tradition unwittingly conceives of human needs in utilitarian terms and is tied to traditions of secular materialism. If we can learn from Simone Weil to recognise the significance of nourishing both material and spiritual needs, we can also look to resources in Jewish philosophy to appreciate the somatic life and emotional and affective needs which she finds it hard to illuminate. Though Weil was often hostile to her Jewish tradition and background, she nevertheless appreciated human vulnerability and relationships in ways that echo Jewish philosophy and which the tradition of secular rationalism tends to minimise. Too often, it sustains a heroic ethic of concealing weakness and vulnerability, especially as men. To admit that we need others is often framed as a sign of weakness and is deemed to be a threat to dominant masculinities.

While drawing on Jewish philosophies and sensibilities to think in different terms about the ways post-modern cultures allow human beings / to thrive and *deepen* their human experience in terms of mind, body, emotion and spirit, we also need to recognise the need to validate the integrity of diverse cultural and spiritual traditions. This is something that Hugo Gryn, late Rabbi of the West London Reform Synagogue, learned from his father when they were both in 'a miserable little concentration camp in German Silesia' grotesquely called Lieberose, 'Lovely Rose': 'It was the cold winter of 1944, and although we had no calendars...my father announced it was the eve of Chanukkah, produced a curious-shaped clay bowl, and began to light a wick immersed in his precious, but now melted, margarine ration. Before he could recite the blessing, I protested at this waste of food. He looked at me – then at the lamp – and finally said: "You and I have seen that it is possible to live up to three weeks without food. We once lived almost three days without water; but you cannot live properly for three minutes without hope!"' (*Forms Of Prayer: Days of Awe*, London: RSGB, 1985, p.500).

We need to learn from diverse spiritual and religious traditions as well as engage critically with their patriarchal and homophobic assumptions. If spiritual traditions are not to find common ground in their struggles against modernity and come together around narrow programmes involving restrictions on abortion and contraception, but if instead we are to engage critically with our responsibilities to future generations, we have to open up a dialogue not only between different Abrahamic religions but also between West and East. In a period of globalisation it is not enough to think in terms of an extension of human rights that are already enjoyed in the West; we have to learn to imagine human dignity in ways that respect the planet and to question the dominance of corporate power. In part, this means learning *how* to listen to each other. Rather than taking for granted the benefits of modernity, thinking that progress lies in a homogenised vision in which we extend these benefits from the West to 'the Rest', there has to be a different kind of dialogue which recognises challenges to Western dominance but *also* learns creatively from the West while voicing its own dreams and aspirations to a West that has learned a new humility.

As we learn to question traditions of secular materialism and begin to recognise the diversity of human needs which different cultures express, we are less likely to think that there is a universal scale against which different cultures can be measured and in which some are found wanting. This is not to suspend judgement or moral evaluation where human rights are being infringed and people made to suffer as we have seen recently in Bosnia, Kosova, East Timor, Afghanistan, Dafur and Iraq. It is to learn something about the difficulties of *judgement* and about the need for people to discover their own diverse voices. For we should refuse to homogenise cultures in a way that often allows a dominant male voice to speak for all and traditional religious authorities to consolidate a power that often needs to be challenged if gender and sexual identities are to be duly honoured and religious traditions reinterpreted to allow for their full participation and expression.

The history of the West was one of dominant white masculinity that could *alone* take its rationality for granted. It legislated what was best for women and children through the institution of marriage which, until recent challenges by the Women's Movement, treated women and children as the 'property' of men. Patriarchial power is often embodied within different religious traditions that insist that 'feminism' cannot belong to their own traditions, that it is an invention of Western cultures that is attempting to impose an order of greater gender equality.

But if you explore the different voices and practices within diverse Abrahamic traditions you discover a diversity of voices and times when women shared much more in the spiritual life of the larger community, and took an active part in worship in mosques and synagogues. The notion that women are already on a 'higher spiritual level' than men and can therefore be excused from certain religious duties and responsibilities is too often a story that works to consolidate patriarchal power and deny women gender equality. So there have to be leanings in different directions; religious traditions *also* need to learn from freedoms that have been hard fought for within Western cultures as they have become more democratic.

As we learn to ask fundamental questions of the West, learning from feminism, gay and lesbian scholarship as well as post-colonial studies, we begin to subvert assumptions of superiority that have for so long been taken for granted. This has to do with opening up dialogues between different religious and spiritual traditions and with secular post-modernity. Opening up a dialogue between Jewish philosophy and Western culture also means *learning* to revise identities in ways that question the self-identity of a secular rationalism that has informed modernity. Jewish philosophies offer embodied conceptions of knowledge as well as ways of recognising the priority, as Levinas expresses it, of ethics in relation to epistemology. We begin to recognise that Western culture needs to learn as much from Jerusalem as it has from Athens. This can help us question whether we really want to exist as disembodied rational selves alone, as we learn within a Cartesian modernity, as we begin to *listen* to our bodies and experience our vulnerability. We can also listen more openly to others with diverse cultures, histories and spiritual traditions as we have learned to listen in different ways to ourselves.

2

A Time for Philosophy

Re-Memberings

What does it mean to re-member ourselves? As life becomes locked into a routine and we take ourselves and those around us for granted, we can easily lose touch with ourselves. It is often unexpected events, such as the death of someone close to us, that make us reflect upon our lives and what matters to us. Otherwise, it seems so easy to forget our own values and where we are with ourselves. We stop asking questions of ourselves and may feel unsettled by the questions asked by others. Rather than thinking about philosophy as something that is abstract and distant from our everyday lives, it can be helpful to re-member that the Greek term 'philosophy' means 'love of wisdom'. This is an appreciation that does not come easily since it has often been forgotten within the philosophical traditions which we have learned to take for granted within the modern world.[1]

We can only make space for philosophy as the love of wisdom *if* we are prepared to re-member the philosophical assumptions that we have grown up to take for granted within our 'common-sense'. We need to take time to consider the philosophical traditions of our families and communities. How did I grow up to think and feel about myself? Did I learn, even if it was never said, that love is something to be earned through individual achievement? Did I feel that I had to prove myself worthy of the love of my parents or was love something that was given unconditionally? Did I learn that love was a scarce commodity so that I had to be careful about who I myself gave it to? How were my feelings shaped by a Protestant conception that, at some level, I was *unworthy* of love and that if others 'really knew who I was' they would surely reject me? Did this mean that I had to learn to live in the shadows, careful about what I could show to others?[2]

Can I remember the person in the family whom I felt could recognise me for *who* I was? Did I feel that I had to learn to speak differently if I wanted to be listened to by the adults in the family? Did I have to assume a different voice if I wanted my father to listen to what I had to say? Did I feel that love could only be expected as a reward for good behaviour or achievement? Did I feel that different people in the family recognised me in different ways or did I feel that nobody offered me the recognition that I needed? Did I turn towards God for recognition that I could not get from the family? Did I ever feel 'I have lost something, but do not know what'. Is this something that I recognise in my searching?

Martin Buber remembers 'In my earlier years the "religious" was for me the exception...' Religious experience 'was the experience of an otherness which did not fit into the context of life....The "religious" lifted you out...The illegitimacy of such a division of the temporal life...was brought home to me by an everyday event, an event of judgement'. A young man had come to see him and though Buber had been friendly and 'conversed attentively and openly with him – only I omitted to guess the questions which he did not put'. Later, he learned from one of his friends 'the essential content of these questions', but he was no longer alive. As Buber remembers: 'I learned that he had come to me not casually, but borne by destiny, not for a chat but for a decision. He had come to me, he had come in this hour. What do we expect when we are in despair and yet go to a man? Surely a presence by means of which we are told that nevertheless there is meaning'.[3]

It seems as if Buber never forgot the meeting. At the time, he had been unable to offer what was needed, which was not a matter of presenting knowledge but 'surely a presence by means of which we are told that nevertheless there is meaning'. It might not have been a matter of what was said, but of the quality of the contact that was being established in the dialogue. This has less to do with what is being spoken than with the *resonance* – 'quality of presence' – that was being established. This has to do with the emotional/spiritual work Buber had to perform for himself because you cannot tell someone about meaning unless you have experienced meaning for yourself.

Parents, for instance, cannot respond to their children's spiritual questions unless they have explored these meanings for themselves in their own individual lives, otherwise their words will often sound hollow and empty. It is not a matter of finding the right words as if it were a matter of knowledge alone, but of being able to *mean* what you say. It is not a matter of intention but rather of being able to share 'meanings' you have struggled to achieve for yourself. But this can involve questioning both the materialist values that you might have been brought up to take for granted, as well as the values that you have inherited from the wider culture. This is what Buber was questioning when he felt obliged to challenge a critical assumption of modernity that 'religious experience' was 'the experience of otherness which did not fit into the context of life...' Within modernity, we grow up to assume that religion is a matter of individual religious belief. It has been transformed into a private and subjective experience that is separate from the public sphere of work, politics and law.[4]

Often the thinking and feelings that we have inherited within modern Western society has been shaped by an Enlightenment vision of modernity. This has involved, as Max Weber realised, the disenchantment of nature.[5] Caroline Merchant also recognised this shift with the seventeenth-century Scientific Revolutions from a traditional organic cosmology in which people came to understand themselves through their relationship with living nature to a mechanistic concept in which nature was regarded as a machine – 'the death of nature'. This means that the natural world was *no* longer conceived as being 'alive' and human beings no longer sought to understand themselves through their relationship with nature. Rather within the mechanistic conception, nature was reduced to dead matter and became the subject of scientific knowledge. Progress came to be identified with the control and domination of nature. People were no longer to re-member themselves as part of the world of nature and creation was to be grasped as a relationship of domination.[6]

When the Russian-Yiddish poet and writer, Abraham Reisen, who settled in the United States in 1908, writes 'I think I have lost something on the way, What it is I do not know' and wonders whether he 'should turn back', he could also be talking about the *loss* of meaning that has accompanied modernity. With the mechanistic relationship to nature that has defined Descartes' dominant conception of 'modern philosophy', nature is no longer a source of meaning and value. Rather human beings are alone in a world that has become disenchanted. Human beings alone have become the source of meaning and value and it is their task to impose their meanings upon a natural world that is otherwise bereft of meaning. In the forests, human beings are unable to hear any echo or find any resonance because the forest has become a 'natural resource' that needs to be 'exploited'. It is as timber that can be sold on the market that the forest has 'value'. Alone in the universe, human beings were supposedly 'free' to give their lives whatever meanings they chose. Meanings were not to be discovered, rather they were to be invented within a post-modern culture. With existentialism, freedom, came with recognition that the world was bereft of meaning.[7]

Meaning/s

Abraham Reisen continues his poem 'I've Lost' with a reference to nature that hints at a connection between meaning, nature and love:
'Already the shadows fall from the trees.
Long falls my shadow.
My heart is unquiet. It cries – turn back!
My loss torments me so'.
He recognises that he has lost something but he does not know what. His heart is unquiet – 'It cries – turn back'. This can be a turning back to childhood where meanings might have been lost. In the Jewish tradition, it resonates with a language of *teshuva* – as a turning back to a tradition that speaks of a personal relationship with God. But, within modernity, it is disquiet that can so easily remain unspoken and unnamed within dominant secular traditions that are often unknowingly framed within the secularised terms of a dominant Christian tradition. There can be the thought that 'I think that I have lost something on the way', but this loss cannot easily be recognised within prevailing philosophical traditions.

Within a Cartesian tradition, meaning lies with individual reason, mind and consciousness. When Descartes says 'I think therefore I am', he is framing a concept of personal identity that we learn to take very much for granted within secular culture. When we are asked to point to ourselves, we learn to point to our minds as the place of our being. We are a mind that is supposedly carried around by a body that is imagined as a machine. This may explain why we can feel angry at our bodies when they seem to 'let us down' if we fall ill. This is a gender-specific experience, in that men and women often learn to relate to their bodies in different ways. Within a Cartesian tradition personal identity is often framed for a dominant masculinity as an instrumental relationship between the living mind and a dead body, since bodies are deemed to be part of a dis-enchanted nature.

Often within Western cultures we feel uneasy in our relationship with our bodies and sexualities, as if they can find *no* place in our understanding of ourselves as rational beings. We learn that it is a matter of 'mind over matter' and that if we 'give in' to our emotions it is a sign of weakness since, particularly for men, it is difficult not to experience emotions and feelings as 'feminine' and so as a threatening sign of 'weakness'. Caught between 'mind' and 'body' there is no space for the heart as a source of meaning, love or wisdom. It can take time and attention to *trace* the different ways in which our thinking, feelings and our relationship to body and sexuality have been shaped through the influence of secularised Protestant cultures within Western culture. We are often blind to these connections and thus to the different influences that shape 'common-sense' because we also disavow religious belief.

Within a secular, liberal, moral culture we learn to identify these thoughts and feelings as 'personal' and 'subjective', since we often assume that our freedom lies in being able to think and feel whatever we want. This makes it difficult to identify *how* we have inherited ways of thinking and feeling – philosophies – that we have never been able to identify or name. We are caught within these diverse traditions, often unable to identify how our personal thoughts and feelings have been shaped through particular traditions, histories and cultures. It takes time and attention to explore values that we might have absorbed from our family, ethnic, racial and class backgrounds. Often it is also difficult to disentangle whether we are living out our own dreams or the dreams that our parents had for us. Within a Second Generation post holocaust or migrant experience it is easy for children to feel they need to fulfil their parents' broken dreams.[8]

There are often unrecognised tensions between the secular cultures we have grown into and the Jewish traditions we have learned about. Unless we can *name* these contradictory impulses, we can find our lives segmented in ways that Buber came to question. Sometimes we assume that through will we can reconcile these different traditions, not wanting to recognise that people can feel hurt also because they feel unrecognised by our responses. Buber learned that he had to engage with the *tensions* between Western traditions that were shaped through Greece and the Hebrew traditions that taught a different wisdom.[9] He had to acknowledge that he was shaped through these different traditions that, like Levinas but in a different way, he had to learn to name.

Otherwise we can feel torn, unable to give voice to the tensions we experience. As Abraham Reisen frames an all too familiar predicament:
'So I stand still in the midst of the road,
Tormented, double-tossed.
I have lost something, but I do not know what.
But I know that I've lost'.
This is not something that people easily acknowledge and it marks an

opening. It shows what people have to learn for themselves if they are to remember themselves. It is not a matter of knowledge that can be passed on, as if it were a matter of knowing that God dwells everywhere and of being reminded of a truth that a person might have forgotten. Rather, we have to prepare ourselves to 'take in' what we are reading and though love can be vital in a search for wisdom, we also have to give *time* and *attention* to our reading. Sometimes we assume that we know the answers, but we have to be reminded of a different reality.

Martin Buber recalls the Chasidic question:

'Where is the dwelling of God?'

This is the question with which the Rabbi of Kotzk surprised a number of learned men who happened to be visiting him.

They laughed at him: 'What a thing to ask! Is not the whole world full of his glory?'

Then he answered his own question:

'God dwells wherever man/woman lets God in'.

They thought they knew the answer to the question which is why they laughed at him. But he was opening up the question 'Where is the dwelling of God?' in a different way. The point is that it is not a matter of will alone, as if people can simply decide to let God in. Rather there is a *process* of exploration.

As Abraham Heschel reflects upon the issues of dwelling, recalling metaphors from nature that have so often been lost: 'Prayer is not a stratagem for occasional use, a refuge to resort to now and then. It is rather like an established residence for the innermost self. All things have a home, the bird has a nest, the fox has a hole, the bee has a hive. A soul without prayer is a soul without a home....For the soul, home is where prayer is...'

This can encourage us to feel at home in our prayers even if we find it difficult to pray.[10] As there is a connection between philosophy and love, so there is a relationship between love and prayer that needs to be explored: 'Through the greatness of Your love I enter Your house'. In our time, we have also to recall the inscription on the walls of a cellar in Cologne, Germany, where Jews hid from the Nazis:

'I believe in the sun even when it is not shining.

I believe in love even when feeling it not.

I believe in God even when He is silent'.

Victor Frankl explores his own survival in a concentration camp: 'What was really needed was a fundamental change in our attitude towards life....We needed to stop asking about the meaning of life, and instead to think of ourselves as those who were being questioned by life – daily and hourly'.[11]

Hearing Experience

Sometimes we can hear what someone has said but find it difficult to listen to what they have to say. It might bring up unexpected emotions that we do not want to encounter in ourselves. We might resent it if they say 'you have not heard what I have had to say' as they recognise that, for whatever reason, we have *not* been able to 'take in' what they have been saying. For some people, it might make little difference because they might never have had the experience of being listened to in their families. A woman might feel that for her whole life, her family never really listened to her. At the time, she did not realise it and it was only later that, in a friendship, she experienced what it was like 'to be heard – listened to' in a way that *allowed* her to feel a sense of disappointment and loss. She realised for the first time what she had been *missing* in the contact she had with her parents as she was growing up, but she had never realised what it was. It was not that she did not have the words to express what she was missing, but that she had little recognition of what she was missing.[12]

Because she was not used to being listened to she was surprised when it happened to her. She realised that, in her own relationships, she often found it difficult to listen because she was more focused upon saying what she had to say herself. It was a new experience for her to be listened to and in time it helped her to learn what it meant to listen to others. Somehow, because she had never really been listened to herself, she had not really learned what it meant to listen to others. She had not had the experience herself but now she had, she knew more about what she valued in relationships. She was grateful to be in a relationship in which she felt she could be heard as well as listening to her partner.

She also knew, as Buber learned, that it was a matter of listening to what was said as well as to what remained unspoken. The 'event' of the young man coming to see him from which Buber learned showed that it was not a matter of language alone. Within the larger secular culture that tended to diminish spiritual needs it could be difficult for the young man to give *voice* to what was troubling him. He might have felt uneasy or embarrassed to frame his distress in spiritual language, somehow wanting Buber to recognise what he was asking for, even if he could not put this in words. It might not have been something Buber could offer because he could not identify the situation as being 'religious', and so assumed that his friendliness would allow the young man to bring forward and express whatever he needed to express. But, at some level, the young man felt that he had not been heard, even if he did not express the fact. He might not have even known that he had been disappointed in the encounter because he might not have known himself in this way.[13]

We might be tempted to say that the young man had not yet learned *how* to listen to himself, but rather than think about this in psychological and individual terms, we need to recognise the ways in which his relationship to himself as much as his relationship with others was shaped within the terms of the larger secular culture. Within an Enlightenment vision of modernity, young men, in particular, can be positioned through an 'external' relationship to themselves, as if they are observers set apart from their own experience. Through the identification of masculinity with a notion of reason radically separated from nature, men often learn to assume a distance from their emotional lives, especially when emotions are interpreted as 'feminine' and thus as signs of weakness and threats to male identities.

This can make it difficult for young men to listen to their inner emotional lives since they assume that their masculinity is affirmed through shaping their emotions according to what is expected of them within the dominant patriarchal culture. For example, a young man does not want to acknowledge feelings of sadness if they reflect negatively on his masculinity. He does not want to know about his melancholy, let alone give voice to it with others, because it could work to demean/diminish him in the eyes of others.[14]

If this means that young men have little experience of 'listening to themselves' because they have grown up within new capitalisms to be so concerned with the image they project to others, this can make it difficult for them to respond to the unspoken emotional needs of others. It can also make it hard for them to give voice to their own emotional needs and narrate what they have been experiencing. Often, they learn to distance themselves from their own experience and can find it difficult to recognise a need to develop more *contact* with themselves through an inner relationship with self.

The difficulties that young men experience are often 'covered over' within a post-modern culture that can encourage both young men as well as young women to identify with work and assume distance from themselves. They might feel sceptical when learning to identify diverse discourses as, for example, thinking about relationships within the family and whether they feel that they have been heard or not. This can immediately be identified in relation to the teachings of Freud and a psycho-analytic discourse. Within post-modern theories, people have become very adept at making these identifications *without* appreciating how, in this respect at least, post-modernism tends to reproduce positionality that echoes rather than challenges an Enlightenment rationalism.[15]

Within post-modern philosophies, the notion of 'experience' has been rendered suspect since it is assumed to be an effect of discourse. Any appeal to experience is taken to be an appeal to a 'reality' that supposedly exists beyond the reach of language. But since reality is assumed to be discursive, there is little space for recognising tension between 'language' and 'experience'. This is a resonance I appreciated in feminist theories and the later work of Wittgenstein. In their different ways, they appreciated that speech can be *empty* and that often we can be dis/connected from what we are saying. Even as we talk, we can appreciate that we are failing to make contact, as if the words fall into the space that has opened up between ourselves and our interlocutor. But we can fail to appreciate that this is happening, especially if we are not used to being listened to, for we can fail to discern a difference.[16]

If we have never really learned to listen to ourselves, it can be difficult to hear others. Education can often leave people feeling dis-placed and unable to re-member themselves and narrate their emotional histories and experience. Post-modern philosophies can help to question a rationalism that encourages people to think that they can assume a universal voice of reason and so speak from nowhere. Uneasy about a rationalist universalism, they encourage people to clarify the 'positions' from which they are speaking. This involves a degree of critical thinking and self-awareness, whereby people can learn to identify their own cultural, class, gender, 'race' and ethnic histories that leaves them with particular backgrounds and traditions.

An awareness of diversity helps to question the authority that a dominant masculinity has assumed in speaking for others. As people become aware of their diverse histories and cultures, so they feel a need to voice their *own* experience and be listened to, rather than spoken for. But this involves being ready to investigate the particularities of one's own history rather than to subsume it into an assimilationist culture. Sometimes, it is only when people feel that others are interested in listening to what they have to say that they can find the appropriate words. Often it is only through establishing relationships of trust that people *can* learn to speak their minds.[17]

Personal / Impersonal

Is it helpful to think that Jewish traditions have consistently articulated a personal relationship with God? How are we to think the 'personal' within a post-modern culture that has become un/easy about personal and emotional life? Does this connect to a recognition that Jewish thought, in Buber even if not so clearly in Levinas, is relational? Does this help us to mark a helpful distinction between Greek traditions that tend towards the impersonal and so an impersonal relationship with God, while Jewish traditions tend to sustain a *personal* relationship with God? If these are helpful questions do they hang together in useful ways, or do we think they need to be approached quite differently, acknowledging the very different ways in which traditions have learned to think about the relationship between 'personal' and 'impersonal'.

Possibly it can be helpful to begin with a question – how can people learn to establish a more personal relationship with themselves? A person might know that difficulties they have in this regard are somehow connected to traumatic histories they have experienced. A man who was forced to leave Germany and take refuge with his family in Britain when the Nazis confirmed their position of power might feel haunted by this past in ways he finds difficult to articulate. He might recognise that whenever he sees the instruction 'Keep off the grass' he is reminded of signs in his childhood that read 'No Jews can sit on the benches'. He acknowledges that it would be 'paranoid' to feel this all the time, but also hears a resonance of the past. Aware that he was born in the same year as Ann Frank and that their family went to Amsterdam while his parents chose to move to London, he can be haunted by the images of children who died in the camps, knowing how easily he could have shared their fate. It is difficult to get in touch with these feelings, but there are times when they surface on their own and he has to deal with them.

Such a man might want to feel more contact with his own history, but also fears opening himself up in this way. Possibly having retired from a profession, he feels a need to occupy himself with study, partly because he fears what might happen if he has 'too much time on his hands'. Part of him wants to learn in order to be able to prevent his history from coming back to him. He might *want* to feel more emotional connection in his relationship but at the same time find it difficult to show his love easily, having grown up in a generation that felt that closeness comes through the sharing of interests rather than in the sharing of feelings. He might also regret that his partner does not share his passion for Judaism and knows that he has to develop more shared interests with her, if their relationship is to be sustained. He wants more personal contact but at the same time *fears* what closeness might bring. Sometimes, in listening to these dilemmas, we can be helped to name our own and so gain a deeper trust in our own experience. This can help us, at the same time, to recognise ways in which this trust can be sustained or undermined within different Western philosophical traditions that we might have unknowingly inherited.

Languages of Soul

There is a famous parable within Jewish tradition that is often repeated. Rabbi Zusya of Hanipol famously said: 'In the coming world they will not ask me "Why were you not Moses?" but "Why were you not Zusya?"' If Zusya had spent all his life worrying that he was not Moses he could have ended up feeling bad about himself. But it could be said that if he had struggled to emulate Moses then even if he had not fulfilled his ideal, he would at least have achieved more than he might otherwise have done. Emulation has its place but it can also have its dangers, for it can make it harder for people to appreciate their *own* qualities – the very qualities that they have to learn to express in order to be Zusya.

If someone has grown up within a Protestant moral culture to feel inadequate as they are, possibly because they have an evil nature, having been 'born into sin' as a Christian tradition might frame it, they might constantly struggle to *be* other than they are. As Max Weber appreciated it, this is the way that the Protestant ethic, working within a secular culture, encourages people to feel constantly that they should have achieved more. Whatever their accomplishments might have been, they can feel haunted by a feeling that they should have done better. Yet often such people will feel unable to identify and name the source of their feelings, assuming that they are individual and personal. Rather than being able to identify some of the historical and cultural sources that help to shape the ways they think and feel about themselves, they will blame themselves for their own inadequacies, comparing themselves unfavourably with others.

In the coming world when they ask 'Why were you not Zusya?', it might take a special awareness for someone to appreciate what they are being asked. They might dismiss the question with the notion 'Of course I was Zusya, who else could I have been?' But this is to misunderstand the question, for it is about spending your time on earth allowing yourself to *become* Zusya. For example, you might have been so concerned to be a 'good daughter' to your parents, that you followed their dreams rather than your own. You might even have mistaken their dreams for your own because you never allowed yourself time to explore your own hopes and dreams.

Said the Koretzer Rabbi: 'We recite in the Shema: "These things...shall be upon your heart. Repeat them to your children...." When these words go forth from your heart, they will truly influence your children for good....' Again these are not things that you can decide as a matter of will. When Jeremiah 29:12–14 says "When you seek Me, you will find Me, if you search for Me with all your heart. I shall let you find Me, says the Lord," he again recognises the importance of the heart'. This is in line with the saying in Exodus Rabbah: 'A person must purify their heart before they pray'. This guidance has been difficult to heed within an Enlightenment vision of modernity that has replaced a language of soul and heart with a concern for thought and reason. Even though Jacob Needleman wrote a text entitled *The Heart of Philosophy*, it was written as a protest against a tradition of 'modern philosophy' that had, in diverse ways, lost its heart. Reflecting upon human identity as a relationship between mind and body left *no* space for the heart as a source of knowledge and little recognition of the spiritual practices that might be called upon to 'open the heart'. Even though the Greek tradition recognised philosophy as a practice of love, it was often sceptical about the place of the heart.

The Hasidic tradition, in the words of Mendel of Kotzk, offers advice that has been emptied of meaning within modernity. But somehow it is still able to speak to us, possibly as a *reminder* that Jewish tradition valued the dignity of human labour that was rarely acknowledged by the Greeks who left labour to slaves: 'He who is about to pray should learn from a common labourer, who sometimes takes a whole day to prepare for a job. A wood-cutter, who spends most of the day sharpening the saw and only the last hour cutting the wood, has earned his day's wage'. The Jewish tradition is full of advice to enable one to pray from the heart. It understands that this is not something that people achieve easily. As Maimonides says: 'To serve God out of love is to fulfill the Torah....But this is a high level of piety, and not every sage attains it'.

Shmuel Hugo Bergman, the Czech-Israeli philosopher and Zionist who taught for many years at the Hebrew University, reflects upon the knowledge of experience when he talks about prayer. He says that 'The one who prays, knows, with the knowledge of experience, that beyond the visible dimensions of the world there is a hidden dimension of our existence in which something of the significance of a man's being is revealed to him, revealed to a greater or lesser degree, in keeping with the strength of the communion. It is a matter of experience, and experience, as is well known, is not debatable' (p.357).[18]

Valuing Experience

William James' *Varieties of Religious Experience* remains a vital text for those concerned with illuminating the different levels of experience. He is concerned with religious experiences and ways in which they are voiced within different religious and spiritual traditions. James was sceptical of the reductionism he recognised in Freud's approach to religious belief. He would have appreciated Bergman's awareness that 'something of the significance' of a person's being is revealed to them. This suggests that meanings are not only invented, as post-modern theories would present it, but that they can also be discovered through establishing a deeper contact with ourselves. In some way, Freud appreciated that the deeper the relationship the individual is able to establish with their unconscious lives, the more universal their insights will prove to be. In this way, he challenges the dismissive attitude towards subjective experience that we have inherited within a science-oriented culture that too easily identifies 'knowledge' with 'objectivity'.[19]

Psychoanalysis appreciates that the way people explore their feelings can help them to acknowledge their values – what matters to them. A young woman might never have mourned for her father because she thought she had a distant and uncaring relationship with him. She might have told herself 'how can I have feelings for him if I never really knew him?' At the same time, she might be surprised at the level of her feelings and it might only be as she allows herself to express her anger at his death that she can get *in touch* with her feelings of loss. This can be a difficult process, as can a person's relationship with spirituality even if Freud rarely acknowledges this. As Kafka put it: 'Many people prowl round Mount Sinai. Their speech is blurred, either they are garrulous or they shout or they are taciturn. But none of them comes straight down a broad, newly made, smooth road that does its own part in making one's strides long and swifter'.[20]

Kafka recognises the difficulties of language and mistrusts those who would speak too easily about spirituality. The road is often difficult and people have to find their *own* way as they deepen their contact with themselves. Again this is a difficult notion within a post-modern culture that often values only the surface of things. We have to be ready to listen to what people have to say and attempt to respond, as Simone Weil recognised, from a similar *level* in our own experience.

In the Sabbath morning service we hear the prayer 'Purify our hearts to serve You in truth'. This resonates with the call 'She should tell the truth and speak it in her heart'. There is a connection between truth-telling and the heart that can be difficult for us to appreciate within a modernity that has identified 'truth' with reason and the mind. We learn to *distrust* the heart because it is so often identified with emotions that are interpreted in Kantian terms as temptations that draw us away from the path of reason. As there is a different vision of emotional life between Hellenistic and Jewish traditions, though they learn a great deal from each other, there is also a different concept of embodied life. Within a dominant Christian tradition that often echoes a Hellenistic tradition in its separation from Judaism, the body is identified with sexuality and the 'sins of the flesh'. A radical distinction has been drawn between spirit and matter, where spirit and mind have been deemed to be sources of goodness while bodies identified with the 'sins of the flesh' have been regarded as evil. As Daniel Boyarin has explored in *Carnal Israel,* this became a crucial source in Christian antisemitism that treated Judaism as incapable of a dis/embodied spirituality.[21]

To quote Simeon ben Lakish: 'To him who wishes to defile himself, the doors are open; to him who wishes to purify himself, aid will be given'. Maimonides calls for something similar when he says 'Wake up and think about your actions. Do not mistake shadows for reality and waste your life chasing after trivial things which do not really help you'. It can be helpful to read this next to Ezekiel 36:26: 'A new heart I will give you and a new spirit set within you. I shall take the heart of stone from your bodies, and give you instead a heart that lives'. The body is not shamed though it is recognised that the heart *can* be hardened against experience. But there is also a sense that, even though people are free to make their own lives, there is a *judgement* recalling Buber's meeting with the young man that cannot be put off until the end of time. Rather as Franz Rosenzweig recognised: 'The shofar blown on New Year's Day....stamps the day as a day of judgement. The judgement usually thought of as at the end of time is here placed in the immediate present'.[22]

Rather than the ethics of self-denial that within a Protestant tradition has taught the sinfulness of pleasure as a distraction, taking people away from acting out of a sense of duty, the Jerusalem Talmud quotes Rav as saying 'A person will have to give account on the Judgement Day of every good thing which they could have enjoyed but did not' (p.373). As Rabbi Nachman of Bratslav also says: 'There are men who suffer terrible distress and are unable to tell what they feel in their hearts, and they go their way and suffer and suffer. But if they meet one with a laughing face, he can revive them with his joy. And to revive a person is no slight thing' (p.373–4).

Visions of Freedom

Maimonides insists: 'Free will is granted to every person. If they desire to incline towards the good way and be righteous, they have the power to do so; and if they desire to incline towards the unrighteous way and be a wicked person, they also have the power to do so. Give no place in your minds to that which is asserted by many of the ignorant: namely that the Holy One, blessed be He, desires that a person from their birth be either righteous or wicked. Since the power of doing good or evil is in our own hands, and since all the wicked deeds which we have committed have been committed with our full consciousness, it befits us to turn in penitence and to forsake our evil deed'.[23]

Though Maimonides sustains a rationalist tradition within Judaism, his vision of reason, freedom and morality is different from the Kantian ethical tradition. As Erich Fromm appreciated, 'there is little of a sadistic superego or of a masochistic ego in the Jewish concept of sin and repentance....people are free and independent. They are even independent from God. Hence their sin is their sin, and their return is their return, and there is no reason for self-accusatory submission'. Fromm recognises that 'The meaning of sin as missing the right road corresponds to the term for repent, which is *shuv*, meaning "to return"...A person who repents is a person who "returns". They return to the right way, to God, to themselves'.[24]

Louis Jacobs also points out that *khet*, a weaker term for sin, comes from a root meaning 'to miss'. As he points out: 'The word is used, for example, of an archer whose arrows fail to hit the target. *Khet* denotes failure to follow the good path, to the lack of character or staying power which prevents a man from arriving at the goal he has set himself....' Jacobs contrasts this with *avon* that 'comes from a root meaning "to be twisted", "to be crooked". It refers to the man whose course in life is deflected from the pursuit of the good...It refers also to the twist in a man's character which seems to impel him to do wrong...' (*Days of Awe*, p.12).

As Adin Steinsaltz, responsible for his own translation and interpretation of the Talmud, recognises: 'Remoteness from God is, of course, not a matter of physical distance, but a spiritual problem of relationship. The person who is not going along the right path is not further away from God but is, rather, a person whose soul is oriented towards and relating with other subjects. The starting point of repentance is precisely this fulcrum point upon which a person turns himself about, away from the pursuit of what he craves, and confronts his desire to approach God; this is the moment of conversion, the crucial moment of repentance' (p.52). There is *always* the freedom to return but again it is also a matter of awareness, as the Chasidic saying recognises 'People cannot find redemption until they see the flaws in their own souls and try to efface them...We can be redeemed only to the extent that we see ourselves' (p.122).[25]

To understand the process through which people lose connection with their own inner light and thus their souls, Rav Kook recognises that 'Though no specific sin or sins of the past come to mind, someone may feel that she is greatly pained, that she is filled with iniquity, that the light of God does not shine upon her. There is no "willing spirit" within her; her heart is calloused; her soul's qualities and characteristics do not go along the straight and desired way that leads to fulfilment in life........She is ashamed of herself and she is aware that God is not within her, and this is her great anguish.....From this spiritual bitterness, repentance emerges as healing by a skillful physician. The sensing of repentance and a deep knowledge of it...comes and streams into the soul' (*Days of Awe*, p.169).[26]

At the same time, we can recall the words of Victor Frankl who writes 'We who lived in concentration camps can remember the men who walked through the huts comforting others, giving away their last piece of bread. They may have been few in number, but they offer sufficient proof that everything can be taken from people but one thing: the last of the human freedoms – to choose one's attitude in any given set of circumstances, to choose one's own way'.

3

Reading, Texts and the
Human Body

Context/s

We read Jewish and Hellenistic texts at a particular moment in time that influences the way we address them. We are inevitably reading them in the shadow of the Holocaust, even though we might carry little awareness of the ways in which this historical catastrophe has shaped our thinking and feeling. In a remarkable essay written as early as 1934 and entitled *Reflections on the Philosophy of Hitlerism*, the French-Jewish philosopher Emanuel Levinas already recognised the urgency of two questions – What is Nazism? And what is its relation to Western rationality? – to the future tasks of thought. Rather than treating Nazism as an aberration, a moment of madness that had captured German culture and politics, Levinas recognised a relationship between Nazism and modernity, something that Zygmunt Bauman was to explore in quite different terms in *Modernity And The Holocaust*. Years before Nazism's genocidal ambitions were to take shape, Levinas exposed the exterminatory logic of its metaphysics. More importantly, he illuminates the troubling relationship between these metaphysics, largely shaped within the terms of a Greek philosophical tradition, and the philosophical categories governing Western tradition.[1]

For Levinas, Western tradition's vulnerability to Nazism is rooted in the historical denigration of the body. The vulnerability of Western philosophy to 'evil' is concentrated in the 'Judeo-Christian leitmotif of freedom' ('Reflections on the Philosophy of Hitlerism', translated by Sean Hand in *Critical Inquiry*, *17* (1990) p.66), as expressed in the Christian doctrine of the soul. It has to do with the ways in which a Western tradition that has largely been shaped through a Platonic/Christian tradition has treated the body as a site of sin and temptation, to be identified with the 'sins of the flesh'. As Levinas recognises, the Christian hierarchy of soul over body, whose legacy is clearly visible in the French Enlightenment's claim to the sovereignty of reason, creates a permanent *distance* between spirit and 'physical, psychological and social matter' (p.66). According to Levinas, who sustains a strong monotheistic critique of myth, the cardinal virtue of such a doctrine is that it liberates the human being from the suffocating grasp of mythic nature, so that their possibilities are no longer legislated in advance by 'a series of restless powers that seethe within him and already push him down a determined path' (p.66).

Growing up with the terms of a secular modernity that has largely been shaped as a secularised form of Christianity, we learn to treat the body not as 'part of' who we are, but rather as separated out as part of dis/enchanted nature. Rather than recognising the body as a source of wisdom and knowledge, the body is *disdained* through its identification with 'animality' that needs to be controlled, through a relationship of dominance between 'mind' over 'matter'. We might catch ourselves thinking in terms of 'mind' and 'matter' without appreciating the source of these philosophical categories. For as 'matter' the body is deemed to be no longer part of a nature that is 'alive', but rather as part of the 'death of nature'.[2]

With the seventeenth-century Scientific Revolutions, the body came to be imagined in mechanistic terms so that moral terms ceased to be available outside of religious discourse. We have learned to accept a distanced relationship with our bodies since, within the terms of orthodox medical practice, they are treated as 'objects' of medical knowledge. Traditionally, as children, we were silenced in the presence of doctors, having learned only to speak if spoken to. Experience of our own bodies is traditionally devalued as 'subjective' and so potentially as an unwelcome interference in the 'objective' gaze of the doctor. This experience is often gender-specific since our relationship with bodies is gender-specific, but people can often identify the relationships of medical power and authority as they feel that asking questions was traditionally experienced as a challenge to doctors. 'Just leave it to me' was the implicit message, 'since where you might have "experience" what I possess is "objective knowledge"'.[3]

The example of health and the ways in which allopathic traditions have assumed a sharp distinction between 'mind' and 'body', thus framing orthodox Western medical practices within modernity, remains vital in helping us to appreciate contrasts between 'modern' and 'pre-modern' through our own experiences of embodiment. As we live in a period of crisis in relation to a dominant medical paradigm, we can draw upon our own ambivalent feelings towards alternative health practices. The relationship between philosophy and medicine remains vital, not least for an appreciation of Maimonides and the crucial teachings of Greek, Islamic and Jewish traditions. It is often through medical practice that we can uncover different thinking in relation to our bodies. For example, in Plato and Aristotle, wherever philosophy is linked to the 'health of the mind' it is in the context of ethics and living a good life, and this is deemed to be inseparable from physical health, something that it often is in Hippocrates.[4]

As the body is dismissed as being the seat of the threat of sin and temptation so there was a radical split within a dominant Greco-Christian tradition between sexuality and spirituality. The body was defined as 'animal' and thus as uncivilised and a *threat* to the possibilities of a spiritual life. It was only through controlling the body and 'rising above it' that people could hope to attain spirituality. As the body came to be disavowed so bodily thoughts, feelings and desires could *not* be acknowledged. Within the dominant Christian discourses the body was denied and was identified as Jewish – as Daniel Boyarin explores in *Carnal Israel* – thus explaining the impossibility of there being a Jewish spirituality since it was chained to the flesh.

While Levinas recognises in *Reflections on the Philosophy of History* that the first break with a tradition of liberal autonomy that shaped a Kantian conception of modernity comes with Marx's assertion of the priority of being over consciousness, this break remains partial, inasmuch as 'to become conscious of one's social situation is, even for Marx, to free oneself of the fatalism entailed by that situation' (p.67). What Levinas wants to stress is that the decisive break with the Western concept of what is human can occur only when 'the situation to which he was bound was not added to him but formed the very foundation of his being' (p.67). In *Recovering The Self: Morality And Social Theory*, I attempted to explore some of the limits in Marx's conception of embodied labour and the way in which he remained partially *trapped* within an Enlightenment rationalism, while at the same time questioning its vision of disembodied knowledge. If Marx had unwittingly been drawing upon Jewish sources and consciously wanted to disavow in his appreciation of creative labour as a means through which human beings could become more fulfilled, this might be an interesting new territory to explore.[5]

For Levinas it is not through the example of medicine but through a more particular discussion of physical pain that he shows the impossibility of the spirit escaping the body entirely. This is a theme that Wittgenstein explores in *Philosophical Investigations*, in which the example of pain is central to this questioning of a Cartesian inheritance that separates mind and body. Through an exploration of physical pain, Levinas shows, according to Cohen, the ineluctable 'rivetedness' of the spirit to the body. As Josh Cohen notes in *Interrupting Auschwitz*, this is the term Levinas uses in his phenomenological description of the impotent desire to escape being in *De L'Evasion* – his essay of the following year.

But this can suggest two things being interconnected and thus can also lead to thinking being constrained within a Cartesian context. Levinas says rather: 'The body is not only a happy or unhappy accident that relates us to the implacable world of matter. *Its adherence to the Self is of value in itself.* It is an adherence that *one does not escape*' (Levinas' emphasis) (p.68). According to Levinas, the West's vulnerability to the ideological and political onslaught of Nazism lies in its *unwillingness* to confront this inescapable fact. It could be through a reconsideration of the relationship of Jewish philosophy to Western culture that recognisable resources might be discovered, as Levinas holds: 'To be truly oneself does not mean taking flight once more above contingent events that always remain foreign to the Self's freedom; on the contrary, it means becoming aware of the ineluctable chain that is unique to our bodies and, above all, accepting this chaining' (p.69).

Some seven years before Nazism's genocidal ambitions were to take their ultimate form, Levinas, as Cohen recognises, 'exposed the already exterministic logic of its metaphysics'. More importantly still, he illuminates the troubling relation of this metaphysics to the governing philosophical categories of Western tradition: 'Nazism's corporealisation of spirit constitutes less a demonic aberration than a strictly symmetrical *inversion* of this tradition. The symmetry between these radically opposed metaphysics points to their shared structure of truth; the elevated Absolute of the Western soul is reflected in the degraded Absolute of the Nazi body. This inversion, moreover, as a permanent possibility within Western rationalsm itself, is inseparable from its history' (p.7). If we are to question Cohen's somewhat abstract Hegelian framing to open up a more complex relationship between Jewish philosophy and Western culture, we can still appreciate 'the inadequacy to the imperative of an appeal simply to restore the violated rule of reason' (p.7).

The significance of Levinas' essay was also appreciated by Giorgio Agamben who, towards the end of *Homo Sacer*, his study of the logic of political sovereignty in the West, credits the essay with being even today 'the most valuable contribution to an understanding of National Socialism' (p.151). As Cohen seems to learn from Agamben, 'if western traditions condition Nazism's metaphysics, then Auschwitz imposes the demand for a thinking of truth which escapes the economy of body and spirit into which Christianity and its demonic other are locked'.[6] It is difficult to go along with Cohen, however, when he seems to be saying, somewhat in contrast to Levinas who hints unambiguously at the complicity of Heidegger's ontology with Nazi politics, that 'If Heidegger provides the point of entry for such thinking, it is because his account of the "indissoluble cohesion" of transcendence and finitude (or of Being and time) rigorously refuses the temptation of biologism' (p.8). Though Heidegger's insights around the recovery of being can help question a Cartesian dualism of mind and body that has shaped modernity, there is a way in which his focus upon an awareness of death and thus on mortality remains implicitly tied to a fundamentally Christian vision of original sin. We might well be able to learn to think differently through Jewish philosophies that, as I have already shown, often resist discourses of sin.

As Agamben recognises, every political community founds itself on the paradox of inclusive exclusion, defining itself through that which it *casts out*. This is no different from the ways in which Western culture, that has traditionally defined itself through its relationship to Christianity, did so through its exclusions of Judaism and Islam. But Western culture and Christianity have often insisted upon appropriating and identifying as their own, ideas, for example, from Genesis and the Psalms that were often identified as 'the Bible' when they were to be welcomed but 'the Old Testament' when they were to be rejected. This complex relationship was shaped differently within different Christianities. During the Protestant Reformation, for example, 'the Old Testament' was to be reclaimed by Luther, which he then followed with a vicious antisemitic discourse when Jewish communities refused to convert to Protestantism.[7] The terms of inclusion and exclusion, as Agamben frames them, have been renegotiated over time, but Christianity has retained considerable power within Europe to appropriate what it has needed for its own purposes.

Texts

As Molly Tuby, a contemporary Jungian analytical psychologist concerned with the analytical study of Biblical narratives, has written: 'Projection is the human propensity to find a scapegoat and to see in that scapegoat all the unpleasant things we fail to recognise in ourselves. This mechanism is one of the few unchallenged laws on which whole schools of psychology agree, ie, if unconscious ideas and emotions are not made conscious, they are projected...'. This is an insight that Freud rediscovered for the West when he said: 'We hate the criminal and deal severely with him because we view in his deed, as in a distorting mirror, our own criminal instincts'. The Baal Shem Tov had long recognised this when he said that 'Sinners are mirrors. When we see faults in them, we must realise that they only reflect evil in us' (*Days Of Awe*, p.450).

Within the terms of a dominant Christian antisemitism, there was an abiding sense that Jews could *not* escape from their bodies, as if this escape from embodiment did not have to be argued for because bodies were *already* identified with 'animality' and thus with the figure of the Devil. As these discourses were accepted as 'commonsense' so they could also shape the terms in which Jewish philosophies sought to defend themselves and frame their relationships with Greek and later Christian traditions. As Zwi Werblowsky recognises in his introduction to Julius Guttmann's *Philosophies of Judaism*, 'The very title of the book contains a programme, and betrays its basic orientation – that of the philosopher of religion...The implied assumption of all such philosophising is that there exists such spheres of reality as art, law and religion, about which one can philosophise'.

He goes on to explain: 'In order to be true to his calling, therefore, the philosopher of religion must hold views on the nature of religion. What is it that gives religion its specific character, making it "religion", as distinct from ethics, morality or art? Guttman's great master, Hermann Cohen, started with a neo-Kantian ethical conception of religion, but in his later work tried increasingly to grasp the specificity of the religious ideal, in which he proceeds by way of an interpretation of Judaism' (p.viii).[8] He also discerns the influence of Schleiermacher and Rudolf Otto's *The Idea of The Holy*, in which they claimed the right of religion to be objectively considered as something *sui generis*, rather than as a phenomenon to be explained through Freud or Marx, through psychology or sociology.[9] He also says that 'perhaps the most important and also the most subtle influence on Guttman's thinking was that of Husserl, whose phenomenology claimed to provide a method of knowing those *a priori* elements and structures which were present, as original data, in human consciousness' (p.viii).[10] This helps focus a concern on religious/spiritual experience in its own terms, something William James, who was sceptical about Freud's reductive accounts of religious belief, is also seeking in his *Varieties of Religious Experience* that so strongly influenced Wittgenstein.

For Werblowsky, it is clear that Guttman 'is not too much concerned with Jewish philosophy or Jewish philosophers, as with the *philosophy of Judaism*. Judaism is something given, a datum, something that is there *before* Jewish philosophers begin to philosophise about it. "Jewish" philosophy consists of the process in which Jewish philosophers throughout the generations take the fact of Jewish religion as they find it, and then "elucidate and justify it"'. I am not sure whether this remains an option *after* the Shoah or whether we are bound to bring different, unsettling questions that Jewish rationalist traditions would have refused. Weblowsky acknowledges that Guttman nowhere explicitly states his own views regarding the essence of Judaism, a phrase Leo Baeck also invokes as the title of his major work, and that 'as an historian, rather than a creative systematic thinker, he preferred his "phenomenology of Judaism" to remain implicit in his work' (p.ix).

Werblowsky does recognise, however, that Judaism draws upon a variety of diverse sources and traditions and was in constant dialogue with Islamic and Christian writings, though as he expresses is in somewhat essentialist terms, 'yet always stamped what it received with its individual and specifically Jewish character'. He also recognises that Guttman retained a rationalist vision of philosophy that explains the *exclusion* from his work of such significant phenomena as mystical and kabbalistic thinking. If this is thinking that is deemed to be 'beyond reason', we have to wonder about its connection with the human body, emotional life and sexuality that could no longer be well reflected upon with such a conception of philosophical reason. It was this very conception of philosophy that was put in crisis and links to Adorno's demand that 'A new categorical imperative has been imposed by Hitler on unfree mankind: to arrange their thoughts and actions so that Auschwitz will not repeat itself, so that nothing similar will happen' (*Negative Dialectic*, p.465).[11]

Inside / Outside

According to Guttman, 'The Jewish people did not begin to philosophise because of an irresistible urge to do so. They received philosophy from outside sources, and the history of Jewish philo-sophy is a history of the successive absorptions of foreign ideas which were then transformed and adapted to specific Jewish points of view' (p.3). We have to explore whether this is a helpful characterisation and whether it is even true of the practice that Guttman adopts. He thinks that such a process first took place during the Hellenistic period. But is he right when he claims that 'Judaeo-Hellenistic philosophy is so thoroughly imbued with the Greek spirit' that it may be 'regarded, historically speaking, as merely a chapter in the development of Greek thought as a whole?' The fact that it disappeared quickly, leaving behind no permanent impact upon Judaism, does not mean that the encounter between Judaism and Hellenism has not had enduring effects upon the ways Judaism has understood its relationship to the West. This was vital to Buber's early twentieth-century addresses on the revival of Judaism collected in *On Judaism* (Schocken Books, New York 1972, ed. Nahum N. Glatzer).[12]

According to Guttman, philosophy had a more enduring effect in the Middle Ages: 'It was Greek philosophy at second hand, for the philosophical revival took place within the orbit of Islamic culture and was heavily indebted to Islamic culture, which, in its turn, derived from Greek systems of thought' (p.3). There is also an issue, not directly addressed through Guttman's approach, about the way Islamic culture was from Mohammed's earliest writings engaged in a dialogue with Judaism. This has been an issue ever since Abraham Geiger's 1833 study, *Was hat Mohammed aus dem Judentume aufgenommen?* (reprinted in 1902, though there was also a later reaction in favour of Christianity as the main source of Mohammed's inspiration). To this, the great influence of Wellhausen gave a lasting impetus.[13]

According to Guttman, 'Since the days of antiquity, Jewish philosophy was essentially a philosophy of Judaism'. Even in the Middle Ages, philosophy rarely transcended its religious centre. 'The religious orientation constitutes the distinctive character of Jewish philosophy, whether it was concerned with using philosophical ideas to establish or justify Jewish doctrines, or with reconciling the contradictions between religious truth and scientific truth' (p.4). As he explains it: 'Armed with the authority of supernatural revelation, religion lays claim to an unconditional truth of its own, and thereby becomes a problem for philosophy' (p.4). He also makes clear that 'earlier periods did not attempt to differentiate between the methods of philosophy and religion, but sought to reconcile the content of their teachings' (p.4). Explaining the direction of his thinking, Guttman holds that 'Appearing for the first time in Jewish Hellenism, this type of philosophy, though not productive of original ideas.....passed to Christianity, was transmitted to Islam, from whence it returned, in the Middle Ages, to Judaism' (p.4).

According to Guttman, 'The distinctiveness of biblical religion is due to its ethical conception of the personality of God'. But he tends to read this 'ethical conception of the personality of God' through a framework drawn from Kant when he says 'The God of the prophets is exemplified by his moral will; he is demanding and commanding, promising and threatening, the absolutely free ruler of man and nature'. He acknowledges that it took considerable time for this conception of God to develop, saying: 'It took a long time before he could shed his primitive attributes as a nature God, making it possible to think of him in purely personal terms' (p.5). But what does it mean to think of God in personal terms?

As Guttman explains it: 'the decisive feature of monotheism is that it is not grounded in an abstract idea of God, but in an intensely powerful divine will which rules history'. But the personal seems to go *beyond* Kant's framework of an impersonal ethic, as Guttman seems to acknowledge when he says that 'This ethical voluntarism implies a thoroughly personalistic conception of God, and determines the specific character of the relationship between God and man (woman)'. Seeming to draw upon Buber, he says 'This relationship is an ethical-voluntaristic one between two moral personalities, between an "I" and a "Thou". As God imposes his will upon that of man, so man becomes aware of the nature of the relationship to God' (p.6).

According to Guttman, 'The omnipotence of the divine will appears most clearly when the world itself is looked upon as nothing but the work of this will. The Creator-God is not part of it, or a link in the world; but God and world face each other as Creator and creature' (p.6). This trait becomes increasingly distinct through the evolution of the biblical idea of creation: 'At first, creation was conceived of as a kind of "making" and "fashioning" by God; in the end, it is the Creator's word that calls the world into existence. The divine act of will is sufficient for bringing everything into being'. But there remains a tension in the way Guttman describes this evolution *with* the personal character of the relationship between people and God. This is not clarified when he draws a radical contrast between 'The personalist character of biblical religion' and 'basically impersonal, forms of spiritual and universal religion that underlies all mysticism and pantheism' (p.6). As Guttman insists on the contrast: 'God is not conceived by them as a sovereign will ruling the universe, but as the hidden source from which all being emanates, or as the inner life-force which pulsates throughout the cosmos' (p.7).

As Guttman puts it: 'Neither pantheism nor mysticism knows a personal, moral communion between God and man; in its place, there is a union with the Godhead' (p.7). There is a danger of confusing pantheism with mysticism, including Kabbalistic mystical traditions that come to be excluded from the realm of philosophical investigation through this identification.[14] Guttman moves too quickly to conclude that 'The living relationship between persons is replaced by the extinction of the personal individuality, which is felt to be the main barrier separating us from God' (p.7). For mystical traditions, 'the divine "ground" or source does not create the world, but rather expels it from its own substance. In religious terms, this means that God is not conceived as the will which determines the world, but rather as a transcendent self-subsistent Being, completely withdrawn into itself'.

Somehow Guttman wants to sustain a sense of the personal relationship between God and human beings, even though we might recognise that this is in conflict with the disdain for the *world of the senses* that is integral to the rationalism he assumes. At some level, disdain for the world of the senses is linked to disdain for the human body since traditionally the body has been the site of emotions, feelings and desires. This is an assumption that Plato makes, but it is also echoed in the Kantian tradition that informs Cohen's thinking. As Guttman puts it: 'The radical distinction between God and the world is blurred even more by all those systems that consider the transition from one to the other as continuous and gradual, and posit an intermediary, supra-sensual world between the Godhead and the world of the senses. Whereas the Creator-God stands over and against the world, his creation, the God of mysticism, becomes the principle underlying the supra-sensual world. Even the ascent of the soul to God is nothing more than the final completion of its way to the supra-sensual or "intelligible" world' (p.8).

Creation/s

Guttman wants to understand the story of creation: 'Nature has lost its divine quality; from the dwelling place of the divine it has itself become the work of God's hands' (p.10). Though we might read the Book of Genesis in different ways, Guttman insists 'This conception of nature dominates the story of creation found in the first chapter of the Book of Genesis. Nature here has a substantial life of its own, but is conceived as inanimate and subordinate to the purposes of God, which, as such, are foreign to it'. This also allows for a particular rationalist understanding of what it means for human beings to be created in the *image* of God.

Reading back from the identification of a dominant masculinity with a conception of reason radically separated from nature within an Enlightenment modernity, Guttman says that 'Man himself, the end and purpose of creation, is not conceived solely as part of nature, but as standing over and against nature, as the image of God. This anthropocentric conception grants man (the gender is significant in a particular way!) the right to conquer the earth, and relegates astral "divinities" to the role of mere luminaries for the earth; it redirects all religious feeling from nature towards the transmundane God. Henceforth, man sees himself as a being superior to the forces of nature which, in natural religion, would be considered as divine' (p.10–11).

Is this a patriarchal reading of Genesis? Is this a philosophical reading and what can it tell us about the relationship of masculinity to philosophy within diverse religious traditions? How does it relate to the more feminist reading of Genesis offered by Avivah Gottlieb Zornberg in *The Beginnings Of Desire*?[15] Is there a tension between Hebrew and Greek that Guttman still willingly acknowledges when he admits that 'This opposition between man and nature has, as yet, no metaphysical connotation. There is certainly no hint of an opposition between the world of the senses and a suprasensual world. Man is a creature of this world, and it is only his character as a person that raises him above things natural' (p.11).

But what is meant by 'only his character as a person'? What does this *imagine* about embodiment and emotional lives? Is this refusal to make a metaphysical distinction between the human world and the world of nature that allows for bodies, sexuality and emotional lives a way of conceiving radically different visions of personal identity, dignity and human worth in a post-Holocaust world? How does this open up ways of drawing upon the sources of Jewish philosophy to question some of the contempt and appropriations that have taken place within Western culture? How are we to re-think the relationship between Athens and Jerusalem?

4

Preaching, Revelation and Creation

Preaching

Leo Baeck, in an essay on 'Greek and Jewish Preaching' that appears in his collection *The Pharisees*, recognises the forms of prophecy in the two and half centuries of Israel's history, beginning with Elijah and ending with the return from the Babylonian Exile, which coincided in India with the masters of the Upanishads and, following them, Gautama Buddha.[1] The authors of the Gathas, Zoroaster and his disciples lived in Persia at about the same time while, in China, it was the age of Lao-Tse and Chung-Tse. This was also the epoch of religious growth and striving in Greece where as Baeck explains: 'Many of them were philosophers as far as the form of their exposition is concerned, but in their aspirations they were really in search of a new religion' (p.109).[2]

As Baeck explains: 'The paths of development of the ancient religious cultures were also largely parallel'. The words were written down and the classical religious literatures thus created, soon to be supplemented by commentaries and edifying discourses. A specific type of teaching evolved which 'no longer proclaimed a new truth but aimed at expounding and spreading the truth already proclaimed' (p.110). This is clearly marked in Greek religion and even more strongly in Roman religion. These official state religions were of a type that appealed to individuals only in their capacity as citizens. As citizens, people were obliged to participate in religious rites and so long as they participated, the state was usually tolerant of everything else. A person's actual religious ideas and theological conceptions remained a matter of indifference. This explains how offences against state shrines were only seen as real crimes if perpetrated by a native of the city.

In the period of the decline of the ancient world when people began to separate themselves inwardly from the state and learned to think of themselves as citizens of the world, the mystery cult with its miracles and philosophy with its general view of the universe and humankind became widely accepted options. But if philosophy were to escape an almost dogmatic character in the different schools, the truth needed to be explained and propagated. As Baeck explains: 'In this respect, the democratic feature given it by Socrates played a determining role. He it was who declared that virtue and piety could be learned; that is, they were accessible to everyone and therefore could and should be preached. This tendency of Socratic philosophy, which was followed not so much by Plato and Aristotle as by the Cynics, is perhaps its most particular contribution to Greek thinking' (p.113). This was different to exclusive doctrines taught by Heraclitus or Pythagoras that held that virtue was *not* accessible to everyone, but was a gift of the gods to the elect.[3]

Living within a German culture that held Greek thought and learning in such high regard, Baeck was concerned to argue for certain similarities between Hellenism and Judaism. As he claims, 'The same democractic feature – one might almost say, the same Socratic manner – characterises Judaism. Here, too, we have the postulate that religion can be learned. It is the Torah, the "teaching". This term implies that it is open to and designed for everyone…Thus Judaism and Hellenism, in virtue of a common didacticism, coincided' (p.113). Greeks had the advantage of formal brilliance and elegance of style in the rhetorical arts. Refusing, however, to concede that this meant the Greeks had philosophy that Jews lacked, as if Greece provided the standard of civilisation in the West against which other cultures had to assess themselves as lacking, Baeck recognised that 'This was an advantage, but it was also a danger' (p.113). This could encourage 'the dominance of the hollow and pretentious conventional phrase, and this often resulted in the sacrifice of real content and conviction. Eloquence was cultivated for the sake of eloquence'. This allows Baeck to conclude: 'It has justly been said that Hellenism died in the cult of the beautiful form' (p.114).[4]

In contrast, according to Baeck, 'Among the Jewish people, this virtuosity was opposed by certain spiritual characteristics and by certain characteristics of the language...our Midrashim display what seems to be an almost studied indifference to artistic form. Only interpolated sayings are given literary polish' (p.114). Baeck also acknowledges 'the great importance of the living oral tradition as against the rigid texts, expressed by the term Midrash – absence of dogmatism, the right, yes, the obligation to explore the Bible and to bring forth from it and form religious ideas' (p.114). Baeck resisted, arguing that Midrash was a form of philosophy, even if a different form of philosophy from traditional Greek philosophy; possibly it was his rationalism that made it difficult to take this further step.[5] At the same time he recognises that the Greeks, too, were probably those 'philosophers' of whose disputes with certain elder scribes the Talmud often tells us. He recognises the many paths through which Greek philosophy entered and helped shape the Jewish world. As he remarks, 'The Jewish sermon was therefore referred to by the same term that designated the Greek one' (p.115). In Alexandria, according to Baeck, 'considering Philo's personality it is not surprising that he should elucidate and sublimate God's words to Moses in such a way that God is made to express Platonic ideas quite explicitly'.

The familiarity that Palestinian preachers enjoyed with Philo's methods is shown in several sermons, according to Baeck, in which the revelation experienced by Abraham is described by an image that emphasises the lofty and miraculous character of the event: 'The Bible says that God led out Abraham. This should be interpreted in the following way: God led Abraham up above the vault of heaven where the Lord dwells, so that beneath his feet he beheld the paths of the stars, the ways that the laws that had been laid down from the beginning'. The Greek word for knowledge is similar to the word for sight, since it is through *vision* that we supposedly know the world. This makes it difficult to acknowledge the ways in which Abraham *hears* the words of God and the ways that the relationship with God within the Jewish tradition is imaged as a personal relationship. There is a midrash that says that on Sinai everyone heard the words of God, even if they each heard differently according to what they could 'take in' at the time. So it is important for the Greek rendering of Abraham to centre upon what he 'beheld' – what he could see stretched out before him. This would make it difficult to appreciate Abraham's arguments with God and ways that he interceded on the behalf of people who would otherwise be punished.

Baeck recognises that those who know Plato's *Phaedrus* will immediately be reminded, word for word, of the marvellous allegory in which Plato, who Baeck describes as 'this greatest of all the Greek "visionaries"', describes the ascent of the immortals at the moment when they 'know': 'For the immortals, when they are at the end of their course, go forth and stand upon the outside of heaven, and the revolution of the spheres carries them round, and they behold the things beyond....In the revolution (the divine intelligence) beholds justice, and temperance, and knowledge absolute...in existence absolut'. The Jewish preacher used the Platonic allegory, as Baeck explains, 'to describe, in the language of the Bible, what he held to be the most sublime of all experiences, the prophetic revelation' (p.116).[6]

Revelation/s

The same sermon also introduces us into a conflict of ideas, for it adds that God said to Abraham: 'He who is beneath the stars, bound up in the earthly, fears them; he who rises above them, into eternity, fears them not. You can be a prophet, you need not be an astrologer'. This is to give the prophet powers of sight but also powers to *ascend* from the earthy domain. There is a danger of echoing a Greek disdain for the earthly that became so powerful within a Platonic/Christian tradition. It is supposedly only if we can escape from the earthly that we can escape from the fears associated with bodies and sexuality that are deemed to be aspects of an 'animal' nature. We find this rationalism present within Plato that assumes in his later writings the divisions of the soul and the need to assert control over an 'animal' nature, later echoed within a Protestant tradition. It is because human beings are 'born into sin' that they have to constantly *prove* themselves worthy. It is only through escaping from the demands of the earthly and the temptations it presents that they can prove themselves through acting out of a sense of moral duty.[7]

In the sermon, Abraham is presented as one who has achieved faith in God and thereby elevated himself above the orbit of the stars. 'In Israel, no star has power', this sermon concludes, and with this declaration, which became a principle, the astrological doctrine of fate was rejected. Even though Jewish thinking remained unmythical for long periods it was still influenced by astrological currents of thought. As Baeck says: 'It is noteworthy that it was with the above-quoted words of Plato that this doctrine was opposed'. But at the same time it is surprising from the drift of Baeck's argument if he is right that 'The feature of his philosophy in which Jewish thinking discovered a kinship is this transcendental impulse, this conception of the world as symbol, and of Ideas as perfect and eternal archetypes of the imperfect and changing world'. This might be considered as an advocacy of Hellenistic Judaism but could equally be explored as a possible source of tension.[8]

In searching for common ground between Hellenism and Judaism, Baeck argues 'not least of all, a common ground with Platonism was found in the biblical doctrine of man's likeness to God' (p.119). The Hebrew texts use the Greek term when reflecting upon the biblical doctrine of humankind's likeness to God. For the Greeks, not everyone was made in the image of God, that was *only* the case with the elect, who were raised up to the level of the gods. The term belonged to the cult of rulers and heroes prevailing in the Greco-Roman world. The language of this cult was later used in the Christian descriptions of the saviour. The specific contribution of Judaism is preserved through ordinary humans being given the attribute that elsewhere is given only to the elect of the elect.

Within a rationalist tradition, it is often reason that is identified as the faculty that alone proves that human beings have been made in the image of God. Through being able to use reason to affirm control over their animal natures they are *able* to affirm their likeness to God. This tends to mean that it is only to the extent that human beings are rational that we can say that they are created in the image of God, thus implying that reason is a faculty that is radically separated from an animal nature. This means that bodies remain identified with a sexuality that is still deemed to be 'animal'. This is interpreted within a dominant Christian tradition as a threat to our human status. It makes it possible to say that people are 'born into sin' and it is only through their moral actions that they can somehow hope to redeem themselves.

A dominant Catholic tradition taught, in contrast to the Protestant tradition that held to notions of predestination, that human beings were free to do good or evil. But if there were a vision of free will, somehow this was always accompanied by a recognition that what was good or evil had been clearly designated so that people were *not* truly free to make these individual decisions for themselves; they had to decide whether they would do what the doctrine had already discerned as 'good' and desist from doing what had already been determined to be 'evil'. There was also a shared sense that people were born into sin and that earthly life was a space in which people would have to prove themselves worthy. This might be a vision of freedom that allows a Catholic tradition to speak about human beings as having been 'created in the image of God', but it is very different from the Jewish tradition that would regard life itself as a blessing. This is a distinction that Mathew Fox draws in his *Original Blessings*, in which he tries to imagine a Christian tradition that is brought back to an inner relationship with its Jewish sources.[9]

The Platonic interpretation of Christianity that deviates from its Jewish sources tends to reinforce a *disdain* for earthly life. This means that human beings have to learn to perceive themselves as being incomplete, if not sinful, tending to frame a particular concept of human life that is less to do with the outpouring of love than it is with making up for inadequacies. As long as people grow up to compare themselves with ideals that exist in a realm of their own, they will be haunted by a sense that their natures are flawed and that they are constantly failing to live up to an ideal that exists in metaphysical space of its own. Whatever individuals are able to achieve in their own lives, they feel that they should have achieved more. They can feel undeserving of love that is being offered to them, considering that if others 'really knew' what they would like, they would surely reject them. This means that, at some level, people are living in *hiding*, uneasy about revealing themselves to others. Constantly comparing themselves with idealised images of themselves, people often feel haunted by feelings of inadequacy.

Being as a Work of Art

In the essay that follows in *The Pharisees*, entitled 'Two World Views Compared', Leo Baeck opens with the striking remark that 'One thing is decisive in Greek thinking – and it is this thinking that formed the Western mind – at least since the time became philosophy: the idea of the work of art. Man, in his intellectual and psychic fear of the mutable, that ocean of nothingness, took refuge in this idea; it was a fear analogous to that which prompted the Egyptians to mummify the body in an effort to make it endure' (p.125). Baeck does not speculate about the source of this intellectual and psychic *fear* or whether it is gender-specific and thus related to a dominant form of masculinity that fears its own mortality, but there is an implicit contrast between reason and emotion that to some extent Baeck seems to share in his rationalism, itself shaped by Greek thought.

Baeck goes on to draw a contrast, saying 'The sensual eye that beholds the world around it is only able to possess the instant, and therefore, as Heraclitus and the Eleatics taught, really possesses nothing. It beholds non-being, for only the ebb and flow reach it, and it sees only something that it will never see again. Such an experience does not disclose the thing or person in itself; it merely goes from one evanescent instant to another, it drifts around in the ever-changing moment that dies as soon as they are born. Only in the work of art, it was felt, can one discover that blissful land of the always-the same; in it is manifested the realm of meaning, of duration, of pure form and personality' (p.125).

Somehow, through a cognition that seems implicitly to be contrasted with emotion and feeling, 'the artist, the intuitive thinker, contemplates and creates...receives and gives the permanent and one, the essence, the thing in itself, which always remains the same. In sensual experience, the casual and shadowlike drift of things passes us by; the work of art confronts us with what is truly seen, because it is always seen: authentic reality, the thing itself, being as such.....or, in the words of Plato, the true form...This is perhaps the best explanation of the Platonic Idea'. This allows Baeck to conclude with at least some evident sympathy that 'In the work of art, in the Idea, change and mutability are transcended; fear of the evanescent gives place to certainty and calm. Here one of mankind's great thoughts has its awakening'. A longing for certainty also haunted Descartes' vision of 'modern philosophy' and it was an aspiration that was to be directly challenged within Wittgenstein's later work *On Certainty*.[10]

As Baeck comes to understand Greek thought, 'Only the work of art *is;* only the work of art is true. Greek thought so completely accepts this proposition that it also inverts it: all being, all truth, is a work of art. To discover and grasp being, one must penetrate the work of art'. This allows Baeck to recognise 'Hence Greek thought is characterised by a broad unity of science and art, by the aesthetic cast and aesthetic mood of all cognition. Mathematics and logic are fundamentally the same as music and the plastic art; and all of them are philosophy. All of them give us true being, the permanent and the timeless....The description of philosophy as "the sublimest music" given in *Phaedo* is not meant merely as a poetic simile...The philosopher, or lover of wisdom, is also the lover of beauty' (p.126–7).

This vision of Greek civilisation haunted the Western imagination and the movement of German romanticism that Baeck grew up with. It allows for a rationalism that does *not* have to break with intuition, even if it distances itself from the body, sexuality and emotional life. As Baeck puts it: 'Hence also the unity of cognition and intuition. Reason intuits the concept; it contemplates justice, prudence, science – and this again is not merely a simile. And, for the same reason, there is also unity of Logos and Eros. The Platonic Eros is an experience of the mind and the soul by which man comes to know the always-the-same through the work of art...Dialectics is essentially the same as the erotic...This Platonic love is less a grasping than a being-grasped' (p.127).[11]

Baeck recognises a further identification when he says 'The Ethos has the same identity with the Eros as the Logos. The highest virtue, the highest perfection, is contemplation and thought, the love for the highest, the being-attracted, the being-seized, that spiritually unites man with the beautiful, the good and the true'. This vision seems to appeal in a way that a more recent tradition of Kantian ethics cannot. As Baeck explains: 'Ethics, as Greek thinking understood this term, is not what we understand by it – something unconditionally imperative, urgent, dynamic – rather it is something intrinsically aesthetic and intellectual, contemplative and reflective' (p.128). As Baeck understands it, 'The same is true of all manifestations of being. There is a world of being, of the beautiful, the true and the good, there is one cosmos, and all spiritual connections with it, those of the Logos, the Eros, the Ethos, of dialectics, mathematics, music, and ethics, of philosophy and of love, are relations to the work of art; they constitute that type of intellectual contemplation for which the mind itself is a work of art and contemplate itself through thought, and so know itself' (p.128).

Baeck feels the attraction of this vision though he can also appreciate that it carries its own weaknesses. It allows him to identify with the *appeal* that Hellenism held for so many Jews, not only in the period of Jewish Hellenism but even through the period of the Enlightenment that has shaped modernity and was to retain significant identification with Greek culture, reason and science. At the same time, Baeck's critical engagement remains incomplete because it remains focussed upon a single, though all-important implication, as he recognises. This is partly because in different ways he remains a child of a Western rationalism that has been shaped through its identifications with Greece. Martin Bernal, in *Black Athena*, has explored the exclusion of semitic cultures that went along with this vision of Greece as the 'cradle of Western civilisation'. Not only was there a need to identify Greece with 'whiteness', thus excluding its relationship with the North African and Egyptian cultural legacies, but there is an implicit rejection of Biblical culture that shapes its own forms of antisemitism. Jews were identified with oriental discourses and there were few ways of bringing Athens and Jerusalem into a relationship with each other.[12]

Hellenism / Mystery

Baeck recognises that 'Being as a work of art is perfect, closed. It is beyond all possibility of becoming otherwise, of developing; it remains what it is. *It is consummated.* It is perfect, and therefore complete; and as something complete, it belongs to the past. Interestingly enough, the Latin word *perfectus* denotes all these three meanings: completed, past and perfect' (p.129). It is as if creation is a completed process, and can no longer be imagined as an *ongoing process* of partnership between

God and humanity where human beings have a responsibility as partners to continue the work of creation. Rather within this Greek vision, 'Nothing is left to man but to behold it, to think it, to be seized by it, to admire it, and to become absorbed in it. The idea of the work of art thus leads to the idea of consummation as the ultimate decisive answer; in it the meaning of everything is given' (p.129).

Drawing a contrast with modern notions of cognition influenced by Descartes and Kant, Baeck recognises 'For us, the term cognition has a connotation of mastering, overcoming, conquering; the Greek Gnosis is veiled in the peace of perfection'. As cognition becomes contemplation so it is something absolutely achieved, and 'If Greek thinking is so rich in a sense of possession, so rich in the certainty of its goal, and so poor in illusions, it is also poor in any attempts to go beyond and to see beyond, poor in enthusiasm and passion, platonic, one might say; and the positive and negative aspects of this thinking are implied in its domination by the idea of final perfection'. Greek ethics offers 'the attitude of the consummated man to the consummated world', which means that 'the task of ethics is to make this idea explicit, and the task of man is to represent this work of art'. This allows Baeck to wonder: 'To what extent the figure of Jesus in the Gospel according to John has the lineaments of the Greek sage is shown in the fact that his life is "offered up" (both to sacrifice and contemplation); as has been justly observed, the figure of Jesus has a statue-like character. It does not move man by the force of its imperatives, it "moved by being beloved"' (p.130). This allows Baeck to conclude that for the Greeks 'The perfected personality is no longer a man but a concept, an ideal' (p.130).

Baeck contends that for the Greeks '...finality, pastness, becomes the ideal, or expressed negatively, the ideal is future-less'. This allows him to draw a contrast with notions of ethics circulating in modern European culture. As Baeck expresses it, 'Properly speaking, it is unethical, at least in the sense in which we conceive ethics, in the sense of an impulse towards the new and coming, which is clearly in contrast to what the Greek world conceived to be supreme...Here ethics becomes contemplation, whether it applies to God or to man, and man thus becomes a god; and because of this, ethics ceases to be ethics' (p.131).

According to Baeck, the mystery cult based on subjective experience and philosophy based on the notion of the work of art represent the two great tendencies in the spiritual and religious life of the Greeks. Baeck as a rationalist is suspicious of subjective experience and notions of trance and rapture that can accompany it. He recognises that 'the mystery cults in which West and East at that time discovered each other contained the faith in a divine power of grace that enters man through the sacrament, frees him from his earthly chains, and makes him divine'. He explains that 'In this world of mystery the experience of redemption is everything…All experience of redemption is psychologically the release from will and the release from reason, the release from everything gradual, from all limitations, from all struggles and activity'.

Here we can discern a scepticism that Baeck probably felt for Martin Buber's explorations of Hasidism that he might well have evaluated in similar terms. But the lines are drawn too sharply and the possibilities of learning from different religious experiences is blocked when Baeck argues that 'It is a sinking into the sea of an all-significant emotion, submergence in the mood in which reality dissolves, in the intoxicating sensation that releases appearances and being from their finite limits – the release from life through the subjective experience. Thinking is pushed back behind emotion and the dreams, the deed gives way to rapture and absorption…Life dissolves into instants of experience, consummated moments; it is only in them that the "I" receives its meaning, only in them that it gains a sense of the ultimate, of fulfilment…The flight from the world of change becomes the flight from life into the world of subjective experience – the apotheosis of the instant' (p.132–3).

The Greek mystery cult and philosophy were able to merge, according to Baeck, because they have an essential feature in common. As he expresses it, 'both live in the possession of what is fixed and final, in the certainty of having it and being it. Contemplation and rapture belong together – the one had ultimate visions, the other ultimate emotions. Even for Plato the one led to the other, but in his case it was only a mutual attraction. They first merged when the church conquered Hellenism, and Hellenism the church. This came to pass under the sign of Platonism. Plato is the father of the church teachers, not only because his state supplied the blueprint for the real structure of the church, but even more so because the church was able to rediscover its mystery in Plato's philosophy'. This is a crucial insight even if it works to *marginalise* consideration of mystical traditions within Judaism itself and the different kind of learning that occurred in France and Spain between Christian gnostic traditions and Jewish Kabbalistic traditions that Gershon Scholem has explored.[13]

Baeck is making a central argument about the relationship between the Church, mainly in its Western forms, and Platonism. He argues that 'In the church the two paths become one. Philosophy and subjective experience, the Gnosis and the sacrament, were synthesised in the certainty of the absolute and consummated man, the redeemer and the redeemed. The two became one: the mystery as work of art and the work of art as mystery' (p.133–4). It was through the church that this alliance survived, as Baeck explains: 'it asserted itself because the church most profoundly and most intimately united the two directions; in the church it triumphed over nations and centuries. The great epoch of the church, the Middle Ages, belongs to it' (p.134).

5

Hellenism, Christianity and Judaism

Scholasticism

In *Two World Views Compared*, Leo Baeck argues that throughout the long Middle Ages, scholasticism 'is the philosophy of finality, the philosophy of concepts that are end-points, answers that are premises. Its faith is in the conclusion, the pre-established syllogism; it deduces final things. Its logic, with marvellous consistency, is the logic of the middle term; the results are known in advance and are presented as the given point of departure; it only has to supply the needed axioms and proofs. All its movement in all its subtlety and richness of its dialectics always takes place in the same space, always in the middle' (p.134).[1]

Within this tradition, truth has *already* been discovered and it is only for people to submit to the truths of Christianity. These were truths that had been seen and if people refused to accept these truths then it had to be because of their blindness. The synagogue was represented as a woman who was blindfold, fumbling her way with a broken stick. Truths are not waiting to be discovered through a confrontation with tradition, but 'Truth is fixed because it speaks of the fixed world'. As Baeck explains: 'It does not build; its art is the art of the locksmith; it only shows how to open all the doors to the house of truth, which stands already erected from the foundations to the roof. It can prove everything; for the truth is final, truth is dogma, and one what is final is true' (p.134).[2]

The house is imagined as a three-storey edifice of heaven, earth and hell. As Baeck recognises: 'The prototype above has its image below, the macrocosm has its microcosm. Everything is given beforehand, permanent, all history is history fulfilled, time completed; what occurs in the future is re-occurrence. Only finality is true and real; the devil has his seat in the becoming, and it must be overthrown'. Here we witness the *finality* of Plato given a Christian expression. People simply have to accept that Christ died for their sins and that they have been redeemed through this action. This salvation is 'true' and 'real' but people have to accept it for themselves. This allows Baeck to recognise the resonance of Platonism when he says 'And to man is given only to contemplate, experience, and acknowledge all this, this final answer...his task is to harbour faith – that medieval Eros – to be seized by it and moved by it, and to be aware in it that he who has it is himself consummated, redeemed'. There is little else that needs to be done, no *process* of *becoming* that involves human beings in struggling with themselves to transform human relationships and create heaven on earth. The truth is given and different realms have to be kept apart. In this scholastic vision '..the idea of consummation, of perfection, finds it ultimate and all-embracing world. Here it became an epoch' (p.135).[3]

In a remarkable passage that seeks to connect the advent of 'the modern' with both science and Judaism, Baeck argues that 'For this reason the Middle Ages came to an end at the point where this idea (of consummation, of perfection) was undermined. The opposition to it came from two sides. First, and this can be only briefly mentioned here, from mathematics. When Kepler replaced the heavenly spheres, that ancient idea of the perfect, by the planetary ellipses – a deed no less decisive in man's conception of the cosmos than that of Copernicus – and when Descartes supplanted Euclid's contained and motionless geometry with an analytical geometry, a new epoch began in the history of knowledge. Statics, in which the infinite is static, increasingly gave place to dynamics...'. But strikingly, Baeck argues that the most important pressure also came from another realm, 'a realm that the church has absorbed and that it thought it had enclosed in its system of finality – the Old Testament' (p.136). We might say 'the Jewish Bible' since the very notion of 'old' suggests that it has been 'superseded' by the 'new', which was the way of positioning Judaism as having somehow outlived its historical purpose and thus unable to speak critically to the conditions of the medieval world, let alone the modern world.

It was no accident that Baeck mentioned, almost in passing, that 'the devil has his seat in the becoming, and it must be overthrown' since as Joshua Trachtenberg explored in *The Medieval World and The Jew*, the

Jew came to be *identified* with the body and thus with the sins of the
flesh within a Platonic/Christian tradition that had disavowed the body.
This allowed the figure of the Jew to be identified with the devil and
portrayed through animal imagery. We find this antisemitic iconography
echoed in Nazi propaganda. But Baeck leaves these issues aside when he
says 'If we come to the Old Testament from Greek antiquity and the
Middle Ages, it is as though we are entering a different world. We leave
the temple of Ideas and the house of the cult and enter the world of life;
the struggle of Ethos and Pathos; from the cosmos of being we come
into the becoming that wants to be a cosmos, from the enclosed space
we emerge upon the endless path' (p.136). Baeck frames the opposition
in different ways that leaves little space for the interaction between
Hellenism and Judaism, but this is because he wants to contrast two distinct world views.

Judaism

Baeck understands Judaism as providing resources for the West to question a Hellenistic world of unchanging perfection. He opens up the
possibility of different ethical traditions where 'Becoming and struggling, the constant preoccupation with the path and the future, with
duty and destiny – this constant *tension* is what is asserted to the meaning of life, the life of the world and of man. It is in this that the soul
conceives its essence. It conceives it in a double experience: that of creation and that of the commandment'. This dual experience was to be
vital for Baeck's understanding of the moral and spiritual life. It helps
define a specifically Jewish contribution to ethics and the meaning of
life. It is not as if with Kant and a Protestant tradition in ethics that the
moral law *waits* to be discerned through an independent faculty of reason, but rather the meanings of the commandments have to be
constantly revealed. People are involved in life as a process of becoming,
in which there is a continuing process of deepening a relationship with
the self and the world.[4]

There are truths that people have to continually rediscover for themselves because they do *not* exist in a space of their own. Ethics is no
longer defined as a matter of living up to ideals and finding that you are
constantly lacking, and thus haunted by a sense of inadequacy. A
Kantian ethical tradition sustains a sense of human imperfection and
inadequacy since people are constantly comparing themselves with ideals that they cannot hope to realise and so affirm their lack.[5] With
Baeck, as with Levinas, people live with a sense of infinity, even though

they might not have learnt to recognise it. Rather than leaving people with a sense of something lacking, it allows them to experience life as a blessing. Baeck expresses it in language that needs to be more inclusive: 'Man here experiences the fact that he belongs to infinity. Infinity bests him whether he goes into himself or beyond himself' (p.137).

In language that can be difficult to follow, Baeck says 'He lives in a space without end, part of it, in a time without conclusion, a piece of it. Space and time here both derive from the one, omnipresent and eternal God' (p.137). Drawing a distinction with Plato can clarify what Baeck wants to express when he says 'For Plato, the transcendent was something isolated, something separated in the beyond; here it is also a beyond, but one that enters man and grows out of him. God, the Holy One, the Other Being, created everything, and He acts and reveals Himself in everything. Everything is in the tension between the infinite and the given, between the world beyond and this world, between the being other and the being one' (p.138).[6]

This is a tension that people can experience in their own lives, within contemporary Western cultures. It is a matter of recognising that *life* is a *process* through which we are constantly forming and creating ourselves. We are being touched and transformed through our experiences, and if we are prepared to face what we have lived through in our emotional histories we can also *deepen* our relationship with ourselves. As we can connect with ourselves more deeply so we can engage in dialogue at different levels. This is 'the long road and leads to the never-attained goal' (p.136), and as Baeck recognised: 'Paul had felt this opposition most profoundly and most tormentingly, and it was from this that he fled to the fixed world of unchanging perfection, which is actually its opposite. In the Old Testament every creative idea is the counter-idea of everything final' (p.136–7).[7]

Creation is not a completed process that was over in six days but is recognised as a never-ending process in which human beings share in the work of creation. As Baeck expresses it, 'Energy replaces art – it is no accident that the Bible condemns the image; it is a thing too fixed and final' (p.138). A Jewish tradition is defined through a sense that '...all energy begets energy'. Nothing is fixed. In the words of an old Jewish saying: 'God creates in order to continue to create' (p.138). Creation is a constant process of birth and people are constantly learning *how* to give birth to different aspects of themselves.

Let me share a personal experience that can possibly help to illuminate these processes. I had a dream that I gave birth to a little girl who was open and attentive. I was looking for a phone to be able to tell my partner but as usual it was busy. I walked around with the baby in my arms trying to find my way back to the hospital. I had recalled that they had taken the baby away for measuring just after the birth and I was disappointed that I allowed this to happen, knowing that my partner would object. Possibly this was a sign of giving birth to a feminine aspect of myself that has been growing over time. It could be an *opening* to a different aspect of self that I am ready to integrate or accept as part of myself.[8]

Baeck refuses to separate the processes of creation from those of revelation, as he says 'Creation and revelation, becoming and become, belong together, the condition one another. The universe with the life in it is caught in the tension between these two elements. The world is neither pure fate nor a pure nature upon which man is dependent, nor is it purely the image of an arch-image that man is supposed only to contemplate and adore. It is God's world, an earthly world and yet God's domain, space yet infinite, time yet eternity – or against, to quote an old Jewish saying: "God is the space of the world, but the world is not his space" and it may be added: He is the time of the world, but the world is not His time' (p.139).

There is a refusal to draw a Greek/Christian dualistic distinction between the 'earthly' and the 'spiritual' in which the earthly is disdained, and God can only be reached through ascending away from the earthly towards the spiritual. Again, God can be found in this world that is the work of creation, but 'the world is not his space' in the sense that God cannot be confined to this world. As Baeck expresses it: 'The world is the creation and the revelation of God, and therefore full of tension. It is characterised both by distance from God and belonging to God' (p.139).

People can experience this for themselves in the world in which they live as well as in the world they create. People play a part in creation through their deeds 'which constitute that world of which a Talmudic hyperbole says that "it is greater even than the creation of heaven and earth". In every act that is demanded of him, man experiences the commandment, and this, too, is the experience of infinity. The commandment for man is God's commandment, born of the infinite and eternal depth, full of divine restlessness and sacred movement' (p.139).

There are always more steps to be taken in life and there is never the peace of final fulfilment. There is always a future in which responsibilities still need to be recognised, as Levinas would stress. There is nothing final or complete, 'nothing perfect in the life of man; in his action, too, he is surrounded by infinity, it irrupts into him, and his path leads to it' (p.140). The pious man, as the Talmud says, is a man 'without rest here or in the beyond'. Baeck shows that he remains influenced by Kant when he says 'The ethical is the categorical, infinite commandment: "Ye shall he holy; for I the Lord your God am holy" (Lev. 19:2); this is the commandment that contains all the other commandments; everything else is only teaching, exhortation, advice' (p.140).[9]

Creation becomes a *human task* as human beings are enjoined to make sure that 'the beyond is to become the here below, the other being this being, the kingdom of God the domain of man' (p.141). Baeck helps to clarify this process when he says a person 'masters infinity by absorbing it in his will, by living it, by introducing it into his life, by making God's commandments an inner acquisition. He brings the beyond down to this world, he brings it down from heaven to earth....he makes God come closer and closer to this world....it is to be found in the Talmud: "God says: My children have prevailed over me"'. As Baeck explains: 'It is seemingly a victory of man over God and yet, at the same time, in reality a victory of God: God's kingdom extends its domain on earth. It is the reconciliation of man with God and God with man. "I will not let thee go, except thou bless me"; such is the expression of the reconciliation'.

The danger that Baeck has in mind that was all too soon to prevail was that 'Where only what is fixed and final constitutes the truth, the principle of unity without exception is dominant – Plato is the initiator of this principle – the principle of the monolithic faith and the monolithic state...'. Judaism offers a hope against such totalistic impulses: 'Where tension is experienced as the meaning of life and lived as life's commandment, there the will to history begins – and all history, is in the last analysis, many-sidedness, interaction, and struggle – there history, with all the sacred unrest that constitutes its life, begins to function' (p.143). If this remains unclear it seems to express a hope at least that 'There is room here for individuals and nations' (p.143).[10]

Baeck offers wisdom that looks towards a multicultural reality when he says 'there are old eyes in which we can read a millennial experience and life, and there are young eyes which imagine that the years they have seen are centuries. There is moral memory and moral inexperience, there is recollection and there is oblivion. When nations and communities do not understand one another, the reason is often that some look at the world in the light of experience, while others question it only in the light of the present. He who wants to grasp the future, the direction of the path, must attempt to see with eyes that are thousands of years old' (p.144). He is *warning* us against visions of perfection in religion or politics where power consists of the ability to possess, dominate and subject because the truth is *already* known, and those who refuse to conform are a threat that needs to be eradicated. The West has inherited these totalitarian impulses present in an otherwise benign Christianity that assume they alone possess 'truth'.[11]

Christianity has been able to offer 'what is always the same, perfection itself, to generation after generation. Century after century can turn to it to contemplate what is permanent and to rejoice in what is complete and final...When it no longer possesses and no longer rules, it has ended; it has no becoming and therefore no returning. When finality dies, its death is final'.[12] A contrast is being drawn here with a Jewish tradition that, paradoxically, rather than being historically 'superseded', *can* still speak relevantly to the predicaments of a post-modern present. As Baeck explains: 'In tension there is no possession. It cannot subject and dominate; it can only realise and re-create. Therefore it can be reborn. He who experiences the infinite and eternal through his life, experiences it endlessly and without conclusion...He does not see God but he sees the path towards Him, the path of the eternal commandment, the never-ending journey that God demands of man' (p.145). In this way, people have the potential to learn that they create themselves and the world 'in order to build a kingdom of God in an earthly existence'.

6

Creation, Ethics and Human Nature

Beyond Reason

Post-Enlightenment Jewish philosophy has been largely a creation of the different philosophical traditions that emerged in Germany. In the shadows of the Enlightenment, mainly through Mendelssohn's writings, there were attempts to affirm the rationality of Judaism so that it could prove acceptable to the modern spirit of the age.[1] This allowed for the development within Western Europe of a tradition of assimilation in which religion was separated from the public world of citizenship and became a matter of individual religious belief. Jewish emancipation was to offer Jews the freedom to exercise legal and political rights within the public sphere, as long as they were prepared to re-express their religious traditions in rationalist terms *as* matters of individual belief.[2]

The terms of rationality against which Judaism had to prove itself were largely laid down through Kant's work and those who engaged with it critically. Hermann Cohen became a central figure in the late nineteenth century who moved from a commitment to the universalism of Kantian ethics to a recognition that Jewish sources potentially allowed for different voices, some of which could question the terms of a Kantian enlightenment rationalism.[3] This tension is still alive in Julius Guttmann's seminal *Philosophies of Judaism*. Julius (Yitzhak) Guttmann had been born into the Wissenschaft des

Judentums movement, a vital tradition of modern Jewish scholarship. His father, who had served as a rabbi in Hildesheim and later Breslau, specialised in the history of medieval Jewish philosophy. Educated in Breslau, he was influenced by the neo-Kantian revival as well as the growing preoccupation of philosophers with sociology.

We can hear the influence of Kant in his presentation of the basic ideas of Biblical Judaism and we *can* feel the tension between the Biblical and the Kantian that is largely set within the secular terms of a rationalist Christian universalism. While recognising that it is 'a modern development' for philosophers to try to clarify the distinctiveness of religion, 'earlier periods did not attempt to differentiate between the methods of philosophy and religion, but sought to reconcile the content of their teachings' (p.4). In this spirit Guttmann holds 'the distinctiveness of biblical religion is due to its ethical conception of the personality of God. The God of the prophets is exemplified by his moral will; he is demanding and commanding, promising and threatening, the absolutely free ruler of man and nature. This conception of God developed only slowly in the history of Israelite religion'.

But this notion of 'his character as pure will', though which God separates from nature, is set within Kant's language. Guttmann acknowledges 'Neither God's uniqueness and superiority over the forces of nature nor his character as pure will were to be found in its beginnings. Only after a long process of evolution did the God of Israel become the God of the world. It also took a long time before he could shed his primitive attributes as a nature God, making it possible to think of him in purely personal terms'. This final transition remains uneasy, but Guttmann needs to illuminate what it means for a Jewish tradition to relate to God in *personal* terms.

Guttman explains: 'This idea of God, not the fruit of philosophical speculation but the product of the immediacy of religious consciousness, was stamped with its definitive character during the crisis which saw the destruction of the kingdoms of Israel and Judea. The destruction of Jerusalem and the exile of the nation were looked upon by the people as visitations of their own God, who became thereby a universal God: the kingdoms of the world were His tools, and He established the course of world history according to His will' (p.5). It seems as if he is also talking about 'religious experience' when he talks of 'religious consciousness', though it remains unclear *how* he thinks about different levels or dimensions of spirituality. At one point he expresses it historically, saying 'Jewish monotheism grew out of this fundamental experience, and through it were established all those religious characteristics that were, in turn, transmitted to Christianity and Islam' (p.5).

But the contrast that he allows is not between an experience of God that we might regard as Hebraic and an idea of God as a perfection that can only be contemplated that we might consider as Greek and later Christian. As Guttmann puts it here: 'The decisive feature of monotheism is that it is not grounded in an abstract idea of God, but in an intensely powerful divine will which rules history. This ethical voluntarism implies a thoroughly personalistic conception of God, and determines the specific character of the relationship between God and man' (p.5). But Guttman wants to be able to present this 'personal relationship' in rationalist terms that seem caught into thinking in Kantian terms, that it is reason as an independent faculty that remains radically separated from nature, that alone allows us to exist as persons in a personal relationship with God. Supposedly it is only as rational selves that we exist as persons who can be 'created in the image of God.' This is what allows Guttmann to say in terms somewhat reminiscent of Buber: 'This relationship is an ethical-voluntaristic one between two moral personalities, between an "I" and a "Thou". As God imposes his will upon that of man, so man becomes aware of the nature of his relationship to God' (p.6).[4]

The tensions in Guttmann's positions and the difficulties it creates for an understanding of the meaning of the 'nearness' or 'estrangement' from God call into question his focus upon the moral will which, in Kantian terms at least, suggests that we act out of a sense of pure will when we are acting *against* our natures, our emotions, feelings and desires. For example, Kant is quite clear that when we visit a relative in hospital out of a sense of moral duty, not really wanting to go because we have never had a good relationship with her, it is a moral act of greater moral worth. In Kant's terms, the fact that we have to act against our 'inclinations' affirms the moral worth of the action. If we want to go because we have a feeling for her and so decide to visit, this action is supposedly of doubtful moral worth because we could be going to fulfil our own selfish desires. As an egotistic action it lacks moral worth.[5]

Kant could only sustain this moral duality through assuming that even though it is quite natural for people to act out of a desire for happiness, such actions have *no* moral worth. But this is to produce an ethic of self-denial since supposedly it is only through accepting a radical split between a moral will and 'natures' that encourage us towards happiness, that we learn to deny our 'inclinations' so that we can act out of a sense of duty. In this way, Kant gives an ethical form to a Cartesian distinction between mind and body, whereby the will is taken to be 'free' because it remains radically split from a 'human nature' that is tacitly linked to the body, sexuality and the sins of the flesh.

Kant gives a secular form to this Christian disdain for the body and sexuality that through their disavowal come to be projected within discourses of Christian antisemitism on 'carnal' Israel. As I argued, in *Kant, Respect And Injustice*, Kant reveals these implicit structures when he affirms categorically that when we think about 'human nature', it is reason alone that allows us to be 'human' while nature remains 'animal'. The contrast between the 'human' and the 'animal' is set as reason becomes the marker of a Western Christian superiority over an 'animal nature'.[6]

Ethics

As Kant thinks about the moral law that can be discerned through an independent faculty of reason, he assumes the suppression of emotions, feelings and desires – inclinations – that can only serve to distract people from acting out of a sense of pure will. As rational selves, we exist *as* moral wills who are able to act out of a sense of duty and obligation. Kantian ethical traditions work to produce a split from emotions, feelings and desires that are taken to be 'selfish' and 'egotistic', and so come to be experienced as threats to sustaining a moral self. People learn to fear their emotions as revelations of an 'animal nature' they need to be able to control. Within modernity there is an identification between a dominant masculinity and a rationality that is taken as a marker of male superiority. A rationalist tradition inherits its own fear of emotions that can show itself as a disdain for mystical and Hasidic traditions within Judaism that appeal to feelings.

Since a Kantian tradition is unable to discern differences between emotions, feelings and desires, gathering them into a homogenised notion of 'inclinations', it becomes difficult to think that moral action is not necessarily a matter of suppressing emotions so that you can act out of a sense of duty. This is a tradition of ethics *as* self-denial, even though Kant has a sense of the ways in which individual perfection through individuals gradually comes to identify spontaneously with the demands of the moral law. This does not allow, however, for the education of emotions and cultivation of qualities that allow for moral development.[7]

There is no space within Kantian ethics to appreciate *how* people might develop feelings of compassion or love of others that makes them want to visit a relative they care for in hospital. This is not a matter of duty and recognises that if someone is visiting out of a sense of duty they are likely to be 'out of touch' with themselves and therefore unable to offer much of themselves in the encounter. They are not present to themselves in the relationship and the person being visited might feel that, in the absence of feelings, they are 'going through the motions'.

Through an act of will, people can make themselves do things they might otherwise not want to do. Sometimes it is important to do this and a way of carrying out responsibilities towards others, even though one might not feel like it. Kant is misleading when he makes this the paradigm of moral action. There is little space for compassion or for love and for recognising that these are feelings that can be developed over time, rather than emotions with which people react to situations. Unless we understand the processes through which people *learn* to establish a deeper feeling of connection with themselves that allows them to feel more compassion for the sufferings of others, we will not have the resources to understand the love or communion with God. This is to question Guttmann's notion that 'Communion with God is essentially a communion of moral wills. The meaning of "nearness" to God or "estrangement" from him is determined by this perspective'. He also feels open to acknowledge, however, 'This purely formal determination still allows of great variety in the relations between God and man'.

This appeal to a 'purely formal determination' is not enough to show the inadequacy of his rationalist framework when he says 'Hosea appears to have experienced the divine will primarily as a loving communion with God and His people. Whereas for Isaiah, the essential stance of man before God is humility before His awesome majesty, the Psalms testify to the feelings of closeness between God and man'. But Guttmann's conclusion that seeks to gather these diverse expressions is hardly adequate when he says 'Despite variations in its material forms of expression, the personalist character of this relationship remains the same throughout' (p.6).

The 'personalist character' is hardly clarified when he says 'God's relationship to the world is conceived along the same lines. He is the Lord of the world, he directs it according to his will, and he realises his purposes within it. His relationship to the world is not grounded in a natural force, but in the unconditional freedom of his will' (p.6). This reflects a Kantian vision of the freedom of will and suggests a dominant concept of masculinity that in the Christian West comes to be reflected in the notion that the father is God's representative within the family. He has the authority to expect that his words will be accepted as law, so that to question them is itself a sign of disobedience.

It can also reflect a particular conception of what it means for masculinity to be *created* in the image of God, for it can encourage men to accept that it is through free will that they should govern their lives. As men learn to assume a relationship of will so they take on a particular physical stance towards the world. This involves a stance in which men expect their bodies to obey whatever demands they make and those around them to conform to their wills. It does not encourage men to learn to listen to what their bodies need or to communicate their emotional needs within relationships. Like God, they expect to be obeyed.

The authority of the moral law that can be discerned through reason alone can be invoked to legitimate patriarchal authority and to present it in impersonal terms. Traditionally, within patriarchal families, the father has learnt to be fearful of engaging more personally with his children since this could threaten the impartiality and impersonality he needs to assume as a figure of authority. Within post-modern Western cultures in which fathers are often looking for more emotionally involved and intimate forms of fethering, they have often needed to question a Kantian inheritance that traditionally supported forms of patriarchal dominance.[8]

Traditionally, fathers were to be owed respect because of the position of authority they held within families, and there was little sense that fathers also had to behave in ways that they earned the respect of their children and that respect was also a two-way relationship. Though Kant was sensitive to issues of autonomy and the social conditions that could make this possible, he tended to assume that people could *abstract* themselves from these social relationships and thus relate to others as rational selves within a noumenal realm. This was also an element in shaping Kant's disdain for Judaism that he assumed to be traditionalist and rule-governed and thus denying possibilities for rational moral action.

According to Hermann Cohen in *Religion of Reason,* 'Kant obtained from Spinoza his knowledge and judgement of Judaism' (p.331). He understood the religion of Israel as a grand strategy to maintain Jewish patriotism in exile through a quasi-legal structure of ritual obligations. As Paul Mendes-Floor has recognised: 'At a deeper stratum of Western consciousness, Kant's conception of Judaism also seems to reflect the Pauline dichotomy between the Christian *kerygma* of love and the Hebrew Torah of law. In certain measure, the significance of Kant's conception of Judaism may be understood as giving a systematic, coherent articulation of the philosophical and theological antagonism that is so basic to Western perception of Judaism' ('Law and Sacrament: Ritual Observance in Twentieth Century Jewish Thought' in *Jewish Spirituality*).

But while we might accept that these dualities have shaped antagonisms 'so basic to Western perception of Judaism', it is not just a matter of *how* Western culture has perceived Judaism but the ways it has helped shape the appropriation of Jewish traditions in order to sustain Christian self-concepts. This has helped to fashion the disdain that Western culture has exercised towards Judaism, as well as to diminish it within the eyes of Jewish people themselves who have learnt to recognise their own tradition through these categories.

When Kant first published his view on Judaism, as Mendes Floor notes, the Jewish critic Saul Ascher ironically observed that Kant's views were bound to lend popular prejudices about Judaism an '*a priori* status' (p.337). But it was also the ways that Kant was to shape through *Religion Within The Limits Of Reason Alone* the ways in which Western culture was to shape its *disdain* for Judaism. It was through the particular form Kant was to give to the relationship between Christianity and Judaism, and the forms of exclusion it legitimated, that Western culture was to come to imagine itself within modernity.

The key category for both Kant's understanding of morality and religion was 'autonomy', which he conceived as humankind's liberation from its demeaning bondage to 'heteronomy'. One of the most insidious forms of heteronomy, in Kant's judgement, was evident in obedience to divine commandments simply because of some external divine authority and this came easily to be identified with Judaism.[9] Heteronomous obedience, Kant taught, falsifies genuine service to God because the will of God can only be followed automously.

Properly conceived religion, for Kant, can only be an inward reality in which faith in God constitutes a trust in the ultimate efficacy and promise of the moral law. For Kant, the only way to knowledge of God is through the autonomous realm of moral conscience or 'practical reason'. Thus, for Kant, authentic religion was synonymous with heeding the 'rational' promptings of conscience, and 'everything which apart from the moral way of life, man believes himself capable of doing to please God', such as prayer and ritual, must be regarded as mere 'religious delusion'.

In stark contrast to the church that has moved towards becoming an invisible church in which obedience to God's moral laws will be 'purely inward', that is, guided by the moral ideal of Jesus and the autonomous principles of practical reason, accessible to every rational person, Judaism exemplifies for Kant a heteronomous religion par excellence.

Specifically, Kant held that, lacking a constitutive moral ideal analogous to Jesus, Judaism does *not* direct its members to serve God through moral duty but rather demands from them an array of ritual and liturgical acts. As a hetero-nomous religion that knows only ritual and prayer, according to Kant, Judaism is indeed *no* religion at all, but a pseudo-religion.

As Mendes-Floor acknowledges in his discussion of Kant, 'the overall thrust of his critique was consistent with his conception of religion and morality. Thus for anyone accepting the premises of the critique it had prima facie a compelling validity: Judaism is, after all, in its classical expression undeniably a religion of rigorously prescribed – that is, heteronomous – religious practices *(mitsvot)*'. In this context it is perhaps apposite to note with Alasdair MacIntyre that in the light of Kant's decisive role in shaping modern consciousness, for many 'who have never heard of philosophy, let alone Kant, morality is roughly what Kant said it was' (p.190). Indeed, Kant's rejection of heteronomy in all its manifestations, especially moral and religious, has become a deeply ingrained aspect of modern sensibility' (p.319–20).[10]

But if anything, this shows the need to investigate the grounding that Kant develops for his moral theory showing the way it is itself tied up within secularised Protestant presuppositions. As I tried to argue in *Kant, Respect And Injustice,* the distinction that Kant seeks to draw between 'autonomy' and 'heteronomy' needs to be radically challenged because it assumes that emotions, feelings and desires are necessarily forms of 'un-freedom' and determination, as for Kant are notions of history and culture. This leaves us with an attenuated conception of the person as a rational self and with a weak conception of 'autonomy' that has proved itself historically incapable of illuminating forms of oppression and exploitation. The importance of ritual practice as a way of establishing a deeper connection with self, rather than simply as routine practice is also connected to a vision of embodied knowledge that *validates* the body and sexuality as sources of knowledge.

In this way, Jewish philosophy can help to enrich traditions of Western culture as it *reminds* people of the forms of forgetting that have allowed for the appropriation of love that was a central concern for Jewish religious teaching, and what the Jewishness of Jesus served to honour and develop rather than to forsake and despise.[11] Only through being able to deconstruct Kant's notion of 'inclinations' can we separate emotions and desires from feelings, and so recognise that it is through a deeper *connection* with feelings that people *can* learn to open their hearts and love others as themselves. The idea of 'love thy neighbour' was central to Jewish religious tradition and love as a defining ideal was recognised as something that needed to be expressed 'with all your heart and with all your soul' in the central prayer of the *Shema*. For love to be 'pure' it does *not* have to be impersonal or dispassionate, as Kant can suggest. This was an embodied love that was not ashamed of its connection with the body and sexuality as signs of impurity and thus of 'sins of the flesh'.[12]

Creation

A focus upon the divine act of will makes it difficult to illuminate the personal relationship that a Jewish tradition imagines with God or the questioning of God's word that has been central to the tradition since Abraham. A rationalist tradition seems to drift towards a Greek conception in which God exists in a separate realm and there is tension between Athens and Jerusalem. There are moments when Guttmann hardly recognises the tension, as when he says 'The omnipotence of the divine will appear most clearly when the world itself is looked upon as nothing but the work of this will'. His argument is concerned to question mystical and pantheistic notions of creation and this shapes it in a particular way, as when he holds that 'The Creator-God is not a part of it, or a link in the world: but God and world face each other as Creator and creature' (p.6).

As Guttmann makes clear: 'This trait emerges with increasing distinctness in the course of the evolution of the biblical idea of creation. At first, creation was conceived of as a kind of "making"or "fashioning" by God; in the end, it is the Creator's word that calls the world into existence. The divine act of will is sufficient for bringing everything into being' (p.6). Somehow this is supposed to allow the relationship 'between God and man' as 'an ethical-voluntaristic one between two moral personalities, between an "I" and a "Thou"'.

But the direction of Guttmann's concerns becomes clear when he argues 'The personalist character of biblical religion stands in the most radical contrast to another, basically impersonal, form of spiritual and universal religion, which underlies all mysticism and pantheism'. He wants to draw a clear line, even if it means disavowing mystical traditions within Judaism, when he holds that 'God is not conceived by them as a sovereign will ruling the universe, but as the hidden source from which all being emanates, or as the inner life-force which pulsates throughout the cosmos' (p.7).

Guttmann needs to insist 'Neither pantheism nor mysticism knows a personal, moral communion between God and man; in its place, there is a union with the Godhead'. The 'personal' needs to be supported with an implicit Kantian notion of the 'moral'. Guttmann makes clear that it does not matter *how* this 'union' is imagined, whether it 'envisages as an essential identity of the self with the divine life of the universe, as a merging of the soul in the mysterious ground of Being' (p.7), since the essential contrast remains that 'The living relationship between persons is replaced by the extinction of personal individuality, which is felt to be the main barrier separating us from God' (p.7).

As with Kant, Guttman is left with a rationalist notion of 'personal individuality' that makes it difficult to illuminate processes through which people *can* learn to establish different relationships with themselves. As Buddhism has always recognised, people can be 'stuck' in their personalities or egos in a way that makes it difficult to feel compassion for others.[13] Despite what they might say, they are constantly locked into their own realities as if others do not really exist for them. This is something that they cannot shift as an act of will and a Kantian tradition that would assume that a higher level of moral individuality is reached as people learn to suppress their 'inclinations', so that they can act out of a sense of duty, can leave people with little *relationship* to their emotional lives. It is the treatment of emotions as essentially 'selfish' and 'egotistic' that makes it difficult to discern differences between emotions and between emotions *and* feelings. It also makes it difficult to pinpoint post-modern traditions of an ethical self that have discerned the limits of rationalist ethics.[14]

Guttmann wants to insist that his distinction between 'the two types of religion' remains valid 'even when they apparently use the same language. The *amor dei* of pantheism and the love of God of the mystic are as different in essence from the personalistic love of God (however enthusiastically the latter may experience the raptures of the divine presence) as is the mystic shudder before the hidden abyss of the divine being from the experience of the sublime majesty of the personal God' (p.7).

This distinction supposedly holds true in the contrast between various types of religion where 'Here, too, it is not just a matter of conflicting ideas, but of fundamentally contrasting religious attitudes. The transcendence of God as personal Creator is foreign to the doctrine of pantheism and mysticism because, according to the latter, the world is not subject to a sovereign divine will' (p.7).

For mysticism, 'the divine "ground" or source does not create the world, but rather expels it from its own substance' (p.8), and 'however much the difference between God and the world may pervade the religious consciousness, the world is at the same time seen as the manifestation of God' (p.8). This allows the conclusion that 'Whereas the Creator-God stands over and against the world, His creation, the God of mysticism, becomes the principle underlying the suprasensual world'.

Nature

Guttmann's rationalism encourages him to insist that even though 'During the Hellenistic period as well as in the Middle Ages, magical practices and, in particular, astrology found their way into Jewish life, but were never able to penetrate the inner sanctum of the religious relationship to God'. It also allows him to hold that 'religion is as different from myth as it is from magic, and the same force underlies its separation from both. The idea of creation marks the point of cleavage between myth and religion, since it excludes any evolution or emanation by which the world proceeds naturally, as if were, from God, and posits the free will of God as sole cause of the world. Here too, the voluntaristic and personalist character of God forms a barrier against mythological intrusions....Nature has lost its divine quality; from the dwelling place of the divine it has itself become the work of God's hands'.

Writing about the Book of Genesis, Isaac Bashevis Singer recalls in his essay for *Congregation: Contemporary Writers Read the Jewish Bible* that 'For Jewish children, to begin studying the Book of Genesis was always an important event in their lives. Jewish children were brought up with the belief that the Torah was the well of the highest knowledge, given by God to Moses, written in parchment by saintly scribes: in the letters with which God had created the world'. Speaking more personally, he acknowledges 'For me, a son and grandson of rabbis, learning the first book of the Pentateuch was the greatest event in my life. I often heard my father recite passages of this book in his sermons to his congregations. I knew already that God had created the world in six days and on the seventh day He rested. It may sound strange, but I began to ponder Creation when I was still a little boy....How can something be created from nothing? God has created the world, but who created God?' (p.3).[15]

Singer acknowledges that 'The more I read, the more questions and doubts assailed me. If God could have created Adam by the words of His mouth, why did He have to cast a deep sleep upon Adam to form Eve from one of his ribs? Some ten generations of early men were mentioned in the Book of Creation, and there must have been wives, daughters, sisters, but only three females are mentioned. I have always heard from my parents that God is a god of mercy. But why did He accept the sacrifices of Abel and not those of his brother Cain? Didn't he forsee that this would cause jealousy and enmity between the two brothers? And why did He create the serpent to lure Adam and Eve to sin with the result that God cursed them, drove them from Paradise, and punished them all with death? Even the fact that God had given the animals to men to be eaten disturbed me. We had a slaughterhouse on Krochmalna Street and I often saw the slaughterers kill chickens, roosters, ducks, geese. And I witnessed those innocent creatures trembling in the hands of their murderers' (p.4).

His older brother Joshua had become 'enlightened' at about the age of 18 and began to argue religious problems with his parents: 'I heard him say, "All religious are based on old books, but these books were written by men and men could lie, distort the truth, or have illusions. If we Jews don't believe in the old books of other religions, how can we know for certain that our books contain absolute truth?" My parents could never give him a clear answer. All they could do was scold him and call him heretic, betrayer of Israel' (p.4).

Singer recalls: 'My older brother confided in me that there was no God. The earth tore itself away from the sun, he said, and it took millions of years before it cooled and began to produce bacteria, plants, animals, birds, insects. My brother used such odd words as "development", "evolution", "accident". He told me that all creatures were born with a survival instinct and had to fight for their existence. The stronger ones were always victorious and brought up new generations, while the weak ones perished and were lost forever. But was this fair? My father and mother always told me that God was a god of justice, on the side of the weak, not only the strong. But I heard my brother remark that nature does not know any compassion; it acts according to eternal laws. He quoted the great Jewish philosopher Benedict de Spinoza, who said that we must love nature with an intellectual love. But how can we love something or someone who knows no pity and perhaps does not love us?' (p.5).

Seventy years later, Singer still feels convinced that, despite what critics have said about Genesis having been written by different people, that 'it was the same master writer who knew exactly where his pen was leading him'. As he admits: 'I would say that although I became disappointed in many beliefs, whether religious or scientific, I was never disenchanted in the wondrous art of these stories....I have learnt that the great storytellers, believers that God takes care of every human being, each and every animal, and that everything that we do, think, and desire is connected with the Creator of all things' (p.7).

Guttmann wants to insist that in the Book of Genesis, 'Nature here has a substantial life of its own, but it is conceived as inanimate and subordinate to the purposes of God, which, as such, are foreign to it' (p.10). But the way we might read people's relationships with their own nature are blocked in the duality and masculine language Guttmann invokes, saying 'Man himself, the end and purpose of creation, is not conceived solely as part of nature, but as standing over and against nature, as the image of God' (p.10). The word 'solely' is telling of a tension that is otherwise not recognised when Guttmann declares 'This anthropocentric conception grants man the right to conquer the earth, and relegates astral "divinities" to the role of mere luminaries of the earth; it redirects all religious feeling from nature towards the transmundane God. Henceforth man sees himself as a being superior to the forces of nature, which in natural religion would be considered as divine' (p.11).

It is the nature of this superiority and the responsibilities that this leaves for people in their relationships with nature that need to be questioned. There is an ambivalence in the text that allows us resources to *question* the modern notion that shaped the seventeenth-century scientific revolution's inheritance that identified progress with the control and domination of nature. There is also little patience in Guttmann's rationalism with Singer's father, who taught him 'that the sky teems with angels, seraphim, sacred beasts, cherubim. They all worship God, sing His praises. God Himself sits on a Throne of Glory and is so loving and merciful that he spends the nights teaching little children who have died prematurely and He reveals to them the secrets of the Torah. But my brother said that these stories were nothing but legends invented by fanatics. He told me that the sky is full of clusters of stars called galaxies...He said that God had no plan or purpose in creating the world...' (p.5).

There seems to be an unresolved tension when Guttmann says so categorically that 'The nature of the Bible expresses the same attitude; nature is looked upon as a manifestation of the majesty of God; any kind of pantheistic feeling is quite alien to it'. He insists that 'Nature remains the work of God's hands, and above the rest of creation there is always present the thought of man's superiority', while at the same time recognising that 'This opposition between man and nature has, as yet, no metaphysical connotation. There is certainly no hint of an opposition between the world of the senses and a supra-sensual world. Man is a creature of this world, and it is only his character as a person that raises him above things nature' (p.11).

This crucially *rejects* the dualism between the earthly that is identified with 'the world of the senses' that is disdained and the spiritual that proved so vital for a Christian tradition. Even though Guttmann's rationalism tempted him in this direction, there are too many vital sources in the Jewish tradition that push towards a different ethical relationship to nature and to 'the world of the senses'. Guttmann is clear, however, that 'It is in the unique historical process and not in the unchanging being of nature that the revelations of God's will and the satisfaction of all religious aspirations are to be found' (p.12).

7

Ethics, Deeds and Love

Histories

The Jewish tradition is historical and keeps alive, within the Western tradition, the possibilities of a *historical* consciousness that tended to be sublated within the terms of an Enlightenment vision of modernity. Even though Hegel refuses the historical claims of Judaism within his Christian view, wanting to see Judaism as having been historically subsumed within the higher ethical universalism of Christianity, there is a sense in which he presents a counter-tradition within the West that acknowledges the historical character of consciousness, thus questioning the otherwise absolutist claims of a Greek tradition of reason.[1] Though Hegel's vision of a universal history also works to deny the integrity of diverse historical and spiritual traditions that can no longer enter into creative dialogue with each other but have to be ordered within a singular hierarchical vision, it could be claimed that Judaism's discoveries of history remain subversive of his intentions.[2] Judaism within its Talmudic readings had always insisted on the *integrity* of *different voices* and has refused the silencing of diversity in the name of a singular vision of truth.

Guttmann's *Philosophies Of Judaism* recognises that 'Biblical religion is essentially historical in yet another sense. It sees its origin in an historical revelation, through which Israel became the people of God. Every subsequent revelation refers back to this parent revelation and bases itself upon it. The prophets do not claim to reveal something radically new, but merely seek to restore the ancient faith of Israel' (p.12). This meant that 'Religious truth was thought of as something historically "given"; development was possibly only by reading new ideas back into the traditional faith' (p.12). The religious thought of the prophets that was nourished by an awareness of a crisis in the life of Israel: 'was centred upon the relationship of God to the people as a whole'.

As Guttmann seeks to explain it: 'God had made a covenant with Israel as a people; the sin of the people had brought down God's punishment upon the nation; but it was the same nation or its remnant that God had promised future redemption' (p.13). This means that the nation and religion were deeply intertwined and, according to Guttmann: 'Even the historical universalism of the prophets adhered to this national "political" view. Humanity, a concept created by the prophets, was a community of nations. The individual, for the moment, was secondary to the people' (p.13).

The problem of the individual appears more clearly with the later prophets. The issue of individual moral responsibility was clarified by Jeremiah and even more so by Ezekiel. As Guttmann explains: 'Every man was responsible before God for his own deeds, and according to those deeds – not according to the merits or demerits of his ancestors – he would be judged'. This meant that 'Divine justice manifests itself in the individual too, and not only in the collectivity of the people though, of course, the relation of individual destiny with that of the nation is never obliterated' (p.13). In post-Exilic literature, after the Jews returned from the Babylonian Exile, the individual assumes greater importance and ethics looks beyond the limited framework of reward and punishment. The idea of a *loving* relationship with God is extended to the individual, especially in the Psalms.[3]

Jeremiah asks the question that has echoed through the centuries of rabbinic literature concerning the prosperity of the wicked and the adversity of the righteous. Some sustained the view, despite contrary evidence, that suffering came as a result of sin, while others considered the sufferings of the righteous as a means of purification for the soul. As Guttman records: 'Deutero-Isaiah introduces the figure of the Servant of the Lord who suffers for the sake of the collective sin of the people...the Book of Job concludes with faith in the majestic and sublime God, who is above and beyond all human questioning' (p.14). Given the rationalist conception of philosophy Guttmann holds to, however, 'this thought is not yet reflection concerning religion; it is the religious consciousness itself, which in its anguish calls to thought for aid. Divine justice becomes a problem for religious thought, which tries to solve it in a mighty struggle...It is characteristic of the book that the final answer is given in the form of divine revelation. The struggle of faith comes to rest in the immediate certitude of divine majesty. The very fact that it is at this juncture that the religious reflection reappears, emphasizes the distinctiveness of biblical religion' (p.15).[4]

This allows Guttmann to affirm that 'Jewish thought is not oriented towards metaphysical questions' (p.15). Rather, as Wittgenstein appreciated, it offered *resources* for the West to question the dominance of a Greek metaphysical tradition, partly through its unease with questions that are removed from any context to be posed in abstract terms alone.[5] As Guttmann explains, the question that became so central to Christianity of how suffering and death came into the world determined Christian readings of the Garden of Eden, but for Judaism, 'Not suffering in general, but rather the sufferings of the righteous, causes us to doubt the justice of God and becomes a stumbling block...Job does not revolt against the magnitude of his suffering...He is driven to rebellion because he suffers without cause, and because he feels himself the victim of God's despotism' (p.16).

Guttmann wants to be able to insist 'Every man apprehends intuitively what is good or evil. The intelligibility of moral obligation implied the rationality of the divine will. Hence God, too, in his actions conformed to moral standards and could be measured by them' (p.16). At the same time, he recognises strains within the Jewish tradition that offer the opposite recognition 'that God was incomprehensible and that his ways were higher than the ways of man, even as the heavens were higher than the earth'. But he wants to be able to conclude 'All this, however, did not detract from the belief in the moral reasonableness of the divine will'. This means, that for Guttmann at least, 'The problem of theodicy is not settled for Job by saying that God is above all ethical criteria, but rather by the recognition of God's utter incomprehensibility paradoxically becoming a ground for trust in the meaningfulness of his providence, a providence of love and justice which is no less meaningful for remaining impenetrable to human understanding' (p.17). As he acknowledges elsewhere, however, it is the experience of *hearing* God's voice that makes the difference. Guttmann needs to believe in the 'intelligibility' and 'essential meaningfulness' of the 'divine will' so that the premise underlying Jewish religious speculation 'is the notion that God's moral will is accessible to human comprehension' (p.16).

Whether we can still believe this in the face of the Shoah, we can recognise that even after the destruction of the Temple 'The faith of

Talmudic Judaism rests completely on biblical foundations'. As Guttmann explains: 'Central to it are the simple and sublime ideas of the Bible concerning a transcendent God, the Torah as the embodiment of his moral demands, the moral nature of the relationship between God and man, the wisdom and justice of divine providence, the election of Israel, and the promise of the coming kingdom of God. No theoretical reflection diminishes the living reality of God'. Judaism was not a matter of religious belief as if deeds were somehow to flow from rationally accepting certain beliefs, but rather it was through *deeds* that people could be brought to an experience of God.[6]

People are not to be taught certain moral principles that were to be accepted as a matter of faith or reason, but they were to be encouraged to *live* in ways that could bring them closer to feeling God's presence. As Guttmann recognises: 'In order to express the consciousness of the presence of God, the religious imagination did not stop even before the most daring anthropomorphisms. In order to emphasise the value of the study of Torah, the Talmudic rabbis describe God himself as studying Torah. The faith that the sufferings of Israel could not destroy, the intimate bond between God and his people, was expressed by saying that God not only lamented over the sorrows that he had brought upon Israel, but actually shared their exile' (p.31).

Even though the passionate violence of the religious ethos of the prophets was to give way, in Talmudic times, to a quieter, more restrained piety bound to history and tradition, Guttmann explains: 'Piety is not so much the mere observance of the divine commandments as the imitation of the divine model. The biblical commandment to be holy even as the Lord God is holy, and the injunction to walk in the ways of God, are interpreted as demands to imitate the divine qualities of love and mercy. The spirit of rabbinic religion is thus elevated above the submission or obedience of will' (p.32). It is doubtful whether Guttmann's rationalism leaves him with the resources to understand *how* this can be achieved, if it is not a matter of will. We can feel the tension and unease when he says 'Its religious activity is rooted in the inner certainty of community with God, yet its piety remains one of precept and duty. Consequently, much stress is laid on moral freedom: man's actions are his own, even in relation to the divine omnipotence' (p.32).

It is a recognition that involves feelings of the heart and an openness to a source that cannot be attained through an act of will that is difficult to express within a rationalist tradition. There is a tension between a Kantian rationalist tradition that wants to think that moral worth can be gained through acting freely as a moral agent in a way that involves the denial or suppression of inclinations and a Jewish tradition that recognises that unless we *act* out of a sense of *feeling* towards others our moral actions will be compromised. Love cannot be ordered; it has to develop in its own time, if it is to develop at all.

These were insights that, through the Renaissance's engagement with Kaballistic traditions, became part of a Western humanist tradition, often expressed in secular terms.[7] These insights also found their ways into Keats and the Romantic movement that sought to give a place to feeling within human life. It is recognised in Wordsworth's Preface to the *Lyrical Ballads*, in the grand elementary principle of pleasure. It is also there in the writings of Blake, Lawrence and Whitman.[8]

Seamus Heaney referred to a similar inspiration that also draws upon sound and hearing, in calling the edited anthology he wrote with Ted Hughes, *The Rattle Bag*. As he explains: 'What we hoped to do was to shake the rattle and awaken the sleeping inner poet in every reader. We proceeded in the faith that the aural and oral pleasures of poetry, the satisfaction of recognition and repetition, constitute an experience of rightness that can make the whole physical and psychic system feel more in tune with itself'. He clarifies what this can mean, saying 'An experience of words and rhythms like these is arguably more than physical. It represents a metaphysical extension of capacity, an arrival at a point beyond the point that has been settled for previously'. (*The Guardian Review*, 25.10.03, p.5.) For Heaney, 'What matters most in the end is the value that attaches to a few poems intimately experienced and well remembered...Such a poem can come to feel like a pre-natal possession, a guarantee of inwardness and a link to origin. It can become the eye of a verbal needle through which the growing person can pass again and again until it is known by heart, and becomes a path between heart and mind, a path by which the individual can enter, repeatedly, into the kingdom of rightness' (p.6).[9]

If the belief in another world, above and beyond time, led to a new evaluation of the present world with the Talmudic saying that this world is like a vestibule in which people should prepare themselves for entering the banquet hall of the world to come, nevertheless, this rabbinic view is very different from the dualistic contempt for the world of the senses that we find in Philo under Platonic influence. As Guttmann insists: 'The Talmud emphatically repeats the biblical affirmation of this *world* and interprets the words of Genesis, "and God saw everything that He had made and behold it was very good," as referring to *both* worlds. The good things of this world, including sensual pleasures, may be enjoyed simply and naturally; only in rare instances do we find any ascetic tendencies' (p.34). Guttmann also recognises, questioning his own Kantian instincts, 'Even more important is the fact that asceticism plays no role in the understanding of ethics' (p.34).

Ethics

The Talmudic teacher who described this world as only a vestibule to the coming world also said that, although one hour of blessedness in the world to come was worth more than all the life of this world, one hour of repentance and good deeds in this world was worth more than all of the life of the world to come. Even if the moral act was understood as, in part at least, a preparation for the future world, it lacked, as Guttmann recognises, 'the negative connotation of separation from the world of the senses. Its meaning was rather wholly positive: to serve God in this world, to fulfil His will, and to build a social order in accordance with His will....fulfilling the will of God in this world is no less communion with God than the state of blessedness in the hereafter' (p.34).

The rabbinic view of the world is also reflected in the vision of human nature. As Guttmann explains: 'The Bible had ascribed a divine origin to the human spirit, but now we find an explicit dualism. The body and soul are seen in sharp contrast. Because of his soul, which is destined for eternal life, man belongs to the superior world of the spirit; in his body, he belongs to the earth. Thanks to his soul, he resembles the angels; thanks to his body, a beast...Man's higher powers, such as his reason and his moral consciousness, are attributed to the soul; his lower passions are assigned to the body. The corollary of man's intermediate position between the higher and the lower world is that, by observing the divine commandments, he can rise to the ranks of the angels, but by transgressing them he descends to the level of the beasts' (p.35).

This remains an uneasy passage with echoes of a Kantian discourse that would also insist in masculinist terms on the 'higher powers, such as reason and his moral consciousness' as if morality can be identified with reason. Guttmann also seems to echo a Kantian disdain for the body and emotional life in his notion that 'lower passions are assigned to the body'. If this disdain seems implicit in the language he uses, he also disavows them when he insists 'But this dualism is far from identifying evil with man's sensual nature. The body is not the ground of evil, and consequently man's moral task does not consist in his separation from the body' (p.35). The clarification that follows is somewhat surprising: 'The warfare between good and evil is fought out *within* man's soul; it is there that good and evil impulses face each other'.

Drawing upon a Kantian discourse, Guttmann says 'They represent two directions of the human will, and man must choose between them' (p.35).[10]

As if caught within an argument with himself that reflects a broader conflict of interpreting a Jewish tradition within a largely Christian culture, even if presented in secular terms, Guttmann seems to be pulled in different directions. The Jewish texts remind him of truths that cannot easily be recognised or expressed within prevailing rationalist moral discourses. He recognises that 'As the source of temptation, sensuality occasionally is identified with the "evil impulse", but in itself is ethically indifferent and had its legitimate sphere of existence' (p.35). He recognises that 'the body is regarded as an essential part of man's God-given nature' and that 'Even the evil impulse is necessarily part of human nature, and the Talmud voices the remarkable demand to love God with both of our impulses – the good and the evil. Here again, the end of ethics is seen not as separation from the world of the senses, but rather serving God within that world, with all available human powers' (p.35). But at the same time Guttmann recognised that these dualistic conceptions *could* easily be turned in the direction of an ascetic contemplative religion and that it provided the opening through which Neo-platonic types of spirituality entered Judaism in the Middle Ages.

Rabbi Akiva used to say 'How privileged we are to have been created in God's image; how much more privileged still are we to have been made aware that we were created in God's image'. But what do we include in this awareness? Does it also include our bodies as well as our minds, our sexuality as well as our reasoning? It is not supposed to make us feel superior to other creatures and thus not involve a denigration of what we share with animals. It supposedly sustains its own humility. As Rabbi Bunam said to his disciples: 'We should all have two pockets, so that we can reach into one or other according to our need. In our right pocket there should be a piece of paper saying, "For my sake the world was created" and in the left, "I am but dust and ashes"'.

By declaring love of one's neighbour to be the supreme ethical virtue, the Talmud does not go beyond the teachings of the Torah, but inquiry into fundamental religious questions has acquired a certain independent value. Of particular interest is the attempt to reduce the entire content of biblical commandments to one principle. The novelty lies in the theoretical formulation that asserts the law to be a commentary on this ethical rule.

Love

In connection with the commandment to love God, the Talmud discusses the difference between those who serve God out of love and those who serve him out of fear. The text argues that observance of the law, even for ulterior motives, was not devoid of value, for through it people could rise to a disinterested observance. Discussing the primacy of learning over the observance of commandments, the Talmud solves the dilemma on one occasion by declaring that the study of the Law was equivalent to the observance of all the commandments, and on another by concluding that not theory but deeds were what mattered. Sometimes it is acknowledged that it is through *deeds* that people will eventually come to appreciate their meaning and so gradually come to serve God out of love.

Guttmann recognises Stoic influences in the Talmud, saying that 'The comparison of the soul to God derives from Stoic metaphysics; the soul fills and vitalises the body as God fills the world, and like God, it sees but cannot be seen. The Talmud incorporates Platonic as well as Stoic ideas, which, divorced from their systematic context, were part and parcel of general Greek culture' (p.40). The Talmud not only knows of the pre-existence of the soul, but also says that before birth the soul knew the entire Torah, *forgetting* it only at the moment of birth. Again, this shows the flow of ideas across diverse traditions. According to Guttmann, 'Here the Torah takes the place of the Platonic Idea, as also in the saying that God looked at the Torah and from this model created the world. The invisibility of God is exemplified by the Platonic parable of the human eye which cannot bear to look even at the brightness of the sun' (p.41).

Rabbi Levi Yitzchak said 'Whether we really love God is shown by our love for one another'. A similar sentiment is expressed by Rabbi Moshe Leib of Sassov, who said to his disciples: 'I learnt how we must truly love our neighbour from a conversation between two villagers which I overheard. "Tell me, friend Ican, do you love me?" "I love you deeply". "Do you know, my friend, what gives me pain?" "How can I, pray, know what gives you pain?" "If you do not know what gives me pain, how can you say that you truly love me?"

To love, truly to love, means to know what causes others pain'.

Max Ehrmann has written the poem:

'Love someone – in God's name
Love someone – for this is
The bread of the inner life, without

Which a part of you will
Starve and die;......'
                              (*The Desiderata of Happiness*, Souvenir Press,
                                          1986 (first published 1948, p.18).

Recognising a need to love as the bread of the inner life goes against
a culture that has for so long taught that love is a scarce commodity that
we have to be careful not to waste. Within a post-modern culture, people have become anxious about committing themselves to love, not
knowing whether they might live to regret it because 'someone better'
might appear in their lives the next day. This can lock both men and
women into a game whereby they are wary of loving, especially if they
fear a relationship that might threaten their ambitions at work. People
might talk of wanting a loving relationship but not be *open* to love in
their emotional lives. They might have lost a capacity to love, by being
so concerned with whether others can be deserving or worthy of their
love. Somehow they can become locked into a narcissistic[11] relationship
with themselves in which others really cease to exist for them.

As E.M. Forster recognised, this is an uncertainty that modernity has
so often refused to acknowledge, preferring to think that if people have
difficulties in loving this is because they have not yet discovered the
right person. Zadie Smith, in her 2003 Orange Word Lecture, 'E.M.
Forster's Ethical Style: Love, Failure and the Good in Fiction', given at
the Gielgud Theatre in London, shared how her love for Forster's *A
Room With A View* could no longer be expressed within the literary
community at school: 'We are as Heraclitus described us: "Estranged
from that which is most familiar". Suddenly this incommensurable
"Love" and this other, more vague surmise – that the novel we loved
was not simply "good" but even represented *a* Good in our lives – these
ideas grow shameful and, after some time, are forgotten entirely, along
with the novel that first inspired them' (*The Guardian Review*,
01.11.03, p.4).[12]

I was struck on reading this because I had felt a similar love when I
had read Forster and had also learned to forget, even though I had not
studied literature. Forster's characters are, according to Smith, famously
always in a muddle: they don't know what they want or how to get it:
'It has been noted before that this might be a deliberate ethical strategy,
an expression of the belief that the true motivations of human agents are
far from rational in character' (p.4). She recognises that 'Forster himself
was conscious of the connection between his style and his ethics in an
interesting way'. He knew *A Room With A View* was, as he put it in his
diary, 'clear, bright and well constructed', but this very clarity bothered

him and made it difficult to finish. The 'undeveloped heart' is the quality, or lack of qualities, that Forster's novels frequently depict. An 'undeveloped heart' makes its owner 'march to their destiny by catchwords', living not through their *own* feelings but by the received ideas of others. They might know what the brain knows, and what other people know, but not what love knows. According to Smith, 'It is Forster who shows shows us how hard it is to will oneself into a meaningful relationship with the world; it is Forster who lends his empathy to those who fail to do so' (p.5).

Smith has learnt to appreciate that central to the Aristotelian inquiry into the Good Life is the idea that the training and refinement of *feeling* plays an essential role in our moral understanding.[13] According to Smith, 'Forster's fiction, following Austen's, does this in an exemplary fashion, but it is Forster's fiction that goes further in showing us how very difficult an educated heart is to achieve' (p.5). As she understands it, 'Part of his project was to step into that Austenite gap where tolerance falls short of love...More than this, he suggested there might be some ethical advantage in not always pursuing a perfect and unyielding rationality' (p.6). Forster's ethical procedure can lead us back to the poet Forster felt had 'seized upon the supreme fact of human nature, the very small amount of good in it, and the supreme importance of that little'. It was through a reading of Keats' letters that Forster found a model for Lucy Honeychurch's way of being in the world. Keats describes it as a quality of 'Negative Capability, that is when man is capable of being in uncertainties, mysteries, doubts, without any irritable reaching after fact and reason' (p.6).[14]

As Smith puts it: 'What Keats conceived of as a positive ethical strategy, Forster recasts as a muddle. It is not by knowing *more* that Lucy comes to understand, but by knowing considerably less....She tells all of them that she is certain of her own heart and mind. But it is by a process of growing less "certain", *less* consistent, *less* morally enthusiastic, that she moves closer to the good she is barely aware of desiring' (p.6). She also reminds us that Forster is the first literary generation influenced by Freud to inherit the idea that our very consciousness is, at root, uncertain and fearful. He recognises that the great majority of people are not like an Austinian protagonist, but that we 'would rather not understand ourselves, because it is easier and less dangerous' (p.6).

Smith knows that 'The heart has its own knowledge in Forster, and Love is never quite a rational choice, as it was for Austen'. He allowed the English comic novel the possibility of a spiritual and bodily life, not simply to exist as an exquisitely worked game of social ethics. She reminds us that 'Elizabeth Bennet's claim at her epiphanic moment is made to herself. It is "Until this moment I never knew myself!" Lucy's claim concerns another person, Mr Emerson. She explains that he "made her see the whole of everything at once". The first is a rationalist's self-awakening. The second is a mystic's awakening to the world'. She also realises that 'Austen asks for toleration from her readers. Forster demands something far stickier, more shameful: love' (p.6).

8

Pleasures, Sufferings and Transcendence

In The Image Of God

What does it mean to be created in the *image* of God? Does it mean that we should learn to be self-sufficient and able to deal with our own emotional lives because God is often assumed to be perfect? According to Philo, God's perfection is complete and 'he is beyond blessedness itself and happiness and whatever is more excellent and better than these'. As 'the Good', God is naturally perfect: 'all perfection and finality belong to One alone' (Rer. Div. Her. 121, quoted in Williamson, p.45). In Det. Pot. Ins. 54, God is described as 'full, in the sense of complete'. Linked with all that Philo says about God's perfect goodness and sinlessness is his belief that God cannot be, and is not, the cause of evil in the universe. 'God,' he says, 'is the cause of good things only; and of nothing at all that is bad...'[1]

This Greek reading of a Jewish conception of God can find its echoes within a rationalist modernity that remains shaped within the secular terms of a dominant Western Christian tradition. Thus a young woman, for example, in contemporary Western culture who had grown up in a family in which anger is disavowed can grow up feeling that anger is an unacceptable emotion that betrays a lack of self-control. She might feel that she should be able to control her anger and that it is only to the extent that she can assert this control that she can think of herself as being 'created in the image of God'. She might have tacitly learned that anger is part of her 'animal' nature that needs to be controlled if she is to exist as a human being. She might assume that it is only through her reason that she can be created in God's image and that every time she 'gives in' to her reason, she is revealing her animal nature. She feels that her anger is a weakness that shows she is falling short of an ideal that she has internalised in her family. Her subjectivity and relationship to herself is *shaped* through this denial of emotions and desires.[2]

As she reflects back on her family and the moral culture it sustained, she recognises that she was always made to feel 'bad about herself' whenever she got angry. This showed a weakness that proved that she was undeserving of love. Even though she grew up within a Jewish family in the mid-West of the United States, she is aware of how notions of original sin – of constantly feeling inadequate, so that whatever she did, she was always left feeling she could have achieved more – had shaped her relationship to herself. Even though her parents said that she was a blessing to them, she never really *felt* this in herself. She felt she was always failing to live up to ideals of perfection that pervaded the family atmosphere, even if they were never openly articulated. Though Philo says that 'Not to commit any sin at all is the property of God, and perhaps also of a divine man' (Virt. 177). Though Philo was thinking of 'Our most holy Moses' (Virt. 175), this resonated, as Williamson recognises with 'Christological statements in the New Testament about the sinfulness of Jesus of Nazareth' (p.45).[3]

Philo inherited a Greek antipathy for anthropomorphism which is what encouraged him to adopt an allegorical method of exegesis. He was *not* concerned with literal meanings that so often spoke about God in personal terms, as when the Talmud insisted that God not only lamented over the sorrows that He had brought upon Israel, but actually shared their exile. Rather Philo was concerned with 'the meanings that lie beneath the surface' that often reveal their true interpretation through a contrast that seems to echo a Greek tradition concerning a life directed towards pleasure and life of a quite contrary kind, a life of self-control and patient endurance which obtains true health and safety (*Agric.* 96–101). When Moses tells the story of Lot's wife, he is not 'inventing a fable', according to Philo, 'but indicating precisely a real fact', the real fact being the inner meaning, which is to do with the intellectual blindness which results from failure to use the mind (see *Fug.* 121). The lazy student disregards his teacher's efforts to train his mind and turns backwards to the hidden and dark side of life and 'so her turns into a pillar and becomes like a deaf and lifeless stone' (p.173).

As a woman reflects back on her family life as a child, she might recognise how she was left feeling as if she was always falling short of a perfection she could never reach. Growing up with a Jewish household had hardly protected her from these prevailing Christian notions. She felt as unworthy as her Christian friends and as much in need to prove herself worthy of her parents' love. She felt that, whatever her parents said, she was expected to do well at school and so prove herself *deserving* of their love. In time she learned that it did no good to 'bottle up' her emotions because she discovered that her inner life was more taken up with anxieties than if she expressed her anger, say, more directly. She felt that she could begin to honour her anger and recognise that it was also made in the image of God.

Pleasure

Reflecting upon attitudes towards pleasure that she learned about in her family made her aware that pleasure was something that could only be justified as a reward for hard work. Happiness had to be worked for and if it came 'too easy' then it was taken to be of little value. She was struck with *how* ambivalent she still felt as an adult about pleasure, reflecting that even in her liberal synagogue it was discouraged on Simchat Torah, a festival that was supposed to be a moment of great joy and celebration. It was as if pleasure was dangerous because it reflected a lack of self-control. People needed to be moderate in their enjoyment because otherwise they would be deemed to be irrational. Because emotions were defined as 'irrational' it became difficult to countenance them. Pleasures were too easily identified with sexual pleasure and the 'sins of the flesh'. Pleasure could so easily lead you astray from following a moral path that was assumed to be a path of reason.[4]

Pleasure comes as a reward for concerted efforts and hard work within a Protestant moral culture. People can allow themselves enjoyment at the end of the week, but sometimes they can only find a certain degree of release with alcohol. In Norway, for instance, there is a tradition of heavy drinking on Friday and Saturday night as if people are so used to a moral culture of self-denial that they can only 'let themselves go' with alcohol. There is a disdain for the world of sense-perception that is somehow linked to pleasure, as if pleasure that comes through the senses is to be disavowed to give way to 'higher' intellectual pleasures. The serpent in the Book of Genesis is identified by Philo as a symbol of pleasure, while Eve is a symbol of life. In not being able to refuse the temptations of sexual pleasure, Eve supposedly brought 'sin' into the world.[5]

Within Christian readings, Eve came to be identified with temptation and so with the 'sins of the flesh'. Mary is often presented as a second Eve, who remains pure and 'untainted' by sexual pleasure when she gives birth to Jesus. It is constantly reiterated that Jesus has to die so that Christians can be redeemed. Through the sacramental wafer and the wine, Christians in/corporate – take into their own bodies – the body and blood of Christ. The *suffering body* of Christ becomes the most pervasive visible symbol of Christian hegemony within Western Europe. Through this symbol, people are re/minded of what they owe to Jesus for having given up his life for their sins. Redemption can only be delivered through suffering and people are to contemplate the suffering body of Christ. People are to be constantly reminded of the sacrifices that were made in their name and the guilt they subsequently carry into the present.[6]

A case was recently brought against the public school in the small medieval town of Ofena in central Italy by Adel Smith, the 43-year-old leader of the Italian Union of Muslims, who converted from Catholicism to Islam in 1987. Smith argued for the removal of the crucifix in his son's classroom because it violated his right to public education free of religious influence. In a 30-page decision, the local magistrate agreed, ordering that the cross be removed. There was widespread opposition to the decision, with opponents suggesting that Italy's cultural foundations in Catholicism were being undermined by Muslims using secular arguments as cover. Smith rejects such notions, saying 'This is Italy's old Catholic fundamentalism coming to the surface. You must not confuse culture with the state and the rights of its citizens. You can keep your crucifixes in your home or your church or around your neck, but not at my child's school' (*Time* Magazine, 10.11.2003, p.57).

Interior Minister Guiseppe Pisanu disagrees: 'The crucifix is not only a religious symbol; it represents 2,000 years of history and culture. Immigrants' culture and religious identities must be respected, but they must also be expected to follow the established judicial and political system of our country. How can a court side with one Muslim parent over the wishes of (all the school's) Italian parents?' The ruling has been appealed by the Minister of Education and a judge has temporarily suspended the original decision, delaying the removal of the crucifix. The Church wants to maintain the status quo, recognising the symbolic power of the crucifix in school classrooms.

If Northern Europe is more characterised by secular cultures, we should not underestimate the difficulties people face in deconstructing the influence of religious traditions that have been rendered largely invisible. In Britain, there is wide-scale ignorance of Biblical traditions so that children often lack the religious references that would make their cultural traditions intelligible. This does not mean, as Foucault came to recognise, that these diverse Christian traditions do not still help to shape the way people grow up to think and feel about themselves. Even if they feel little conscious identification they *can* still feel that it is only through suffering that they deserve pleasure, or that dwelling upon their emotions has to be a form of self-indulgence because as moral selves they should be selfless.[7]

Transcendence

Philo is discussing the possibilities open to man in view of the fact that, in a sense, his mind is 'a god to him'. He describes how the human mind lifts its gaze beyond the material world to reach out after 'the intelligible world', and sees therein the surpassingly lovely Ideas. As Williamson puts it: 'Whether the solution which Philo adopted did anything more than, as Bultmann suggests, substitute one version of transcendence, in terms of the opposition between matter and spirit, for others is a matter for discussion. But Philo certainly believed he had found a solution' (p.106). 'The problem of the sheer transcendence of God', according to Williamson, 'created a situation within which, without finding a solution to the problem, Philo could have written nothing about God, since he could know nothing about him' (p.106).

Williamson suggests a solution is to be found also in Philo's expounding Exodus. 25:7, where it states 'For if, O mind, thou dost not prepare thyself of thyself, excising desires, pleasures, grief, fears, follies, injustices and related evils, and dost (not) change and adapt thyself to the vision of holiness, thou will end thy life in blindness, unable to see the intelligible sun' (p.106). But there is an alternative: 'If, however, thou art worthily initiated and cast, be consecrated to God and in a certain sense become an animate shrine to the Father (then) instead of having closed eyes, thou wilt see the First (Cause) and in wakefulness thou wilt cease from the deep sleep in which thou hast been held. Then will appear to thee that manifest One who causes incorporeal rays to shine for thee…For the beginning and end of happiness is to be able to see God'. As Williamson seeks to explain, 'ascent to that ultimate visio Dei is possible for men only because God has expressed his inward thought in his Logos, which is, among other things, the sun of the transcendent world of Ideas' (p.106).[8]

Without intending to infringe his Jewish monotheism, Philo calls the Logos 'the second God', in whose image man has been made (*Quaest,* in *Genesis* xi:62). The description of the Logos as 'the second God' Philo deduces from the statement 'in the image of God He made man' in *Genesis* ix:6. Williamson recognises that 'To regard the Logos as an intermediary in the proper and fullest sense would perhaps involve a departure from the Jewish view of God as a living God, himself active in the world and history – a step not taken by Philo. It cannot be emphasised enough that the Logos for Philo is God's Logos, the incorporeal Word or Thought of God, not a distinct and separate being having its own divine ontological status, subordinate to God' (p.107). The 'Logos is also the Thought of God expressed in such a way that man can apprehend and comprehend it'. This means, according to Williamson, that the 'Logos is a bridge between God and mankind because it is the divine rationally impressed upon the natural order, in so far as it is capable of receiving it, and yet closely united with God as flowing from his essence' (p.108).

Philo uses the idea of the creation of the world by God, using his Logos as his instrument (*organon*) to express his belief that the universe – except for the physical body and the irrational element in man – is a reflection of the ideal pattern in God's mind. This shows the ways in which Philo has absorbed a Greek rationalism and its disdain for the body and emotional life that in significant ways contrasts with Talmudic Judaism. In *Leg. All.* 1.65, Philo states, in his allegorical exposition of *Genesis* ii:10–14, that 'River' denotes generic virtue, goodness. This issues forth, he explains, out of Eden, as the Wisdom of God, and this is the Reason (Logos) of God. This is a clear statement identifying Wisdom and the Logos, a process, according to Williamson, 'no doubt justified in Philo's mind by the fact that Scripture assigns to Wisdom attributes and functions also assigned to the Logos' (p.105).

We can read about the 'wisdom' that comes out of the mouth of God, which allows Williamson to make a telling observation serving to link a dominant masculinity with a prevailing rationalist tradition when he concludes: 'So, there was already within Judaism language about Wisdom which was so close to what was said elsewhere about the Logos so as to justify the virtual abandonment of the feminine term. Wisdom, (Sophia) and the adoption of the masculine noun, Logos, became much more useful because of its masculinity to both Jewish and Christian writers in the first century AD' (p.105).

Philo avoids the use of the term *nous* for the divine Mind, and uses instead the word *logos*, almost certainly as Williamson argues, because he wanted Logos to be reserved for the Mind of God and *nous* to denote, as in Aristotle, the human rational faculty, or mind. Even though Philo's language frequently personifies the Logos in relation to the act of creation, so that the Logos can appear as a kind of kind personal agent performing the actual work of creation, Williamson insists that when the 'The instrumentality of the Logos in creation is clearly stated in *Spec. Leg.* 1.81: "And the image of God is the Word through whom the whole universe was framed"...The Logos, it needs to be stressed over and over again – especially for Christian readers of Philo's work – is the Logos of God, God's Logos' (p.111). He recalls Philo's words in *Som.* 11.45, where Philo says of the material universe that 'when it had no definite character God moulded it into definiteness, and, when he had perfected it, He stamped the entire universe with His image and an ideal form, even His own Word'. As Williamson insists, 'The Logos here is referred to as if it were an instrument in God's hands rather than an Agent through whom he performed the act of creation' (p.112).

Williamson reads Philo in largely Greek terms in saying that there is a rational plan which governs the life of the universe, and to be affirming that the Logos 'is simply the instrument through which the divine purpose is carried out'. God, he says, 'directs the affairs of men through the operation of that rational law which is bound up in every constitution of the world' (Drummond, 1888: ii:200) (p.112). In *Sacr. AC* 51, Philo refers to 'the right reason which is our pilot and guide', a reference, according to Williamson, to 'the rule of "right reason" in human life; though it is certainly the case for Philo that "right reason" (orthos logos) in man is a reflection of the divine logos at work in the universe' (p.112). In *Rer. Div. Her.* 119, the Logos is called, among other things, the *spermatikos*, the divine Logos, which 'implants its seed' within men. This allows for Williamson in *masculinist* terms to say 'All men, therefore, participate to some extent in the life of the Logos. Man was made a likeness and imitation of the Word, when the Divine Breath was breathed into his face' (*Op. Mind.*, 139; cf. *ibid.* 146): 'Every man, in respect of his mind, is allied to the divine Reason, having come into being as a copy or fragment or ray of that blessed nature' (p.114).[9]

If it is men alone who can take their reason for granted within a Classical Greek tradition, we can discern the process through which the feminine, through its identification with emotion, comes to be disavowed and disdained. For when Genesis talks about people being created in the image of God this comes to refer exclusively to their rationality, and can be read as *already* affirming a control or suppression of emotions, feelings and desires that are deemed to be 'irrational' and thereby threats to male reason. This is a move that Talmudic Judaism resisted, though there has been a strong tradition of Jewish rationalism that would sustain a patriarchal tradition. But given the place of the *shekhina* in the tradition and the different ways in which Genesis has been read within a Jewish tradition, it is quite wrong for some feminist scholars to argue that patriarchy in Christianity has its sources in Judaism, so that through the 'eradication/superseding' of its Jewish sources, Christianity can be 'purified' of its patriarchal elements that somehow exist as 'alien' and 'foreign' elements within it. In so many ways, this serves to echo forms of traditional Christian antisemitism.[10]

Philo's understanding of the Genesis narrative, as being of man as created in the image of God, relates to the Logos as God's *eikon*. Williamson exposes the workings of Platonic assumptions, saying 'men become sons in the fullest sense only by fellowship with the Logos, which means living the life of reason (and abandoning the life of the flesh, the body, since the body is, in effect, a tomb for the human soul: see *Spec. Leg* iv:188. It is Logos that brings man to repentence and salvation by entering the soul and making man aware of his sins, bidding them to be cleared out in order that that Logos might be able to perform the necessary work of healing' (*Deus Imm.* 134–5; cf. *Rer. Div. Her.* (63–4)).

There are other echoes that Williamson also acknowledges that seem to question an ethic of self-denial and a masculinity that is identified with self-sufficiency. These refer to the need for physical and spiritual *nourishment* that a Greek tradition recognises, with its emphasis on happiness and where ethics – for Aristotle at least – are connected with human flourishing. If the Greeks had a strong sense of the obligations that people have as citizens they did not have a word for duty, as it is has been framed within Kantian terms, in radical opposition to the pursuit of happiness.

Kant is clear, for example, that if you enjoy playing with your children this is less morally worthy than if you are playing with them out of a sense of duty. It is the split between duty and happiness that the Greeks did not accept. Plato's *Republic* questions the notion that justice can be thought of as a relationship of exchange between self-sufficient individuals. Rather, he acknowledges the ways in which people *need* each other and that justice is connected with the moral relationships we establish with each other. Even though Plato expresses his vision within hierarchical terms, he recognises that individuals are 'social beings' who can only thrive *in* relationships with each other. But there are different orders of men and women, citizens and non-citizens, who have specific obligations to perform.[11]

Within the dominant narratives of Western philosophy and political theory, there is a recognition of the relationship between a Greek tradition and the later Christian tradition that developed in relation to it, but there is relative silence concerning Jewish and Islamic traditions within the West. In relation to ethics, Judaism tends to be identified with the Ten Commandments and thus with foundational obligations that can supposedly not be questioned. This echoes the traditional notion that Judaism is concerned with punishments for breaking the commandments, while Christianity supposedly introduces a discourse of love, mercy and compassion. Judaism is placed within a dominant Christian narrative that projects its fears of 'Carnal Israel' and silences its *own* disdain for the physical body, desire and sexuality.[12]

The tensions Philo inherits in trying to bring together a Platonic reading of Jewish sources are revealed in his disdain for the body and thus the rationalist terms in which he expresses nourishment. How do we understand the relationship between 'material' and 'spiritual' needs, and what forms of nourishment do we need to flourish? This could be a meeting point between the Greek and the Jewish – between Athens and Jerusalem – because there are tensions within both traditions around issues of pleasures, physicality, sexuality and ethics.

It is within a particular strain of Platonic/Christian tradition that we discover with particular intensity a duality that argues that it is *only* through the disavowal and suppression of an 'animal' bodily nature that we can hope to receive spiritual knowledge and nourishment. Rather than food being used to nourish the body, the body has to suffer denial so that it can be 'purified' and ready to accept spiritual nourishment. It is through starving the body that control is affirmed, as Kim Chernin has explored in *Womansize* where she explores the dominant Christian sources that still pervade a secular post-modern anorexic culture.[13]

As Philo reads the mysterious 'bread of heaven' referred to in Exodus, it is 'the Divine Word, from which all kinds of instruction and wisdom flow in a perpetual stream'. He calls the Logos 'the heavenly nourishment', the 'ethereal wisdom' poured upon minds that delight in contemplation. The effects of feeling upon the Logos are ethical, as well as mystical, according to Williamson, for, as Philo continues, 'This Divine ordinance fills the soul that has vision alike with light and sweetness, flashing forth the radiancy of truth and with honied grace of persuasion imparting sweetness to those who hunger and thirst after nobility of character' (*Fug.* 137–9). This indicates a Greek tendency towards spiritualisation in which the allegorical readings that Philo offers tend to discount the need to *nourish* the body as well as the soul. This distinction itself needs to be re-visioned, as if it were *through* nourishing and listening to the needs of the body that the soul can also be nourished. Purification within Jewish traditions usually disavows suffering of the body.

But if Williamson fails to acknowledge this he does, at least, recognise that 'This passage reinforces what is said elsewhere in Philo's works to emphasise the practical and active aspect of the life of the Jew who shared in Philo's mystical and intellectual form of Judaism. In *Cong.* 70, Philo stresses the importance of deeds and actions, this being only one of the many passages in which the ethical character of Philonic Judaism is exhibited' (p.114). Where the Sabbath Morning Service calls for the congregation to 'Purify our hearts to serve You in truth', there is a recognition that it is not through the suppression or denial of emotion that this can be done.

Rather than think that the aspiration to holiness can be achieved through an exercise of will alone, there is an awareness that it is through good *deeds* and actions that a process of transformation takes place. It is not through disdaining an 'animal nature' and thus through the ethics of self-denial that the heart can be 'purified'. If this involves a transcendence of negative emotions such as anger or hatred, this is best achieved, as Freud makes clear, through developing a relationship *with* our emotions and feelings rather than suppressing them.[14]

Talmudic Judaism, as Guttmann understands it, preserves the activist character of the Jewish tradition. As he explains in his rationalist terms: 'Religious life was still centred on the divine "commands", in which God addressed himself to the human will, and showed the way of communion between man and God. Human destiny is conceived in different ways. Piety is not so much the mere observation of divine commandments as the imitation of the divine model. The biblical commandment to be holy, even as the Lord God is holy, and the injunction to walk in the ways of God, are interpreted as demands to imitate the divine qualities of love and mercy. Love of God and faithful trust in him are considered the foundation of the right observance of the commandments' (p.32). This passage deserves to be quoted again because it questions the ways in which Judaism has been portrayed within the dominant Christian discourses of the West, and the ways in which it is so often forgotten within secular discussions of morality. This allows Guttmann to insist 'The spirit of rabbinic religion is thus elevated above mere submission of obedience of the will' (p.32).

Even though I would question the appeal to the will, I would agree with his emphasis on moral freedom where it is up to people themselves to freely choose whether they obey the commandments and whether thereby they want to move towards a closer communion with God. Guttmann recognises a resonance between the commandments and a Kantian vision of the moral law that helps explain the focus he gives to will. This means that he also disavows the body, sexuality and emotional life. It allows him to say 'Its religious activity is rooted in the inner certainty of community with God, yet its piety remains one of precept and duty' (p.32).

We are left thinking that it remains a matter of will whether commandments will be obeyed as if morality remains, in Kantian terms, a matter of individual moral actions. This leaves us with a limited conception of the moral self as a rational self, and thus with a narrow vision of what it means to be 'created in the image of God' or 'to be holy as the Lord God is holy'. We are left wondering whether, in our emotions and desires, we are *also* created 'in the image of God', and how accepting that life is a blessing rather than a sin might help us to move towards feelings of love that would make it possible to 'Purify our hearts to serve You in truth'.

9

Language, Ethics, Culture and Denial

Languages Of Soul

Within an Enlightenment vision of modernity, we have generally learned to dispose of a language of soul that is often confined to the religious sphere. Within a Cartesian tradition, we have learned to think of the mind, reason and consciousness where we might have once spoken more easily of the soul. We learn to wonder about the relationship between mind and body as a defining issue within 'modern philosophy', and assume that this expresses whatever was meaningful in the relationship between 'soul' and 'body'. Within a Jewish tradition that was anxious, within modernity, to affirm itself as 'rational' and 'moral' in terms of a secular rationalism that was largely expressed in the secularised terms of a dominant Christian tradition, the *soul* came to be regarded as a *metaphor* to be invoked in ancient prayers that were not expected to speak critically in the present. The fact that the Jewish morning prayer involves giving thanks to God for delivering us a soul that was pure and that prayers recognise that the soul leaves the body at night to return as we awaken in the morning became a matter of individual religious belief.[1]

Within modernity, it became difficult to voice what these prayers seemed to be communicating because they spoke out of a biblical tradition that in so many other ways appeared archaic. Within the prevailing modernist split between public and private spheres, religion was framed as a matter of individual religious beliefs alone. In Germany, for instance, Jewish emancipation meant that Jews became citizens with legal and political rights 'like everyone else'. The only 'difference' that was acknowledged was between Germans who went to church and those who happened to go to synagogue.[2] If religious tradition continued to provide the foundations for secular ethics, it was made clear that ethics could be derived from reason alone. As students learned about philosophy in the university, they learned about a Greek tradition and, later, a secular tradition of ethics whose Christian sources tended to be minimised. It was only as I recognised that Kant, Kierkegaard and Simone Weil were all, in different ways, speaking out of Christian tradition that I could position my own relationship to my philosophical writings.[3]

Jewish students were often left in a schizoid position, as they were rarely encouraged to identify the university as Greek and so *name* the silence in relation to Jewish traditions that they faced. Rather, Judaism became generally invisible within the history of philosophy and sometimes the Jewish philosophers even colluded in the invisibility when those such as Guttmann argued that philosophy was somehow *external* to Judaism which was not itself a philosophical tradition. Sometimes this was meant as claiming that Judaism is not an exclusively rationalist tradition, but then nor is philosophy in that it has been influenced by diverse sources.

Jewish scholars often learned to judge their own traditions through the eyes of a dominant culture that had itself absorbed the notion of Judaism as 'lacking' because it was particularistic, concerned with the moral destiny of a particular nation rather than being universalist and thus open to humankind. This became another way of claiming the inferiority of a Judaism that had been reduced to silence through having been 'superseded'. As Hegel repeats, Judaism had somehow outlived its historical usefulness and whatever value had been the value of its tradition had been absorbed in the synthesis that had emerged through Christianity.[4]

In Christian tradition, which Hegel secularised but never abandoned, Judaism's transformation into Christianity was central to its narratives of salvation. Supposedly, this is the moment when the redeemer appears in human history and is rejected by his own people. Thus it is that the Jews surrender their own divine mission in favour of Christianity, which absorbs their message while negating its flaws and raising it to a higher, more universal and thus an ethical level. It also tacitly influenced how Marx felt about his own Jewishness, namely, as something that needed to be transcended through an emancipation that was framed as 'human'.[5]

Yirmiyahu Yovel, in *Dark Riddle: Hegel, Nietzsche and the Jews*, recognises how 'Hegel internalised the pattern of this Christian metaphor. He even made it a model for his concept of *Aufhebung*, a concept which means that something is negated by not being annihilated; rather, its essential content is preserved and raised to a higher level of expression. For the mature Hegel, this is a basic pattern of reality and history. Every cultural form makes some genuine contribution to the world of the Spirit, after which it is sublated (*aufgehoben*) and disappears from the historical scene. Yet the Jews continued to survive long after their *raison d'etre* had disappeared – indeed, after they no longer had a genuine history in Hegel's sense, but existed merely as the corpse of their extinguished essence. But how could it be that Judaism evaded the fate (and defied the model) of which it was itself the prime example?' (p.24). This became part of the 'dark riddle'.

Somehow Judaism had persisted as a relic of Antiquity that survived the Middle Ages, the genuinely Christian age, and now enters the modern world to claim its rights within it. Hegel was willing to grant these rights, but he did not know what to do with the Jews in modernity *as Jews*, nor could he explain their survival. If they were to be assigned a place, this could not be specifically as Jews, as Mendelssohn had demanded, but *as* individuals and human beings in general, as Enlightenment rationalism had promised. As Yovel reminds us, 'A special antisemitic genre developed within the Enlightenment movement itself' (Voltaire, Reimarus, Holbach and others). Jews were referred to negatively even by their best friends. The philosemites of the time (like the later Zionists) wanted to 'cure' the Jews by changing their degenerate conditions, but they did not deny they were degenerate. A prominent advocate for the Jews, Abbé Grégoire, described them as 'sunk in moral and physical degeneration'. Lessing defended Judaism, not as such, but through the Jewish capacity to *overcome* Judaism and manifest the nobility of their 'universally human' soul (p.31).[6]

It was Gotthold Ephraim Lessing, the celebrated humanist and the writer of the play *Nathan The Wise*, who best expresses the instincts of the Enlightenment instincts in relation to Jewish emancipation. He had written a free-thinking, rational theology and given the ideas of toleration and the universality of the human race a vivid artistic expression.[7] The young Hegel was profoundly influenced by *Nathan The Wise* and quoted it more often than any other. In Lessing's popular play, Nathan, an emancipated and educated Jew, was based on Moses Mendelssohn, the philosopher and chief spokesman of the Berlin Enlightenment (*Aufklarung*), author of *Jerusalem* and friend of Kant. The young Hegel was also inspired by Mendelssohn's *Jerusalem*, particularly its arguments for religious toleration, while rejecting the second part that implied that Judaism, because it is free of religious dogma, was more suitable as a basis for the Enlightenment than Christianity.[8]

In *Jerusalem,* Mendelssohn shows that Judaism imposes *no* dogmatic belief as a condition for salvation. In Judaism, there are no revealed truths, only a revealed constitution or basic laws. As Yovel points out: 'Kant, abusing this idea, read Mendelssohn as testifying that his people's religion was merely political and devoid of moral content' (p.44). As Yovel points out in a helpful note: 'Mendelssohn had not said anything of the sort. There is nothing in Mendelssohn's position which denies the moral nature of many Jewish commandments; but what gives Judaism its distinctive character are neither its true beliefs nor its moral insights (which are universal), but the specific customs and ceremonies which the Jews were ordered to keep, and in which their fidelity to their identity is centred' (notes, p.202).

The young Hegel follows Kant, as Yovel acknowledges, in 'turning a great Jew he admired into a witness against his people'. Mendelssohn has seen Judaism's merit in that it had no dogmas and was free of the contradictions between the truths of revelation and those of reason which afflict Christian rationalists. Hegel turns this merit into a defect. 'What deeper truth is there for slaves than that they have a master?' he asks sarcastically. 'If the Jews have no truths, it is because a people of slaves is incapable of grasping truth. Truth requires freedom, but the Jews are unable to live outside the master-slave relationship. They understand only commands, so truth too has to take the form of a command for them. The claim that there is only one God appears in Judaism as a commandment, even as the supreme law of the state' (p.44).

Lessing was more tolerant within the terms of an Enlightenment rationalism. In Act 2, scene 7 of *Nathan the Wise*, Nathan meets a young Templar knight who has saved his daughter from a fire and wants to get closer to the noble young man. As the knight establishes a personal relationship he shifts from designating him as a Jew, and thus by his contemptible nation, to calling him by his proper name, as an individual. Yet the knight explains frankly that his heart abounds with hatred for the Jews. He attacks their alleged arrogance, their sense of religious superiority. As Yovel intercedes: 'The young Hegel could have been this knight' (p.45). What is Nathan's answer:

'You can loath my people as much as you like. Neither of us has chosen his people. Are we our people?

'What does people mean, then?

'Is a Christian or a Jew more Christian or Jew than a man?'

This is Lessing's Enlightenment view which means, as Sartre was later to investigate in *Anti-semite And Jew*, that the Jews' humanity must be discovered and acknowledged, as Yovel expresses it, 'not through the mediation of his or her Jewishness, but rather by *ignoring* that Jewishness and uncovering some "universal man" beneath it' (p.46).[9] He recognises, as Sartre also did, that 'implied in this abstract liberal approach is the demand that the individual renounce his specific identity as a condition for his humanity to be discovered and acknowledged' (p.46). Yovel does not really explore the implications of this insight as a critique of liberal tolerance, as Sartre is willing to do, but then Sartre was left with a negative vision of Jewishness as imposed by the antisemite, a view that he later renounced as he came to a fuller appreciation of Jewish history and culture.

Yovel recalls that Hegel liked to quote another passage from *Nathan The Wise*. Nathan is telling the cloister-brother how years ago he saved and adopted a Christian girl after his wife and child had been murdered in a pogrom. To which the good friar responds "Nathan! Nathan! You are a Christian! By God you are a Christian! A better Christian has never existed!", and Nathan answers: "What makes me a Christian for you, makes you a Jew for me". This could be read in different ways and after the Holocaust it carries a particular resonance. It could at some level be an affirmation of love as part of a Jewish ethical tradition, thus questioning an appropriation by Christianity of an ethic of love.

We might also wonder about the difference between those who adopted Jewish children and thus rescued them by bringing them up as Christians and those who were careful to bring them up, as best they could, with a knowledge and feeling for their own Jewish customs and traditions. But Yovel presents the issue more directly and he is probably right to say: 'Again, we have the same idea: peoples and religions are external shells. True religion – universal humanity – can hide under many names but needs none. This, too, could have taught Hegel that he may hate the shell while loving the person beneath it' (p.47).

Confessions

The difficulties that Western culture has had in coming to terms with Jewish philosophy is also recognised in different ways by Wittgenstein who, for a time, was struggling with issues of his own Jewishness. In 1937, as Hitler was consolidating his power in Germany and antisemitic legislation was working to isolate Jewish people in Germany, he came to a number of close friends and said he wanted to 'make a confession'. Rush Rhees has explored the matter: 'In his letters and in notes he wrote down for himself he said he wished that he might become a different man – that he could be rid of self-deception regarding his own failings and, in this way, lead a different life. Becoming clear about himself, recognising, for example, that in his relations with other people he had been performing for himself in a character that was not genuine, was difficult: not because he wasn't clever enough to discern it, but because he hadn't the *will* and could not recognise this. He could not become clear by intellectual examination and argument with himself but only by doing something he found difficult, something that needed courage – such as writing out a confession to show his friends'. In *Personal Recollections*, edited by Rush Rhees, Wittgenstein is said to have written about the experience in a notebook: 'Last year, with God's help, I pulled myself together and made a confession. This brought me into more settled waters, into a better relation with other people, and to greater seriousness. But now it is as though I spent all that, and I am not far from where I was before. I am cowardly beyond measure. If I do not correct this, I shall again drift entirely into those waters through which I was moving then' (p.192).[10]

Even though Wittgenstein had been baptised a Catholic and not brought up within Jewish traditions, it was important for him to acknowledge his Jewish ancestry and correct the false impressions he had given to his friends. This was not because of an intellectual commitment to truth but because, somewhat paradoxically, he was acting out of an insight about *life* and *its* relationship to *truth* that had possibly been nourished within Jewish traditions. At some level, it was an understanding of truth that separated Athens from Jerusalem, though it was also present in Greek tragedy, particularly in Sophocles. Three weeks after the previous remark, Wittgenstein wrote: 'What one writes about oneself cannot be more truthful than one *is*. This is the difference between writing about yourself and about external objects. What you write of yourself is as elevated as you are. Here you don't stand on stilts or on a ladder, but on your bare feet'.

About two months later, in February 1938, he wrote: 'If you are *unwilling* to know what you are, your writing is a form of deceit... If anyone is unwilling to descend into himself, because this is too painful, he will remain superficial in his writing'.

Wittgenstein is rejecting a transcendent option offered by Plato and insisting upon what might be called a *grounding* of our thinking in our lived experience. Within a post-modern culture in which we have often learned that we can create our own identities and shape identities as performances, it can be difficult to grasp what *can* be involved in coming 'to know what you are'. This is not a matter of intellectual acknowledgment but of learning how to *attune* to yourself so that you are sitting in a different relationship with yourself. As Stanley Cavell appreciates in *City Of Words*, this explains the resonance that Wittgenstein felt with Freud and the ways they somehow shared a sense that one needed to resist a temptation to escape from oneself and that was such a powerful temptation in Western celebrity cultures, in which people are constantly encouraged to compare themselves with celebrity figures and in some ways to live through them.[11]

This was not a personal issue for Wittgenstein but was potentially revealing about the relationship between Jewish philosophy and Western culture. In developing his thinking about Jewishness, Wittgenstein was very much influenced by Weininger's seminal *Sex And Character*, although there were crucial differences.[12] Though Wittgenstein might have acceded to Weininger's reflection that 'If a Jew could understand what being Jewish really is, he would have the solution to one of the most difficult problems: being Jewish is a much deeper riddle than the run of antisemitic catechisms supposes, and the more deeply we think on it the less likely it seems that it will ever be without a certain obscurity' (quoted in Rush Rhees, p.197). He adds: 'So the Jewish question can be resolved only in the individual case, each single Jew must try to answer it for his own person'. As Rhees comments: 'But Weininger said that for a Jew the "solution" would be an "*overcoming*" of what was Jewish in himself. And Wittgenstein said nothing of the kind' (p.197).

As Rush Rhees understands it, 'For a time, at least, Wittgenstein tried to get clear about what was Jewish in himself and his work. His reading of Weininger may have been one stimulus to this – I cannot say. But his examination of himself – what he wrote in trying to see clearly the position of the Jewish people in Europe and to recognise in himself certain traits he could see in them – was something Weininger never could have written' (p.198). One of these remarks in *Culture And Value* draws directly upon an analogy with bodies that has featured strongly in shaping the contempt that Western cultures have felt towards Jews and Judaism. In 1931, directly after the remark 'Rousseau's character has something Jewish about it', Wittgenstein writes: 'It is sometimes said that man's philosophy is a matter of temperament, and there is something in this. A preference for certain similes could be called a matter of temperament and it underlies far more disagreements than you might think' (p.20).

Directly after this, we have the following: 'Look at this tumour as a perfectly normal part of your body! Can one do that to order? Do I have the power to decide at will to have, or not to have, an ideal conception of my body?

'Within this history of the peoples of Europe the history of the Jews is not treated as circumstantially as their intervention in European affairs would actually merit, because within this history they are experienced as a sort of disease, and anomaly, and no one wants to put a disease on the same level as normal life (and no one wants to speak of a disease as if it had the same rights as healthy bodily processes (even painful ones)).

'We may say: people can only regard this tumour as a natural part of the body if their whole feeling for the body changes (if the whole natural feeling for the body changes). Otherwise the best they can do is *put up with* it'.

It is as if Western culture would have to come to a very different feeling about itself and its histories of violence, colonialism and white supremacy after the Second World War and the Holocaust *if* it is to allow due recognition to Jewish and Islamic philosophies, cultures and traditions. This would be to challenge its traditions of hospitality as Jacques Derrida explored the subject in his later writings, as well as its vision and aspirations for itself.[13] As Wittgenstein continues in the same vein, it involves rethinking its traditions of tolerance: 'You can expect an individual man to display this sort of tolerance, or else to disregard such things; but you cannot expect this of a nation, because it is precisely not disregarding such things that makes it a nation. I.e, there is a contradiction in expecting someone *both* to retain his former aesthetic feeling for the body and *also* to make the tumour welcome' (p.20–21).

Wittgenstein can help us appreciate the importance of acknowledging the different criteria that we need when we evaluate or judge, so that we do not evaluate people according to criteria that are not appropriate. We cannot simply construct identities for ourselves at will as a post-modern culture can suggest through disavowing the history and culture we have inherited. Often we have to come to terms with what 'we are carrying' if we are not to live in denial and if we want to have a chance of *changing* the way we feel about life. As Rush Rhees recognises, 'when Wittgenstein speaks of the natures of different people – in some sense what these various people are – he is able to speak of the "lie" or *Lebenslüge* of trying to be what one is not: which represents something different for one person and for another. Weininger leaves no room for this.

Wittgenstein would emphasise that one man's nature and another's are not the same, and that what is right (or imperative) for one man may not be right for another' (*Ludwig Wittgenstein: Personal Recollections*, p.208). In a remark that could indicate contempt or Jewish self-hatred, Wittgenstein notes: '...if he could only feel *contempt* for what he is, this would be or come close to "wanting to be what he is not"; or, at best, "regarding his life as though this – that he has such a nature – were of no consequence". The "autobiography" would not be an account of *his* life but of something else. He would never *understand* his life' (p.210). A remark made in 1947 echoes this earlier 1931 passage when he says '...If a man does not lie, he is original enough. In fact, it is a beginning of genuine originality if he does not want to be what he is not'.

Ethics

As Levinas writes in *Beyond The Verse: Talmudic Readings And Lectures*, 'We Jews who wish to remain so know that our heritage is no less human than that of the West, and is capable of integrating all that our Western past has awoken among our own possibilities. We have assimilation to thank for this. If we are contesting it at the same time, it is because this "withdrawal into the self" which is so essential to us, and so often decried, is not the symptom of an outmoded stage of existence but reveals something beyond universalism, which is what completes or perfects human fraternity. In Israel's peculiarity a peak is reached which justifies the very durability of Judaism. It is not a permanent relapse into an antiquated provincialism'. In this way, Levinas is responding to both Hegel and Marx, though he has as yet not said of which ethical values and relationships of justice the world is reminded by Judaism.[14]

Levinas recognises that people need to make *explicit* this particularity so that others can appreciate what it stands for. For Levinas this means 'It still needs to be translated into the Greek language which, thanks to assimilation, we have learned in the West. Our great task is to express in Greek those principles about which Greece knew nothing. Jewish particularity still awaits its philosophy. The servile imitation of European models is no longer enough'. This involves identifying the diverse issues with which Judaism is concerned while recognising, as Levinas knew, that 'The search for references to universality in our Scriptures and texts of the Oral Law still comes from the process of assimilation. Those texts, through their two-thousand-year-old commentary, still have something else to say' (p.201).

Within European modernity there was a general *disavowal* of the language of the soul, as philosophy was cast as a secular discipline of reason, radically separated from nature. The language of the soul belonged to religion if it belonged anywhere and it was generally regarded as 'irrational'. It might be mentioned as a source of inspiration in music and the arts but otherwise it tended to be repressed. Religion became the sphere of life that was supposedly concerned with the perfection of individual souls and was regarded as a private and personal matter.

In contrast, through its Greek expression, philosophy came to be regarded as impersonal and universal because these were supposedly the characteristics of reason. At university, students still learn to disavow the 'I' because the personal has become devalued and marked as subjective and anecdotal, and therefore supposedly incapable of operating as a source of knowledge. It also echoed the Protestant disdain for the personal as linked to the 'selfish' and the 'egotistical', something that needed to be silenced and eradicated if people were to learn to be obedient to the moral law.

In the construction of the Judeo-Christian tradition there was a suppression of the critical voices of Judaism that had sought safety through an alliance with the powerful. There was an emphasis upon what these different religious traditions *shared* and thus a focus upon the shared humanitarian values of peace, tolerance and justice. The notion that the voice of God is impersonal, universal and rational, imposing commandments that needed to be obeyed, also tended to minimise critical differences between religious traditions that were seeking some form of accommodation.

But it remains critical in the Jewish readings of Genesis that God asks 'Where are you?' and receives the reply '*Hineini* – here I am'. This call to the person who is asked to respond personally to God is echoed at critical moments in the Biblical text. This reminds us that God is calling to individuals to show themselves and speak personally. It indicates a personal relationship with a personal God that people such as Jonah sought to avoid. They fled because they did not want to respond to this appeal to the individual. They did *not* want to hear the language of the soul or listen to its echo within themselves.

Personal Ethics

In *The Altruistic Personality*, Frank and Pearl Oliner investigate those who risked themselves to save Jews during the war. They discovered that it was not those who had been university-educated and who were in the professions who most likely spoke out and took action to rescue their Jewish neighbours. There seemed to be little relationship between traditions of universal ethics and the capacity of individuals to take moral action. Rather it tended to be those who had relationships with parents who encouraged them to develop their *individual* moral conscience who were more likely to engage in the risks of rescue. They had developed an ethic of personal responsibility and they felt when the knock on the door came, they could not do otherwise but help. They often did not regard themselves as morally exemplary figures but as people who had a strong sense of their individual morality.[15]

Lawrence Langer has argued that this has revealed a *flaw* in a Kantian tradition that identifies morality with an impersonal concept of reason. It allows people to argue that they are against mistreatment of fellow citizens in principle but that the Jews should not be allowed to be citizens. Somehow a Kantian tradition had not nourished seeds of resistance but had allowed people to 'hold on' to their principles, while *failing* to take action to prevent the oppression of Jews whom they came to accept as 'other' – as a threat to the 'health' of the German nation. With the widespread adoption of eugenics as merely being 'common sense', tending to identify medical and ethical discourse, it proved relatively easy within German culture to isolate and marginalise the Jewish community. There was an ethic of rights and principles that tended to see individuals as representatives of more general cases. A Kantian tradition somehow proves itself unable, except for a few exceptional individuals, to sustain an ethic of care and compassion because it tended to see people as rational moral agents, rather than as people who were in need of love and care.[16]

A Jewish tradition, in contrast, outlines particular responsibilities towards the widow, the orphan and the bereaved, recognising that these situations can leave people with a particular need that has to be addressed. If people have responsibilities for others, they have particular responsibilities for those in distress. This has tended to be regarded as a 'weakness' in a tradition that shows it to be more particularistic and thus supposedly less concerned with universal duties and responsibilities to people in general. This is a misreading that Philo appreciated because he felt torn between a Greek tradition that tended to focus upon the impersonal and the universal as opposed to the particular responsibilities that a Jewish tradition felt a need to name, though he felt that there did not necessarily have to be a contradiction.

Philo could not accept the Stoic view that virtue excludes emotions where the Stoic ideal is *apatheia* – absence of feeling or emotion. The

early Stoic philosophers had argued that all emotions are irrational and
that the wise person should therefore seek to excise them from life. Philo
recognised that some feelings and emotions were good and virtuous.
Some emotions such as mercy and compassion are urged upon people.
He accepted that 'Moses governed his anger by his reason' (4 *Macc.*
2:17). People had to learn to curb and control their emotions, but not
to eradicate them. Philo also disagreed with the Stoics over their notion
that all emotions are equal. To Philo, since some laws are weightier than
others and some less serious, some sins involving emotions or feelings
are less grave.

As Williamson records: 'Piety and holiness are great virtues; piety,
faith, holiness and justice are all in turn equally designated queen (or
leader, or chief) of the virtues. In the light of traditional Jewish teachings, Philo allied himself with the Peripatetics against the Stoics in
regarding some emotions as virtuous and useful' (p.204). Philo believed
in the biblical virtue of 'righteous anger' and, prompted by Exodus
32:27, speaks of 'the impulse of righteous anger' as 'accompanied by
an inspiration from above and a God-sent possession' (*Fug.* 90). He
also talks about 'love of humanity, of justice, of goodness, and hatred
of evil' as qualities which Moses alone attained in combination (*Vit.
Mos.* ii:9). For Philo, hatred of evil was something the Bible taught men
to feel.

Philo tended to believe that absence of passion is possible only for
exceptional people such as Moses 'for no moderation of passion can sat-
isfy him', but it is unclear whether even here it is as much of an ideal as
it is for the Stoics. For the majority of people, such as Aaron, progress
towards perfection is gradual and virtue seems to consist in the moderation of emotion. As Williamson puts it: 'To this argument Philo adds
the conclusion that an emotion controlled by reason becomes a virtue –
eupatheia (a good feeling), a Stoic term used by Philo in his own way'
(p.206). The way of God, which the virtuous may tread, is the only
route along which 'good feeling and virtue' can both walk (Abr. 204).
There is not the same kind of tension between virtue and happiness that
was later to be found within a Kantian tradition.

A Moral Path

Freud helps identify the emotional suffering that can be produced
through the Stoicism echoed within a dominant Christian tradition. As
people learned to disregard their emotions, they created schisms within
themselves as they denied their emotions, feelings and desires. This

meant that people became estranged from their inner emotional lives, and often felt *split* between their inner emotional turmoil and the way in which they felt obliged to present themselves to others. As people became estranged from their inner emotional lives so they could assume an externalised relationship with themselves. They found it harder to listen to themselves, fearful they would hear voices of an animal nature, learning to identify with selfless ideals within a dominant Christian tradition that was shaped through a Stoic disdain of emotional life.[17]

An ethical tradition of self-denial can make it difficult to identify the harm that people do to themselves, say for example, when they allow themselves a sexual relationship that they feel to be inappropriate. It is not that they think in universal terms that it is always wrong to engage in pre-marital sex but that this relationship does not 'feel right' to them. It is only through learning to *trust* their feelings that they might make the correct decision. It is not an issue that they might be able to settle through reason alone since they might have no reason to reject the sexual partner in question, possibly when others feel it would be a good match. But a woman may feel that it is wrong *for her* and if she goes ahead she might feel bad about not having trusted her feelings. Her instincts might have told her to refuse even if she had no clear reason for doing so. She might feel regretful as a result and, unless she is able to express her regret, she might feel divided against herself, as if her head were saying one thing and her heart another. She might feel that she had to learn to listen to herself more closely, knowing that when she acts against herself in this way, it seems to leave a shadow around her.

Part of listening to her inner voice might be in recognising that what might work for others might not work for her. She has become aware that morality is not a matter of conforming to rules that we might legislate for ourselves in Kantian terms; it also involves learning how to develop and deepen a relationship with one's emotional inner self. That is something that Freud partly recognises when he defines psychoanalysis as a listening cure. Through feeling listened to, in a way that might be quite unfamiliar for someone who realises that he or she has never really been listened to within the family, could cause one to experience more of what it means to listen to yourself.

Psychoanalysis can provide an emotional *space* in which people feel listened to in a way that allows them to talk more personally themselves. They might feel that they have never really voiced what they feel or desire because they have grown up to conform to the expectations that others have of them. They might also have been fearful of their own emotions as indications of an 'animal nature' that affirms just how unworthy they are.

Through affirming that people have a right to their *own voice* and a recognition that it takes time for people to establish a relationship with an inner emotional life they have learned to ignore, people can feel more able to question a moral culture of self-denial. But psychoanalysis can work to separate the emotional and the psychological from the ethical in a way that both the Greek and Hebrew traditions might question in their different ways. Freud tended to identify morality with the superego that was connected to the father's authority within the family. He recognised that the superego could foster the repression of sexual desire, but did *not* name the different ways in which this might work within different religious traditions. Freud can now encourage us to identify the soul with the personality, thus making it difficult to identify the different kinds of harm/injury that can be done to a person. He tends to foster a notion of 'psychological damage' that can work to isolate the 'psychological' into a sphere of its own.

Drawing on a Greek tradition and a reading of Sophocles and Homer, Simone Weil questions this psychologism and looks towards a Christian language of affliction in order to illustrate the *harm* that can be done, say to a young girl who is dragged into a brothel against her will. Weil is ready to think of rape, not in terms of a liberal language of an infringement of rights that she thinks tends to assume the person is left intact, but as a violation of the person – of the soul – from which it is difficult to recover.[18] Though she disavows her Jewish heritage, Weil could have equally looked to the Jewish Bible for sources of affliction. It could also possibly have helped her question her own personal aspirations towards being 'reduced to matter', so that she could serve as an 'instrument of God' that for her flowed out of her developing commitment to a Christian tradition of self-denial. She learned to reject her own body and its desires and looked towards impersonal suffering in ways that also served to devalue personal suffering. Conceiving of God in impersonal terms, she became wary of a God who addressed people personally.

Fulfilment

If life is deemed to be a blessing, it might be possible to find fulfilment in this life rather than assume that we have to sacrifice ourselves in this life to find fulfilment in 'a world to come'. The emphasis that a Kantian ethical tradition places on duty and obligation draws a sharp distinction between duty and happiness. Seeking happiness has no moral worth, though as Philo makes clear, Judaism recognises that virtue and happiness *can* co-exist.

Philo insists that 'in no other action does man so much resemble God as in showing kindness' (*Spec. Leg.* iv:41–77), adding that there can be no greater good than to imitate God. As people act out of a sense of compassion for others they are acting out of a sense of their own feelings for others. This is not something that can be achieved as a matter of will, but neither does it mean that *feelings* such as compassion should be confused with emotions that in a Kantian tradition are considered to be changeable and unreliable. Some people might feel compassion quite spontaneously, while for others it is something that they might only achieve *after* years of working on themselves emotionally.[19]

As Williamson explains: 'Following Plato, Philo divides the virtues into the earthly and the heavenly, the former being a copy or imitation of the latter. The heavenly virtues, or virtues of the soul, consist of virtues such as "prudence, temperance and each of the others" (Sobr. 61), while the bodily virtues comprise "health, efficiency of the senses, dexterity of the limb and strength of muscle" and such as are akin to these' (*ibid.* p.208). This shows a valuing of the body that Philo often denied. The basic distinction made by Philo is between divine intellectual virtues that have God as their object and human moral and bodily virtues. In respect of faith, which for him is one of the key virtues, Philo differs from other philosophers, for to them faith was not a virtue. For Philo, faith involves belief in revealed truths and trust in God's promises.

It is the faith that good, and not evil, will be done to us that is cherished by Simone Weil as a fundamental feeling that people are born with. It is a trust that is often *broken* when a woman is raped. It is a violation that cannot be understood in personal terms, in the sense of an injury to the personality. Rather it is a violation of the soul that can mark a life forever. This is a language of soul that a utilitarian culture fails to appreciate. If we are to understand the injustice that people do to each other, we need to understand different levels of harm.

As Philo puts it, humanity means giving help to those in need and is a virtue 'nearest in nature to piety' (Virt. 51). He says that Moses possessed humanity and fellow-feeling through a 'happy gift of natural goodness' (*ibid.* 80). The pious man, according to Philo's ethics, is the humane man. Acknowledgement of the holiness of God and just dealings with other people go hand-in-hand. Clustered around humanity are its fellow-virtues: concord, equality, grace and mercy. As Williamson concedes: 'Philo's elevation of humanitas, as well as the lofty place he gives to justice is an expression of his fundamentally unchanged Jewishness' (p.211).

Simone Weil was also thinking about justice but she does not connect it to questions of happiness and fulfilment. This is something we can find in the thinkers of the Counter-Enlightenment who, in different ways, were questioning a Kantian inheritance of the moral self as rational self. These were thinkers who could value pleasures in this world as much as the sacrifices that needed to be made for others. They questioned a culture of self-denial as Isaiah Berlin recognises in his writings on Vico, Herder and Herzen. Though he was not seeking in any way to claim them for a Jewish tradition, we could still say that their sensibility was in tune in significant ways with Biblical insights that the West might otherwise have forgotten. It was a challenge to an Enlightenment vision of modernity that framed human nature in rationalist terms and identified morality with an independent faculty of reason.[20]

Berlin recognised the value of a tradition of Counter-Enlightenment, though he tended to express his work in the history of ideas rather than as a challenge to prevailing philosophies. As Bernard Williams suggested in his memorial talk for Berlin, it was possibly nearer the truth to say that though Berlin long regarded himself as having abandoned the difficult terrain of philosophy, he was, in some degree, searching for different ways of doing philosophy – ways, I suggest, that may resonate with a Jewish tradition he otherwise rarely connected to his intellectual work. As Williams expresses it: 'In fact, I do not think that he did leave philosophy, He merely left what he took philosophy to be. His conception of the subject had been formed originally in those discussions in Oxford before the war which were shaped by the agenda of positivism...it saw philosophy as a timeless study, which had no interest in history (except perhaps marginally, in the history of philosophy itself)' (*The First And The Last*, p.122).

As Williams goes on to explain: 'If what Isaiah wanted to do was really history, then, in his view, it could not be philosophy. Isaiah agreed with this himself, and that is why he said that he had left philosophy, and why did he not notice that he had discovered or rediscovered a different kind of philosophy, one that makes use of real history'. He also recognises that 'Analytic philosophy has been much taken up with defining things. But as Nietzsche said, "one can only define things that have no history". Because that is true, all the things that Isaiah found most interesting – liberty and other political ideals...such things do not have definitions or analyses but only complex and tangled histories, and to say what these things are, one must tell some of their history' (p.122–3). Though Berlin talked less of justice than he did of freedom, he felt a need for a vision of humanity that

recognised emotional life, so long discounted within a rationalist tradition. Though he was sceptical about psychoanalysis, he sought ways of
illuminating moral life that broke with the traditions of self-denial and
possibly unconciously drew upon biblical traditions he rarely acknowledged. In some way he was exploring voices that indirectly allowed for
a renewed conversation between Jerusalem and Athens.

10

Traditions, Bodies
and Difference/s

Traditions

Within modern Western cultures, many people are growing up with little connection to religious traditions having been raised in largely secular cultures. Though their grandparents might have been practising Christians, they themselves often have little feeling for religious tradition and little sense of how the Western culture they take for granted has been largely shaped through Christian and Greek traditions. They often have even less awareness of the ways in which Western culture has also been shaped by Judaism, often mediated through Christian and Greek culture.

They might be only dimly aware that as Alexander moved east in his conquests he brought Greek culture to 'civilise' the lands of the Orient. It was through a fusion of the Orient and the Occident that Hellenism was constructed. As Milton Steinberg has written in *Judaism and Hellenism*: 'From India to the Hellespont, from Egypt to the Black Sea, people of diverse stocks learned to speak Greek, came to dress like Greeks, to worship like Greeks and to think like Greeks'. But as Martin Bernal shows in *Black Athena,* it is only in the nineteenth century that Europe comes to a self-conception of itself as having its beginnings in a predominantly white culture, disavowing as we have said the connections that Greece had sustained with Egypt and Phoenicia.[1]

As Steinberg argues: 'The Jews, alone in the ancient world, had a sense of the dignity of the life of every human being'. Learning that human beings are each created in the image of God, they learned that each individual was consequently of infinite moral significance. This showed itself in a reluctance to inflict capital punishment and through attempts to mitigate human slavery by protecting the rights of the bondman in such a way as to make the possession of a slave economically unprofitable. Hellenistic literature does not contain any discussion of the morality of human bondage: 'they reveal an inner moral disquietude, tend to end either with a rationalisation of the status quo or with advice to slaves to find their freedom in inner self-emancipation'. The Hellenistic social structure was built upon brutal slavery and so often we pass over in silence the justifications we find in Plato, and particularly Aristotle, as if this failing, as Simone Weil at least recognised, did not compromise their ethical theories in devastating ways.[2]

Greek society was founded on violence and in it the world belonged to the strong. From Plato through to the Stoics, compassion for the weak and dispossessed is rarely to be discerned in Greek thought, even though it was the Stoic legalists who first voiced the axiom that all human beings are, by nature, equal. Plato felt few qualms in consigning the masses to bondage in his ideal state. Aristotle insists that some human beings are naturally slaves. The Stoics generally despised the great masses of humans as *typhloi* or blind fools. According to Steinberg, 'Only the Jew has a doctrine of charity and sympathy for the oppressed. Only they had the feeling that the human being attains truest humanity in the giving of oneself to those who falter in the struggle for existence' (p.121). In Judaism you hear the sentiment that 'If you see a righteous person persecuting a righteous person, know that God is with the persecuted...and even when the righteous persecutes the wicked, by the very fact of persecution, God is with the persecuted'.

In his *Culture And Anarchy,* Mathew Arnold conceived of Western civilisation as a balance between the polarities of Hebraism, meaning Judaism and its offspring, Christianity, and Hellenism and its offspring, the Renaissance and modern science. As he argues: 'Hebraism and Hellenism – between these two points of influence moves our world...though it never is evenly and happily balanced between them'. Arnold conceives it in terms of a nineteenth-century aspiration towards progress but refusing its materialism: 'The final aim of both Hellenism and Hebraism, as of all great spiritual disciplines, is no doubt the same: human perfection or salvation. Still they pursue this aim by very different courses. The uppermost idea with Hellenism is to see things as they really are; the uppermost idea with Hebraism is conduct and obedience'.

The focus is upon being able to see things 'as they really are', *as if* a singular truth is revealed through Platonic forms that can give the essential meaning of things.[3]

In this way, language was supposed to represent an independent reality and there was a correspondence between language and things in the world that it represented. This Greek vision haunted Western Philosophy and as Socrates had contested various definitions in order to reach an essential truth, so reason was recognised as a faculty through which a universal truth underlying a diversity of appearances would be revealed. Possibly Wittgenstein's frustration with Socrates shows another way in which his philosophy can be considered to be Hebraic rather than Greek, when the latter says for instance, in *Culture And Value*, 'Reading the Socratic dialogues one has the feeling: what a frightful waste of time! What's the point of these arguments that prove nothing and clarify nothing?' (p.14). As he explains on another occasion, 'but that is the difficulty Socrates gets into in trying to give the definition of a concept. Again and again, a use of the word emerges that seems to be incompatible with the concept that other uses have led us to form. We say: but that *isn't* how it is! – it *is* like that though! and all we can do is keep repeating these antitheses' (p.30).

In *Conversations with Wittgenstein*, M. O'C Drury recalls another remark about Socrates that says something more about the methods that Wittgenstein was developing that could possibly be considered 'Hebraic', and helps to clarify the difficulties he experiences in relation to Socrates. Wittgenstein says to Drury, after listening to a paper he had written: 'You know I rather like it. You are doing the sort of thing of I am working at, trying to see how in actual life we use words. It has puzzled me why Socrates is regarded as a great philosopher. Because when Socrates asks for the meaning of a word and people give him examples of how that word is used, he isn't satisfied but wants a unique definition. Now, if someone shows me how a word is used and its different meanings, that is just the sort of answer I want' (in Rush Rhees, *Ludwig Wittgenstein: Personal Recollections*).

Arnold was more sympathetic to Socrates and a Greek tradition and recognised 'the Greek quarrel with the body and its desires is that they hinder right acting and thinking'. He recognises that 'to get rid of one's ignorance, to see things as they are, and by seeing them as they are to see them in their beauty, is the simple and attractive ideal, which Hellenism holds out before human nature....They are full of what we call "sweetness and light". Difficulties are kept out of view, and the beauty and rationalness of the ideal have all our thoughts'. He tends to accept that we relate to the world *through* knowledge and seek to bring knowledge and ethics into relation with each other. He consolidates a distinction between knowing and doing that is part of what Wittgenstein feels a need to challenge.

While for Arnold 'The governing idea of Hellenism is spontaneity of consciousness, that of Hebraism, strictness of conscience. The difference, whether it is by doing or by knowing that we set more store, and the practical consequences which follow from this difference leave their mark on all the history of our race and of its development', this points to a significance that led Wittgenstein to think of his later philosophy as 'Hebraic' rather than Greek. He was no longer involved in a search for an underlying structure of language, as he was in the *Tractatus*, as if, when language works well, there is a single relationship between language and the world it represents. Wittgenstein had lost confidence in this vision and rather than treating ordinary language as lacking when it is set up against an ideal of language, he recognised that it is through *everyday use* of language that meaning is achieved. He was concerned with the different uses of language in diverse language games and thought that we had to honour and learn from these different practices.

In this way you could say that Wittgenstein's later *Philosophical Investigations* marked a shift, in some way, from Greek to Hebraic, and that its explorations of truth through the diverse uses of language is in the spirit of the Talmudic tradition that refuses a vision of singular truth, and through its methods celebrates the existence of different truths between which we cannot choose as a matter of reason alone. Hillel and Shammai offered, within Rabbinic Judaism, different paths and, even if a choice was being made in practical life, this was not because one position was true while the other was false. Somehow the text had to value these different truths, recognising that they might come into their own in different moments of life. It was part of a recognition that truth is not singular and that, if we choose to take a particular path, we can discover, possibly later in our own lives, a need to return to particular experiences in life now that we are able to grasp the particular impact that they had upon us. We might find ourselves drawing upon different ways of thinking, possibly long abandoned, because they help to illuminate changes we feel we can make in the present.

As Arnold recognised: 'Hebraism differs from Hellenism (while the Greek thinkers sought restful contemplation of eternal truths), Hebraism has always been severely preoccupied with an awful sense of the impossibility of being at ease in Zion; of the difficulties which oppose themselves to the human pursuit or attainment of that perfection of which Socrates talks so hopefully and so glibly'. But this is where

Arnold's conception of Christianity as an offspring of Judaism has to be questioned, because the notion of sin that he wants to invoke does *not* account for the diverse difficulties we face and the ways in which Christianity refers to people being born into 'original sin' so that life is so often a testing ground for a salvation that can only be realised in a world to come. It is 'this worldly' vision that sets Judaism apart from 'otherworldly' traditions within Christianity.

Arnold thinks in terms of a perfection that remains Greek in inspiration, but he does acknowledge that 'Under the name of sin, the difficulties of knowing oneself and conquering oneself which impede man's passage to perfection, become, for Hebraism, a positive, active, entity'. But this threatens to subsume Judaism within a dominant Christian self-conception in which people are caught up in a struggle against their sinful natures. We have to recognise critical differences between moral traditions, particularly in their relationship to the physical body and their emotional lives. These are distinctions that Arnold *cannot* appreciate within his vision when he says 'by alternations of Hellenism and Hebraism, of man's intellectual and moral impulses, of the effort to see things as they really are and the effort to win peace by self-conquest, the human spirit proceeds' (p.126).[4]

Though Arnold gives public recognition of a Jewish tradition through his identification of Hebraism, it can again become subsumed through a relationship with Christianity that is imagined as having superseded it. The focus upon deeds and actions potentially allows for a different reading of Christianity that can potentially *restore* its connection to its Jewish sources, but the focus upon sin works differently. The recognition of difficulties that a Greek tradition of detachment thinks it can transcend retains a powerful echo through Western philosophical traditions. It questions the ease with which Christian visions of equality, as in respect what I explored in *The Moral Limits Of Modernity,* so often allowed for people to abstract themselves from social relationships of power and dominance. Wittgenstein also tends to assume that people have equal access to these diverse language games.[5]

Christianity inherits a Greek vision of detachment that shapes its universalism and thus its claim to *moral superiority* against a supposedly particularistic Judaism. Christianity has been able to disdain a Jewish tradition not only for its 'blindness' – shown in its supposed inability to see the self-evident truths of Christianity – but it has failed to take responsibility for the ways in which traditions of Christian antisemitism have helped shape Western traditions of philosophy and social theory.[6] A Greek tradition seeks an eternity that it cannot find in the world of particulars. It searches in the realm of essences, universals and logic that

Wittgenstein learned to question in his later writings. At least through his recognition of Hebraism, Arnold was part of a humanistic tradition that could value diverse legacies.

Difference/s

As a woman who grew up in the United States thinks back on her upbringing, she realises how formative was her parents' unwitting decision to send her to a Christian summer camp. She was obliged to attend prayers and it was only when she said that she was Jewish, while at the time having little sense of what this meant, that she experienced herself as being different. But it was the pity with which others related to her that left her feeling that in the eyes of the others she was deemed to be *lacking*. They expressed the hope that she might find her way to Jesus. She was upset because she had never experienced herself as different in this way and it sparked her desire to know more about her own tradition. She had to deal with the fact that the wider culture carried a vision of historical progress that believed in a singular vision of truth, so that whatever Judaism taught it had somehow been historically disproved. She was made to feel that whatever she might have learned, it was a lesser truth and that she was missing out on 'the truth' that Christianity alone offered.

Growing up as Jewish within a largely secularised Christian culture can encourage you to *see* yourself through the eyes of the dominant culture. Not only have forms of Judaism felt the pressure to prove themselves acceptable according to prevailing conceptions of rationality, they have often distanced themselves from their own mystical and spiritual traditions that they have learned to see as irrational within the terms of a dominant scientific rationalism. Within an Enlightenment vision of modernity that has shaped religious belief as a matter of private and individual perfection, there is often a radical break between the Greek traditions that inform educational theory and the practices and the privatisation of Judaism that is rarely given public recognition.

Within modern philosophy, there is little space for Jewish traditions that are defined as 'religious' and therefore as offering little to philosophy that conceives of itself as a rational and universal discourse quite different from the particularistic concerns of different religious traditions. This helps produce a 'dual consciousness' as people might grow up with feelings for a particular tradition but feel silenced when it comes to sharing the critical insights it potentially offers to prevailing traditions. In this sense, Levinas is right that our education remains Greek.

However, he mistakenly thinks the task remains to translate Hebrew insights into Greek, rather than show the different possibilities for *life* that it offers and ways in which they find an echo in the present.[7]

If you grow up in a Jewish tradition within the West, you can find it difficult to name the tensions you feel between the insights of the prayer book and the secular education you receive in school. We may find that we are already Greek and that the tensions between Athens and Jerusalem produce a schizoid split between different spheres of life that remain silent in respect of each other. We might assume, without recognising a Greek source, that thinking is higher and purer than doing, and thus find it unsettling to read Mordechai Gafni when he writes 'For the Jew there is no greater sin than the sin of detachment. The ideal is the full embrace of the concreteness of being. God is in the details. God is in the ferment of our lives'. We might already think that this reflects a lack, that Jewish philosophy has been less concerned with universal statements about the nature of reality and, even after reading Wittgenstein, find it hard to appreciate Gafni when he says 'Their vision is almost always of the particular individual and his or her own choices. For the Jews eternity resides in the human encounter with the moment. God, the source of the eternal, is revealed in the infinite depths of the human personality no less than in the mathematical theorems of Pythagorus' (p.128).[8]

The Talmud describes God who is attendant and empathetic to the joys and pains of human beings. The Jewish God is personal and cares deeply about all of God's creatures. The Jew believes in a God who cares even if that has been tragically tested through the Shoah. As Gafni says: 'Our God knows our name. The mandate of the Hebrew man is *imitatio dei*, to be like God. To be like God is about moral commitment to the betterment of the world and deep existential empathy with all who suffer. To be like God is to have a passionate social vision, which addresses all facets of humanity. It is to be concerned, engaged and attached' (p.128). Since for the Hellenist, God is a force in the universe, an unmoved mover, Gafni can say 'The notion of a God who cries is blasphemous to the Hellenist. The notion of a God who doesn't cry is blasphemous to the Jew' (p.128).

Speaking as a Jew, Gafni acknowledges: 'Athens was a great city, but we are children of Jerusalem. Jewish eternity resides in the infinite value and holiness of our personal story and our potential for change'. He realises that to *become* you have to be ready to risk failing, and that change, by definition, involves instability and that this means 'Balance needs to be disrupted when it fronts an excuse for fear of growth and change'. He is not arguing against balance and stability, but warning against the danger of them making us unwilling to genuinely struggle with ourselves and the world. As he warns: 'There is something comfortable about the Hellenistic vision – all is harmony, life never really touches me and I don't have to pay the price of becoming....Maybe we need to become unstuck from the tired idea that our life is what it is. Our life is what it could be'.

I felt uneasy as I wrote 'speaking as a Jew', since this can so easily be read in an essentialist way. When Gafni says 'Athens was a great city, but we are children of Jerusalem', does this exclude the possibility of people who might have been brought up in different traditions or none, choosing to adopt Jerusalem as their own city? If this is always possible we also have to recognise that these are *not* discrete spaces that we move between, even if they can represent discrete traditions. It is important to realise the way these cities interelate and have learned from each other and the ways in which, in the West, we remain the children of diverse creative spiritual and sexual traditions, being pulled in different directions. Often if it is not clear how Jerusalem has continued through its focus upon acting and ethics to be heard within the philosophical traditions of the West this is also because we have otherwise been deaf to its presence.

What was striking in the later Wittgenstein was his recognition of this influence, even though he knew little about the tradition himself. It was his concern with how meanings emerged through the practices of everyday life rather than through ideals that were set apart and worked to make people feel constantly inadequate for failing to live up to these ideals. Language itself was deemed to be inadequate, for it only dimly reflected the purity of Platonic forms. Wittgenstein had learned to question visions of purity and perfection that had long haunted Western culture. But again this meant an appreciation of different traditions for what they have to offer. It did not mean that people had to decide between them, but it could mean that Christianity would have to radically *rethink* its own foundations and history and the ways it had been shaped through a disdain for its Jewish sources that has proved so historically destructive, not only in relation to Christian antisemitism but through the West's relationship to itself and its others.[9]

Christianity has inherited a vision of itself as the bearer of a singular truth that does not easily allow for recognition of the dignity of difference. Rather, difference was taken as indicating a *lack*, a falling away from truth. The West has yet to come to terms with its imperial and colonial pasts in which it so often framed 'others' as 'less than human'. Christianity was an integral part of the civilising mission of the West that deemed others to be 'primitive' and uncivilised. Often the cross was carried next to the gun as it was recognised that colonialism could not be established through the force of arms alone but would also involve the shaping of hearts. This was part of a civilising mission that was known as the 'white man's burden' and thus as a moral obligation to those who could not make a transition from nature to culture, from tradition to modernity, without help. It was only through accepting subordination to their colonial masters that they could *hope* to move towards modernity and progress. This encouraged people to identify with the Christian West and shape their own traditions accordingly.

Bodies

Within a Greek tradition, the body remains a threat. Though one may be seriously concerned with justice and with the needs of others, individuals often learn to aspire to overcoming their need for others to reach a state of perfection where they no longer feel dependent in any way, including in relation to their own bodies. In this way, they can focus on the intellectual contemplation of eternal truths. Philo felt torn between the God of Aristotle and the God of the Bible and this is shown in his ambivalent feelings towards the body.

Following the Stoics and Aristotle, Philo also distinguishes between the contemplative intellectual virtues that have God as their object and practical, moral virtues. But in respect of what is for him one of the key virtues – faith – Philo differs from them because for them faith is not a virtue. Faith also involves trust in revealed truth and trust in God's promises. Prayer is also a virtue he wants to recognise when he says 'each of the virtues is a holy matter, but thanksgiving is pre-eminently so' (Plant, 129 – quoted in Williamson, p.211).

But in Philo's explicit dualism between body and soul we might be tempted to say that he is 'more Greek than Jewish'. According to Ronald Williamson, in *Jews In The Hellenic World*, 'Influenced by the Orphic views of Plato's *Phaedo*, Philo regarded the body as a severe hindrance in its striving for virtue, as dragging it down from its true functions and aspirations into a world of sense and passion. The body is for him at times thought of as the tomb of the soul' (*Leg. All.* 1:108; *Spec. Leg.* iv:188).[10] He describes the soul as 'imprisoned in that dwelling-place of endless calamities – the body' (*Conf. Ling.* 177). In one passage, he calls the body 'the grave of the soul' (*Quaest. In Gn.* iv:75) (p.212).

But even if Philo encouraged his readers to 'live with the soul rather than with the body' (*Abr.* 236), he still had to accept the pull of a Jewish tradition when he acknowledged that 'we consist of body and soul' (*Spec. Leg.* ii:64) and that, according to Williamson, 'the life of virtue has to be achieved on earth within the human frame. For Philo men could not but be *in* the body, though to achieve virtue it was imperative that they should not be *of* it'. This echoed his refusal of a Stoic tradition that would treat all bodily emotions as immoral and bad. Even if people have to learn to subdue the body and its emotions if they wanted to live a moral life, it is not a matter of rejecting the embodied lives we inherit. People had to learn to curb the passions of the body if they wanted to be able to live a life of virtue.

As David Winston has argued in 'Philo and the Contemplative Life', reprinted in *Jewish Spirituality*, 'In making the Logos the primary manifestation of the deity, Philo was naturally constrained not only to reject all anthropomorphic descriptions of God, but also to insist on His absolute rationality and on His insusceptibility to irrational emotions of any kind' (p.210). In ascribing pity (*elos*) to God, he departs from the Stoics who had classified pity as a species of grief (*lype*), which is one of the four primary passions. There is also a darker Platonic inheritance that encourages Philo to think of the body as a corpse so that people walk about during their lives 'always carrying a corpse' (*Quaest. in Gn.* iv:77). It is this vision of the corpse that echoes in the sense of 'being dead while alive' that haunts Christian culture in the West. It is later echoed in the writings of Simone Weil when she talks about a need to reduce herself to matter so that she can serve the will of God. It is in tension with a Jewish tradition that would treat life as a *blessing* in which individuals would seek an intimacy and nearness to God. Through evil deeds, we find ourselves distant and in danger of suffering a moral death.[11]

From Philo's perspective, the body is a corpse, 'the dwelling place of endless calamities' (*Conf.* 177), and is symbolised in Scripture by Er: 'For this reason, in the matter of Er too, without evident cause, God knows him to be wicked and slays him (*Gen.* 38:7). For he is not unaware that the body, our "leathery" bulk (Er means leathery), is wicked and a plotter against the soul, and is even a cadaver and always dead. For you must not imagine that each of us is anything but a corpsebearer, the soul rousing and effortlessly bearing the body, which is of itself a corpse.'

According to Philo, moreover, the body is the source of both *agnoia*, lack of knowledge, and *amathia*, fundamental ignorance, for '...the chief cause of ignorance is the flesh and our affinity for it. Moses himself affirms this when he says "because they are flesh" the divine spirit cannot abide....those who bear the load of the flesh are unable, thus weighed down and oppressed, to gaze upward at the resolving heavens, but with necks wrenched downward are forcibly rooted to the ground like four-footed beasts' (*Gig.* 29–31).

Philo seems to think that it is through the gradual removal of the psyche from the sensible realm that it *ascends* to a life of perfection in God, and in these moments seems to echo a Platonic notion that it is only with *death* that the soul entombed in the body is able to return to its proper place. Sometimes the sojourn in the body is represented as a period of exile, as when Philo says 'For the soul of the wise man when it comes from above, from the ether, and enters into a mortal and is sown in the field of the body, is truly a sojourner in a land not its own, for the earthly nature of the body is an alien to the pure mind and subjects it to slavery and brings upon it all kinds of suffering' ('Quaestiones et Solutines' in *Exodum* 3.10).

For Philo, Abraham comes to represent the virtue-loving soul in search of the God who arrives at a more purified understanding of the divine. The migration of Abraham to the realm of the intelligible is reflected in the alteration of his name from Abram to Abraham and is vividly described in Philo's allegorical interpretation of *Gen.* 12:1–3: 'And the Lord said to Abraham, Go forth from your native land and from your kindred and from your father's house, to the land that I shall show you…'. Intent on purifying man's soul, God initially assigns it as its starting point for full salvation and its migration from three regions, body, sense/perception and speech. 'Lord' is a symbol of body, 'kindred' of sense/perception and 'father's house' of speech. The words 'Go forth from these' are not equivalent to 'Disengage yourself from them in substance', since such a command would be a prescription for death. The words are equal instead to 'Make yourself a stranger to them in your mental disposition; cleave to none of them and stand above them all…Go forth, then, from the earthly matter that envelops you. Escape, man, from the abominable prison, your body, and from the pleasures and lusts that act as jailer…Depart also from the sense/perception of your kin….migrate also from speech…so that you may not be deceived by words and expressions and be severed from the authentic beauty that lies in the matter disclosed. For it is absurd that shadows gain the advantage over objects, or a copy over originals' (*Mig.* 1–4, 7–12).

According to Philo, theoretical virtue is indeed perfect in beauty, but its practice too is a prize to be striven for. In *Decal.* 100, he bids people always to follow God who had devoted six days to *praxis* and the seventh to *theoria*, thus bringing the practical and the contemplative into a healthy relationship with each other. Elsewhere he seems more open to a different relationship between body *and* soul, saying that body and soul want to relieve each other, so that while the body is working, the soul enjoys a respite, but when the body takes its rest, the soul resumes its work. In this vein he seems to acknowledge a Jewish tradition that allows for *joy* to be realised in this life so that virtue does not have to involve self-denial. Philo says that there is one reward the virtuous person can receive here and now – the great reward of joy.[12]

The performance of the Law confers joy upon people as a present experience. It is not salvation that involves denial of present joys. Philo writes that 'there is no sweeter delight than that the soul should be charged through and through with justice, exercising itself in its eternal principles and doctrines and leaving no vacant space into which injustice can make its way' (Spec. Leg. Iv. 141). Philo speaks of the servant of God feeling more joy in that position than if he had been made king of all the world (*Rer. Div. Her.* 7). This links in to Philo's recognition that a crucial element in ethical teaching is the idea of the imitation of God. God is also described by Philo as 'the husband of Wisdom, dropping the seeds of happiness for the race of mortals into good and virgin soil' (*Cher.* 49).

But this is imagined in gendered terms, as he goes on to explain how God removes from human life 'degenerate and emasculated passions which unmanned it and plants instead the native growth of unpolluted virtues' (*ibid.* 50). In gendered terms echoed in Williamson's words, 'Man can live with "high hopes" of the descent of the divine potencies which will descend with laws and ordinances – but laws and ordinances accompanied by the divine powers to live by them' (*ibid.* 106). Philo contrasts haste to fulfil a promise to a fellow man and delay in fulfilling a promise to God, 'who lacks and needs nothing' (*Spec. Leg.* ii:38).

It is also the vision of self-sufficiency that can be offered through this conception of God to human beings that a Jewish tradition often questions. As David Hartman recognises in 'Moral Uncertainty in the Practice of Medicine', in *Joy And Responsibility*, the God of the Bible, unlike the God of Aristotle, is described almost exclusively in terms of the divine *relationship* with human beings. Hartman explains the contrast in relation to an ideal of self-sufficiency: 'The God of Aristotle was an object of intellectual contemplation. Only God who could be conceived of as a Creator, as acting at a particular time, could give Law to humanity and could be conceived in terms of a relationship' (p.124).

Intellectual perfection in Greece involved independence and self-sufficiency, later echoed within modernity as an ideal of masculinity, and thus a liberation from human relationships that demanded intense emotional involvement. By contrast, *interpersonal love* places the lover in a context in which one is *vulnerable* and dependent, precluding the possibility of absolute control and self-sufficiency. As Hartman explains: 'the relational perfection found in the biblical tradition leads humans to accept dependency as a permanent, positive feature of the human condition' (p.124).[13]

In choosing a covenantal relationship, God in effect, as Hartman understands it, chooses interdependency. This covenantal relationship is largely absent in Philo. It also questions the Greek conception of the body that we so often read in Philo, as Hartman explains: 'If to be fully human is to give up the quest for self-sufficiency, and if to be whole one must learn to love, to accept dependence and to be able to say, honestly, "I need you", then spiritual liberation must consider the significance of the human body. The Greek tradition must be turned on its head. The human body can humanise us and dispel our delusions of self-sufficiency' (p.125). As Hartman explains it: 'The source of human hubris can often be traced to the exaggerated emphasis on the intellect at the expense of recognising the limitations of the body. The body gives persons a sense of humanity and dependency, and hence, teaches humanity' (p.125).

Hartman recognises that 'In hunger and in need, in the interlinking of sexual desire, love and self-transcendence, in disease and in decay, the body is an important spiritual teacher. To gain spiritual wholeness, the human soul must make contact with the body' (p.125). Rather than rejecting the mortality of the body in the face of an everlasting soul, it is through *accepting* the vulnerability of the body that we can appreciate the soul. It is through the body that the soul learns to deal with everyday life and so can grow into a deeper contact with itself. This refuses to acknowledge death as liberation for the soul, for it is only through contact with the body that the soul can *deepen* its relationship with itself. Hartman expresses a similar idea: 'To the degree that people are alienated from the rhythms of their body, to that degree are they out of touch with the spiritual outlook of the biblical tradition' (p.125).

Love, Friendship and Hospitality

Reason's Illness

In his exposition of Wittgenstein's thought *The Claim Of Reason*, Stanley Cavell interprets Wittgenstein as finding a 'truth in scepticism', even if it is one that the sceptic distorts and misunderstands. As Putnam expresses it: 'It is true that we do not "know" that there is a world and that there are other people, in Cavell's interpretation, but not because (this is the sceptic's misunderstanding) we "don't know" these things. In ordinary circumstances, circumstances in which neither doubt nor justification is called for, our relation to the familiar things in our environment, the pen in our hand or the person in pain we are consoling, is not one of either "knowing" or "not knowing"'. Rather, Cavell suggests, it is one of *acknowledging* (or, sadly, failing to acknowledge). Our task is not to aquire a 'proof' that 'there is an external world' or that our friend is in pain, but to *acknowledge* the world and our friend' (Introduction, p.10).[1]

How are we to understand this acknowledgement and what is the difference in the acknowledgement we might give to friends, neighbours or strangers? This is a question that can only be framed within the context of everyday life where we discover the different demands that are being made upon us. As Rosenzweig sees it, the philosopher is a being who is incapable of accepting the process of life and what he calls 'the passing of the numbness wonder has brought'. Such a relief comes too slowly, according to Putnam. The philosopher, according to Rosenzweig, 'does not permit his wonder, stored as it is, to be released into the flow of life. Of necessity, he must hook the "problem" from where he stands. He has forcibly extracted it through "object" and "subject" from the flow of life and he entrenches himself within it. Wonder stagnates, it is perpetuated in the motionless mirror of his meditation; that is in the subject. He has it well-hooked; it is securely fastened, and it persists in his benumbed immobility. The stream of life has been replaced by something submissive – statuesque, subjugated' (*Understanding The Sick And The Healthy*, p.40–41).

As Putnam recognises, a number of critics of the traditional metaphysical enterprise have noted that the philosopher seeks an imaginary position, one outside the flow of time. This is also an insight that Antonio Gramsci develops in his *Prison Notebooks*.[2] The male philosopher seeks to view everything, even himself, as if he were not *in* it; to view it 'from sideways on', as John McDowell has put it in his paper 'Non-Cognitivism and Rule-Following' (reprinted in *Mind, Value And Reality*, p.207). By describing this imaginary position as a place outside the demands of life and the flow of time, Rosenzweig suggests that this sort of philosophy stems from a 'fear to live' (p.102).[3]

It is the fear of death that has so often shaped a western philosophical tradition formed within the terms of a secularised, but often unacknowledged, christianity that makes it difficult to live life and so to think meaningfully in the face of our own mortality. As Rosenzweig explains, as he moves towards the conclusion in his *Understanding The Sick And The Healthy*, 'We have wrestled with the fear to live, with the desire to step outside of the current, now we may discover that reason's illness was merely an attempt to elude death. Man, chilled in the full current of life, sees...death waiting for him. So he steps outside of life. If life means dying, he prefers not to live. He chooses death in life. He escapes from the inevitability of death into the paralysis of artificial death'. The difficult task Rosenzweig has accepted is to help people to release themselves from this paralysis, knowing that this means helping people to face their own deaths. As he explains: 'By teaching him to live again, we have taught him to move towards death; we have taught him to live, though each step he takes brings him closer to death. Each step that he takes is accompanied by fear. This is not as it should be; the courage to face life should still all fear' (p.102).

Rosenzweig suggests that *if* people can face their own mortalities then they will allow themselves to think philosophically in different ways. He questions the kind of philosophy that has emerged in the West when the philosopher 'separates his experience of wonder from the continuous stream of life, isolating it'. According to Rosenzweig, 'This is the way his thought proceeds. He does not permit his wonder, stored as it is, to be released into the flow of life. He steps outside the continuity of life and consequently the continuity of thought is broken. And there he begins stubbornly to reflect' (p.40). But life cannot be stopped in its tracks and our thinking has to reflect life *as* a *process* that is to be lived. Life is not within our control even though a rationalist modernity might want to suggest otherwise.

Loving Others

As I explored in *The Moral Limits Of Modernity*, Kant was caught between wanting to acknowledge the significance of the love we owe our neighbours and his sense that love as an emotion remained, at some level, a threat to reason. He felt easier with a notion of respect that is grounded in a notion of law. In different ways his thinking about ethics was developed out of reflections on law. This is clearest in relation to the demand for impartiality. Kant tends to think of love as a 'rational emotion' because it is still important to sustain love within his moral vision. But at some level he remains *uneasy* about the love we can feel for others. This is shown in his writings on sex and marriage, in which love seems to fall into thinking of the contact between bodily organs, so that within marriage people have a contract to make use of each other's sexual organs.[4]

At some level, Kant sustains a disdain for emotional life and never really allows us to offer hospitality to our emotions, feelings and desires. These 'inclinations' are defined as aspects of an 'animal nature' which needs to be suppressed, controlled and denied, since they play *no* part in shaping and defining our humanity. Rather, Kant sustains the radical distinction between reason and nature that insists that it is only through an independent faculty of reason that we can discern the moral law. It is only as rational that we are 'human' and it is only through reason that we *can* exist as moral selves whose actions can be deemed to have moral worth. This helps form a particular vision of human development through which our 'inclinations' gradually come to have less hold, and we more easily identify ourselves with the demands of duty and moral law. This shapes a vision of individualisation as transcendence.[5]

The notion of personal identity as a rational moral self that informs Kantian ethics gives limited hospitality to emotions, feelings and desires. Rather, we learn to deny emotional and spiritual lives as we learn to discount emotions and desires as being threatening to our identities as rational selves. Often, we are so used to excluding and rejecting emotions that we grew up with, as we learn to identify rationality with control that they have little relationship to our sense of emotional lives. Freud appreciated the time and attention that it takes for people to *build* bridges towards emotional lives that they have suppressed within a rationalist culture. Often we learn within a rationalist culture that we can only allow emotion if we know it to be rationally justified.[6]

The dissatisfaction with a Kantian rationalism that possibly characterises an embedded Jewish philosophy dates back to the early reception of his work and as Putnam mentions, in his notes to *Understanding The Sick And The Healthy*, Rozensweig's criticism of German idealism is presaged in the philosophy of Schelling in his last period. Logic or 'pure thought' cannot explain existence, as Hegel has attempted to do. Schelling said: 'The whole world lies, as it were, in the nets of understanding or of reason, but the question is *how* it came into these nets, since something else and something *more* than mere reason, indeed, even something striving beyond these limits, is evidently in the world (*Sammtliche Werke*, vol. X, 143 – quoted in Putnam, *ibid.* p.111).

But Hegel at least comes to appreciate the weakness in Kant's ethical rationalism and the kind of ethical constructionism it has encouraged. In his early writings on theology there is already an awareness that Christianity can foster a tendency to rationalise emotional experience. As Yovel explains: 'In particular, Hegel denounced the "spirit of mourning" in which Christians conduct this celebration (the sacrament of the *hostia*)'. The Greeks celebrate with joy, whereas Christianity cultivates suffering and is plagued by a peevish spirit. For the Greeks, 'misfortune was misfortune, pain was pain', whereas Christianity has 'for the sake of suffering humanity...piled up such a heap of reasons for comfort in misfortune...that we might be sorry in the end that we cannot lose a father or a mother once a week'. (Hegel's *Jugendschriften*, p.22. Yovel uses Kaufmann's translation in *Hegel*, p.59.)[7]

When the young Hegel moved from Berne to Frankfurt and wrote *The Spirit of Christianity and its Fate*, he became concerned with issues of 'religion and love'. He was beginning to distance himself from Kant and make his peace with Jesus. Kant had argued that duty and love cannot be united in a single concept, because love cannot be commanded. This was because love had to be separated from emotions and Kant could not draw a distinction between emotions and feelings, but assumed they were all to be gathered as 'inclinations' and set against reason. For Kant, love was a rational feeling and thus could be separated from the physical body and sexuality that was still tacitly identified with *Carnal Israel*.

If Kant argued that duty and love cannot be united, for Hegel, Jesus, through the single dictum 'love God above all and love thy neighbour as thyself', knew better. Hegel could not acknowledge that the importance of love *affirmed* the Jewishness of Jesus, rather than constituting a break with Judaism, as Church fathers sought to insist. As Hegel sought to understand it and as Yovel explains: 'The religion of love makes it possible to live morally and maintain a sense of emotional plenitude rather than be torn, as in Kant, between one's life and one's duty. Kant had banned all natural drives and human needs from morality, whereas Jesus' religion of love expressed human needs in their noblest form, and is capable of restoring the unity between man and his Other, his feelings, and the world' (p.33).

Even if I agree with the sentiment; it is expressed too generally and the issues around a dominant Christian appropriation of love are left unexplored. Yovel is clear that 'the religion of love makes Judaism look even worse to Hegel, since he shares the tradition which saw Judaism as built on seclusion and hatred of all other nations. Judaism also supposedly lacked the element of beauty, the essence of Greek religion which Christians learned to absorb but Jews reject fanatically' (p.33). He is also helpful when he suggests, 'It is interesting to see how Hegel used his critique of Judaism as a lever for distancing himself from Kant. Jesus' principle of love is now set against the Kantian "Ought". All human legislation that mediates between contradictory interests is based upon an Ought, says Hegel; as such, the law is not part of nature but imposed upon nature as a command' ('The Spirit of Christianity' in *Early Theological Writings*, p.209 – quoted in Yovel, p.34). For Hegel, as Yovel remarks, 'This is true of Kantian moralism and Jewish legalism alike' (p.34).

Hegel now attributes to Kant the sources of the 'positivity' he had previously ascribed to Jesus. Hegel recognises that Kant's morality is so abstract that all particular acts of duty must take their content from contingent circumstances, so that a residue of 'positivity' remains in Kant's morality that is ineradicable. As Yovel seeks to explain: 'Thus a moral system which claimed to be pure and universal is affected by contradictions between its form and its content. Hegel says that this contradictions "shock us" because this makes it possible to stamp all kinds of arbitrary, occasional actions with the seal of absolute morality, while disqualifying as immoral – or at least as morally irrelevant – "all human relations which do not unquestionably belong to the concept of (Kantian) duty", be they love, solidarity, familial links, etc. "Woe to them all", says Hegel ironically, "from the morality of the Ought!"' (*The Spirit of Christianity*, p.212 – quoted on p.34).

Some of the differences that we find explored between Kant and Hegel *show* the tacit acknowledgement of the ways in which antagonism and contempt for Judaism help *form* the conceptual structures which are often taken for granted within contemporary philosophical writing that tends to disavow a historical awareness. According to Derek Parfit's *Reasons And Persons*, for example 'each of my momentary selves, my "time-slices", has the right to be considered a different individual'.[8] As Putnam presents it, 'the idea that the self that will be called "Hilary Putnam" in a week's time is in any sense more "identical" to me than is the perfect stranger thousands of miles away is just a persistent illusion'.

According to Putnam, 'this view is just as metaphysical as the view it opposes, the view that there is some self-identical entity, some "substance" in traditional metaphysical terminology which is present as long as I am, and which is my "essence". In traditional religious thought, and also in the psychology of Descartes and other Rationalist philosophers, this substance was identified with an immaterial soul...' (Putnam's Introduction to *Understanding The Sick And The Healthy,* p.7). But the question still remains of *how* we are to understand human emotional growth and moral development and the ways in which they can be related to each other. This could have to do with allowing the soul to manifest itself more openly and freely within our everyday lives and relationships.

Rosenzweig would have questioned Parfitt's claim that it makes no sense to think of oneself as the same person at different times. Indeed, he thinks that thinking this way is essential to our lives. As Putnam puts it: 'This is another way of making the point that "common sense in action" has no choice but to rely on the language game. For Kant, rational thought itself depends on the fact that I regard my thoughts, experiences, memories, etc. as all *mine* (that is, the fact that I prefix the "I think" to all of them, not just at the time but also retrospectively)' (p.8). As Putnam reminds us: 'We are *responsible* for what we have thought and done in the past, responsible *now*, intellectually and practically, and that is what makes us *thinkers*, rational agents in a world, at all. Kant, like Locke, can be seen as making the point that the "game" of thinking of my thoughts and actions at different times as *mine* does not depend on a metaphysical premise about "self-identical substances", and is nonetheless a game that we cannot opt out of as long as we are engaged in "common-sense in action"'.

But Rosenzweig would possibly have been less concerned to sustain Putnam's rationalism, though he would have recognised Putnam's awareness that for Rosenzweig 'a proper relation to God no more depends on a *theory*, on an intellectual conception of what God "really is", or a grasp of the "essence" of God, than a proper relation to other human beings or to the world *depends on* a theory of man or the world'. Again, a comparison with Wittgenstein may help in grasping the thought. In *Culture And Value* we have the following remark about religious belief that makes it clear that for him, too, a religion, if it is to have any value, cannot be a *theory*: 'It strikes me that a religious belief could only be something like a passionate commitment to a system of reference. Hence, although it's *belief*, it's really a way of living, or a way of assessing life. It's passionately seizing hold of *this* interpretation...It would be as though someone were first to let me see the hopelessness of my situation and then show me the means of rescue, until, of my own accord, or not at any rate led to it by my *instructor*, I ran to it and grasped it' (University of Chicago Press, Chicago, 1980, p.64).

Wittgenstein often felt the 'hopelessness' of his situation, but he never turned to an explicit religious belief. However, he recognised that his emphasis upon the concrete details of everyday life and his suspicion of idealisations that characterised Greek thought meant there was something 'Hebraic' in his later thinking. He was concerned with our finitude that thought we should *not* seek to escape, or 'rise above' it, as Kant puts it. He discovered a need in his own life to 'make space' for acknowledging a Jewish inheritance that others might have thought he had disavowed. He felt a need to be truthful with friends, even though he often found it difficult to come to terms with his own emotions and desires.

Wittgenstein was aware of the hold that an Enlightenment rationalism continued to have within modernity and this was partly why he felt that his later writings could not be appreciated.[9] But he never grasped this as a possible tension between Greek and Hebraic inheritances. The withering of his inheritance and the moves towards more abstract forms of moral theory in the 1990s has shown his fears to be at least partly justified. At the same time there have been significant tendencies in a different direction with the development of 'virtue ethics'.

As Norman Malcolm recognised, Wittgenstein appreciated that we can instinctively reach towards others in pain. We can reach out to comfort others. For Wittgenstein this was a 'natural' human response to the suffering of others.[10] This was not an altruistic concern that we perform in accordance with a principle that we should help people who are suffering. Rather, Wittgenstein is tacitly subverting the rationalism that underpins a Kantian ethic and is preparing the ground in which we can recognise our care and compassion as a *human*, almost instinctive, response to the pain of others. This is part of Wittgenstein's questioning a philosophy of mind that is informed by Greek rationalism when it assumes that these connections are made through the rational workings of the mind and then applied as a matter of principle. It might well be that a Protestant moral culture educates our emotions and shapes our experience and dispositions so that we inhibit responses we might otherwise make to others.

In this way, Wittgenstein helps to question rationalist visions of 'the human' that frame the placing of emotions, feelings and desires as *threats* to reason and thus to our status as rational moral selves. In Kant, the emotions are distractions that 'take us away' from being able to deliberate clearly. But as Carol Gilligan has shown in *In a Different Voice*, in her empirical work with young people who are attempting to decide, for example, what to do about an unplanned pregnancy. She shows that though men often want to settle this as a matter of principle that can then be *applied* to their individual cases, women more readily think that it is a matter of exploring whether the relationship they have with their partners is strong enough to sustain a pregnancy. They want to know, as part of an ethics of care, what their partners are feeling about them, their relationship and the pregnancy before they feel able to make a moral decision. Often it is only through exploring the difficult emotions, with both partners being prepared to do the 'emotional work' of exploring their complex emotional responses, that people feel *able* to think clearly about the situation. Often it is only when we can feel clearly, allowing us to express and so release the anger and disappointment we carry, that we can 'move closer' to being able to express what we want to do.[11]

Traditionally, men in modern Western cultures have found it difficult to express their emotions and share their feelings with their partners. Often they have learned to exert control over their emotional lives, assuming that it is through control that they can affirm their male identities. Sometimes they might be anxious 'not to hurt others', so they find themselves being accommodating to what others would expect them to feel. With the strength of a post-feminist culture, women sometimes experience similar difficulties, having learned to rationalise their own experiences. Often they do not know what they are feeling and, like men, they have grown fearful of dwelling upon their emotions within a moral culture that treats taking time with emotions not as an individual responsibility but as a form of self-indulgence.

Unless we learn to question the ways in which our gender-specific experience and identities have been shaped within a rationalist moral culture, we can inherit a fear of intimacy that is difficult to overcome.

As individuals within intimate relationships we can recognise ourselves as alone, standing next to our partners but really, at some level, unable to 'let them in' – offer them hospitality within our emotional lives. Often, men find it particularly difficult to share their vulnerability, experiencing this as a threat to their male identity. They might *want* to be 'more open' with their partners, but recognise, unlike Kant, that this cannot happen as a matter of will alone. We often grow up assuming that we can 'put the past behind us', so that we are often deaf to the ways unresolved emotional history calls us back to deal with unresolved emotions.[12]

Friendship

Sometimes people really want a partner with whom to share their lives, but because they have not dealt with the emotional baggage they carry, they have not really created a space for a loving relationship. Often within a Kantian tradition we learn to reject emotional life as threatening our status as rational moral agents, so that we never learn *how* to offer hospitality to our emotional lives. Since we cannot be 'open' in this way emotionally with ourselves it can be difficult to be 'open' in our relationships. This can also shape the way we act in friendships, since it can be difficult to 'let someone in' and thus show hospitality if you cannot really 'let yourself in'.[13]

But it can be difficult for people to recognise in a rationalist culture *how* they have become estranged from their emotions. At one level, people feel they are not missing anything significant since it makes it easier to live life according to reason alone. In another way, people say they have no difficulty, say, in expressing anger, as if this somehow proves they have a relationship with their emotions. Often men, at least, become angry because they cannot allow themselves to be vulnerable, something they experience as a threat to their male identities. Often they get angry as a form of displacement and thus as a way of concealing more vulnerable feelings of loss, sadness or fear that it would be more threatening to acknowledge. A man might be completely unfamiliar with his fear, unable to really identify the emotion, especially if it were not an emotion which he was permitted to express in childhood.[14]

Often men who have grown up to assume control of their emotional lives will only allow emotions, say of anger, when they already know in advance that they can rationally justify the anger. At other times, they might pride themselves at being 'in control' of their emotions. Freud knew that this repression can be a form of deadening, where people surrender their own spontaneity and vitality. All their actions might be carefully controlled and they might be so used to policing their emotions that they no longer recognise that they have an inner emotional life at all. If they can recognise their inner emotions they do not think these can ever be shared with others. Even in their friendships, they might feel the need not to 'burden' others with their emotions and feel that they should be able to *deal* with their inner emotional conflicts whenever they arise.[15]

Even though we might very much want a close friend, we might find it difficult to accept that others can really 'be there' for us. This can affect how vulnerable we can make ourselves to others, especially if we feel that our dependency might be used against us. We might feel grateful that we have a friend but feel unable to make use of the friendship. Within a moral culture in which men are encouraged to be self-sufficient, it can be difficult to *show* our vulnerability to others. We might communicate in indirect ways that show a need, but do not allow us to ask directly for the support that we need. Sometimes we just need others to listen to us, but this can be difficult for us to acknowledge since it can be experienced as a threat to our male identities. Often men from diverse class, 'racial' and ethnic backgrounds can more easily reach out to others when they are feeling good about themselves, but find it difficult to make a phone call to friends when they are down. It is hard enough acknowledging that you feel depressed but can feel too risky to share this with others when, at some level, you fear they might take advantage of you.

Nietzsche writes on friendship in *Human, All Too Human,* in which he talks about 'Anticipating ingratitude. The man who gives a great gift encounters no gratitude; for the recipient, simply by accepting it, already has too much of a burden' (p.323). He talks about friendship as a *gift*, both in terms of friendship as a gift which we offer to others without expecting anything in return, thus questioning a utilitarian vision of friendship in terms of exchange, and at the same time recognising that some people have a gift for friendship which others can lack. He writes tellingly that 'In many people....the gift of having good friends is much greater than the gift of being a good friend' (p.368). He is aware of the difficulties of 'being a good friend'. He knows that being a good friend can involve more than feelings of care, concern and sympathy for others. Sometimes we have to confront friends with difficult truths about themselves that they do not want to hear.[16]

In thoughts which in some way echo what Kant has to say about the difficulties of self-knowledge that we have because of our finitude, Nietzsche is also aware of our rationalisations and self-deceptions.

Sometimes we hold on to friendships because we do not want to realise that the relationship no longer works for us, or has really died. At these moments we can be called upon to speak more truthfully about what has been going on in the friendship, if we want to give it a chance for recovery. Nietzsche had been deeply affected by the breakdown of his friendship with Wagner, realising that he could no longer befriend a person with such anti-semitic views. Once he came to know these views, he could not sustain the friendship.

Nietzsche knew that people had limited self-knowledge and that they often hid things from themselves and from their friends. Often we *conceal* things that at some level we know about ourselves. In this way, Nietzsche questions an Enlightenment rationalism that too often assumes that people are engaged in a search for knowledge. Like Freud after him, Nietzsche appreciated that we often conceal what we do *not* want to disclose to others, as well as ourselves. Sometimes friendships can be held together as an unspoken pact against facing truths and people rely upon their friends to sustain these self-delusions. But this is a friendship that will *harden* from the inside and will eventually be reduced to an empty ritual. It is a relationship in which neither party can grow and in which individuals can be stuck in a denial that needs to be broken.

Rather, Nietzsche recognises that we need friends who will also be ready to tell us what we do *not* want to hear, but can rely upon a good friend to tell us. A friend will 'be there' for us in difficult times when we need the support of a caring other who knows us, but will also risk anger and rejection through telling us what we do not want to know about ourselves. For Nietzsche, this connects to how he understands the ease with which we conceal and deny truths about ourselves. Later, in *Human, All Too Human*, we have the remark again expressed in gender-specific terms: 'Self-observation. Man is very well defended against himself, against his own spying and sieges; usually he is able to make out no more of himself than his outer fortifications. The actual stronghold is inaccessible to him, even invisible, unless friends and enemies turn traitor and lead him there by a secret path' (p.491).[17]

Often as men there are parts of ourselves that we know little about and have very little relationship with because we have learned to identify masculinity with control over emotions, feelings and desires. With Nietzsche this is expressed through an elitism in which, supposedly, it is only the 'noble' who are capable of giving and receiving the gift of friendship. In this way, friendship does not have to do with rules that can be impartially applied by anyone as rational selves. For Nietzsche, most people will feel unable to accept being bound in gratitude and so will be unable to accept the responsibilities of genuine friendship. In a remark which connects nobility with gratitude, he says 'A noble soul will be happy to feel itself bound in gratitude and will not try anxiously to avoid the occasion when it may be so bound.......while cruder souls resist being bound in any way, or are later excessive and much too eager in expressing their gratitude' (p.366). They will supposedly be expressing a gratitude that they do not really feel.

As Graham Smith has written in a paper on 'Nietzsche's talent for friendship' that he presented at the *Ethics Of Altruism* Conference, and from which I have taken these quotations, friendship is a gift given freely with no expectation of return. But Nietzsche also holds that it is only those who are 'noble' who are capable of giving and receiving the gift of friendship. This means, as Smith acknowledges, that there is little 'room for genuine concern and sympathy for others'. It might be that Nietzsche places an emphasis on the harder responsibilities of friendship that a prevailing liberal vision too easily ignores. He insists that pity can be no basis for friendship, whatever a Christian ethical tradition supposes.[18]

Nietzsche recognises that friendships involve expressing difficult feelings towards others that are too often put aside for fear of losing a friend. It is not a matter of living up to an abstract ideal of friendship, as a Greco-Christian tradition can sometimes suggest, but of exploring the everyday complexity of relationships that we find in some Biblical narratives and which Jewish philosophies can somehow teach us to value. This means that, for instance, we can often swallow the anger we feel at being let down by a friend, out of an unspoken fear that they might reject us if we express the anger we feel. In this way we learn to be *false* to ourselves, as we refuse to give hospitality to our own feelings of anger that can too easily be experienced as threatening. At some level, we fear being left isolated and alone. Often, people live in fear of losing the friendships they have, so they keep their negative thoughts and emotions to themselves, not wanting to 'hurt' or 'damage' the friendship. They do not appreciate how they can be undermining a friendship through this kind of behaviour.

In an interview with Lynn Barber for The Observer Magazine, *Life*, Christopher Hitchens shares how it was a sympathetic letter written by Martin Amis when his mother had committed suicide in Athens that was the start of their friendship. He shares a contemporary narrative of friendship. In Jewish tradition, this could serve as a contemporary ethical story or midrash.[19] A former girlfriend had phoned him to ask him how he was because she said that there had been a letter in *The Times* saying that a woman with his mother's name had been murdered by her lover in a hotel room in Athens. The police had believed at first that it was murder because there was blood everywhere. But then they found a suicide note addressed to Christopher saying, in effect, 'You will understand one day'.

As Lynn Barber explains, Hitchens says: '"You only really need one friend, who is your counterpart, who knows everything about you, and that's Martin. Martin is the one that I love, who means everything to me". Amis, in turn, says he loves Hitchens because, "He's incredibly funny, and he instructs as he delights". He also says "The Hitch is an incomparably good friend ...Having him for a friend during bad times is like having a hundred friends – he'd do anything for you". They consoled each other through their respective divorces and mid-life crises and loss of their fathers' (The Observer Magazine, *Life*, 14 April 2002, p.14).

There is another story of friendship that Barber also tells. As she introduces it: 'Hitchens claims to believe in Einstein's injunction to "remember your humanity and forget the rest". But once in a while, he throws up these steel barricades marked "principles" or "not being a hypocrite" behind which he can behave with truly Trotskyite ruthlessness. This was most apparent when he attacked – some would say betrayed – his old friend, Sidney Blumenthal, in 1999. Blumenthal worked for the White House and testified in the Lewinsky hearings that he had never tried to smear Lewinsky as a stalker. Hitchens said not so; he remembered a lunch in which Blumenthal had done precisely that, and he went and signed an affidavit to that effect. In theory he could have sent Blumenthal to prison for perjury: it was a sharp end to a long friendship' (p.14).

As Barber goes on to explain: 'Some of Hitchen's friends were so shocked they dropped him. He says he doesn't know precise figures, but: "There are people I realise I haven't heard from and there may be many more I haven't guessed at.....I don't know how many – but, I hope, a lot. Put it this way: I don't want it to be over, I'm afraid of it blowing over. Because I should have pulled the chain on him (Blumenthal) much earlier than I did – there was a long period when I was a hypocrite, when I thought I could still think of him as a friend"'. Barber also observes that: 'In fact, the Blumenthal affair was strikingly reminiscent of Martin Amis's sudden termination of his friendship with Julian Barnes. Perhaps this is why they over-sentimentalise their own friendship' (p.14). Possibly this is also a particular feature of male friendships, especially as they are focussed upon the singular best friend.

When Lynne Barber pressed Martin Amis to name Hitchen's faults, he said: 'Let me think. He's quite tough, you know, steely. He perhaps is a bit rough in argument sometimes, rougher than I would be. And he'll give a waiter or a cab driver a pasting (if they were disobliging), in a way that I wouldn't. He's physically brave, too'. Hitchens would be happy with this version: he admires toughness (p.14). The unspoken theme of masculinity is not far from the surface and may give a particular shape to male friendships. He talks about the regret he feels at not having served in the armed services and thinks maybe this is why he seeks out dangerous places such as Beirut or Belfast or Bosnia.

He remembers in 1978 having written a long piece from Beirut for *The New Statesman* and his father ringing up and saying 'Read your piece on Beirut. I thought it was very good'. Barber records Hitchins saying '"Well thank you!" because I didn't get much of that – or did I miss it, or want it, or that I didn't know that I did, anyway. Then he said, rather gruffly, "I also thought it was rather brave of you to go there", and hung up the phone. I had never expected to hear anything like that from him, because he'd been in Arctic convoys. I'd always thought I'd rather disappointed him by not being good at cricket or rugger. So it was an amazing unsought compliment. But then I thought to myself, "Maybe that's what I have been secretly wanting, to have that validation"' (p.14).

12

Dialogue, Responsibility
and Ethics

Dialogue

Martin Buber, in *The Way Of Man: According to the Teaching of Hasidism,* shows the influence of the Hasidic movement that was spreading across the Jewish communities of Eastern Europe at roughly the same time as the European Enlightenment, which was to inform the thinking of Moses Mendelssohn. Rather than assuming that these movements, coming from the East and inspired by the example of the Bal Shem Tov, were 'backward' and 'uncivilised', so that if they wanted to make a transition from nature to culture, from tradition to modernity, they would have to accept the supremacy of a rationalist Enlightenment, Buber understood how much they also had to teach. He had an ear that could listen to what they had to say, and he refused to categorise them as 'primitive' and thus as lacking the means to progress. He appreciated how much they could also *teach* Western culture.[1]

Writing in the early years of the twentieth century, when there was a crisis in European rationalism and a recognition that positivist traditions within the human sciences had their limits, Buber was able to hear the different voices that had emerged out of Hasidism in Eastern Europe. They offered the possibility of renewal for Jewish philosophy and thus the chance to open up a different kind of conversation between Jewish philosophy and Western culture. They helped to question traditional ways in which the West had come to understand its own modernity as setting a singular path that others would be destined to follow, if they wanted to make a transition from tradition to modernity.

Buber was learning something different, not only about a spiritual movement within Judaism, but about the possibilities that it opened up for a different kind of reflection on the history and philosophy of what had often been too easily defined as 'western culture'. Not only did it promise to question the ethnocentric assumptions of a European modernity, but it allowed for a different kind of conversation to be initiated between Judaism, Christianity and Islam in their complex relationships with a European modernity. Rather than there being a *singular* truth that Christianity had so often claimed as its own, there was multiplicity of different paths. It was through Hasidism that Buber was learning a respect for difference but also a recognition that individuals had to explore their *own* paths, and thus had the potential of going beyond the vision of themselves as 'rational selves' that had shaped European visions of modernity.

Buber wanted to remind us of something different that could be discovered in Hasidism and promised to open up dialogues between different civilisations and cultures that cross the traditional boundaries of 'Western culture':

'All people have access to God, but each person has a different access. Humanity's greatest chance lies precisely in the unlikeness of people, in the unlikeness of their qualities and inclinations. God's all inclusiveness manifests itself in the infinite multiplicity of the ways that lead to Him, each of which is open to one person. When some disciples of a deceased zaddik came to the "Seer" of Lublin and expressed surprise at the fact that his customs were different from those of their late master, the "Seer"' exclaimed: "What sort of God would that be who has only one way in which He can be served!"

'God does not say: "This way leads to Me and that does not", but He says: "Whatever you may do may be a way to Me, provided you do it in such a manner that it leads you to Me". But what it is that can and shall be done by just this person and no other, can be revealed to him only in himself....

'Everyone has in him something precious that is in no one else. But this precious something in a person is revealed to them only if they truly perceive their strongest feeling, their central wish, that in her or him which stirs their inmost being.

'By no means, however, can it be our true task in the world in which we have been set, to turn away from the things and beings that we meet on our way and that attract our hearts; our task is precisely to get in touch, by hallowing our relationship with them, with what manifests itself in them as beauty, pleasure, enjoyment. Hasidism teaches that rejoicing in the world, if we hallow it with our whole being, leads to rejoicing in God'.

Speaking

Martin Buber's writings on Chasidism have spoken to me since I was very young, growing up in the refugee Jewish community in north-west London in the 1950s and 1960s. Somehow, he was able to illuminate the *silences* that we grew up to take very much for granted, living as we did in the shadows of the aftermath of the Holocaust. Our parents did not want to share their traumatic experiences because they wanted to protect their children who represented the future for them. So our lives were determined by a catastrophic event that was to remain largely unspoken in those days. Their survival was to be given meaning through the lives, if not the achievements, of their children. The horrors of the past were constantly *present* but they were not to be spoken about. As children, we inherited a sense that our parents 'had suffered more than enough' and we learned not to add to their sufferings. While we were still young we learned not to ask too many questions. We learned that the past was a territory we should not enter.[2]

At some level we knew that the Jewish tradition was a tradition of questions and that it also talked about the moral obligation to remember the past. But at the particular moment we were growing up we learned that questions were *not* to be asked and that we could not expect to speak with our parents about the memories they carried. Rather, the past was a book that was closed to the present. What this meant was that, growing up in the shadows of the Shoah, death was never really far from us, for often we bore the names of those who had perished and been murdered. It was through naming that the souls of the dead were to be allowed to continue to live through us in the present. This connected, intimate and personal relationship between the lives we were living in the present and the dead relatives who were being memorialised through the names that we bore as our own.[3]

In many ways this remained a silent dialogue in which the dead were allowed a continuity into the present. Sometimes we carried the histories of these souls into the present, as if there was another voice that strove to be heard. It was at moments when, as boys, we might be called up to read from the Torah in synagogue that we would be reminded of the names we had. Sometimes this was recognised as a difference between what was still called your 'Christian' name, which was your 'first' name and thus the name that you showed to the world. I was called 'Victor' because I was born in 1945, the moment of victory for England that at the same time was the moment of realisation of the terrible destruction of European Jewry.

My first name carried this double inheritance as it also served as a form of protection – as well as hiding – through its identification with a shared historical moment.

We also had what were called 'Jewish' names, our Hebrew names that were called out in synagogue, along with the Hebrew names of our fathers. My Hebrew name was Jacob and this set up its own forms of identification with the Biblical Jacob who was to become Israel. But it also helped to shape the promises and dangers in the relationship that I had with my older brother Johnny, for, like Jacob, I was to be the second son. Often these 'Jewish' names only came into play within particular religious contexts. Otherwise they remained largely concealed, though they also held open the possibilities of a *dialogue* between the different names we carried, between what was shown to the world and what was lived through our relationships with others and the names that remained largely hidden and concealed. There were the possibilities of an inner dialogue between the 'Christian' and the 'Jewish' names we carried. This could help to form a particular experience of 'double consciousness' that already framed an implicit relationship between Jewish philosophy and western culture.[4]

It was much later that the dialogue between the different Christian and Jewish traditions we inherited became a possibility for us as we grew up in the somewhat stultified Anglo-Jewish community of the 1950s. We were more than ready to pay the price of assimilation. We readily accepted the terms of an Enlightenment modernity which promised that 'the other' could become like 'the same', as Levinas was to express it. It was also Levinas who was to consider the possibilities of a dialogue between Athens and Jerusalem, thus 'making visible' and open to dialogue aspects of the diverse cultural and religious traditions that had shaped our subjectivity.

This was often difficult to formulate because the relationship between Jewish philosophy and Western culture had been shaped in ways that worked to silence Jewish history, culture and philosophy, which was perceived as only available for investigation within the context of religion. The terms of secularisation and questions about the ways modernity had been shaped through a dominant Christian tradition could hardly be voiced within the self-conception of disciplinary boundaries, possibly this partly explains my restless journey between philosophy and social theory that refused the fixity of disciplinary boundaries.[5]

For me, Levinas helped to create an intellectual space in which what was excluded as 'religious' and thus privatised within an Enlightenment modernity could be *recognised* as an intellectual, moral and spiritual legacy. It helped me recognise a relationship to a Jewish philosophical tradition and how it had always been for me in dialogue with the powerful Christian tradition with which I had learned to identify within philosophy through its secularised forms within modernity. It was only through *naming* the Kantian ethical tradition I was working with *as* a secularlised Christian tradition which had offered me a limited hospitality that I could complete the *Moral Limits Of Modernity*. This was a naming that Derrida was also to approach in relation to Kant in his later writings.[6]

Naming

Living within a refugee community that did not want to really recognise itself as such made it difficult to name our experience as we were growing up. Often, aspiring middle-class Jewish parents who had come to London as refugees before the Second World War sent their children to private schools when they could afford it, and did their best to forget their own experiences so as not to spoil their children's chances of belonging. It was as if as children we had *no* background though we knew that our parents had come from elsewhere, but often they treated their experiences as exclusively their own, as if they had 'nothing to do' with us as children. At some level, they feared that their history could harm their children's chances of belonging so they often excluded their children from them, feeling that they could not be shared. Rather, as children we were assured that since we 'were born in England' this somehow *proved* that we 'belonged' here, so that we inherited English history as our own and felt that we were owed hospitality by the dominant culture.

But often this hospitality came at the price of forgetting Jewish history or learning to treat it as a separate and privatised 'religious' history. So it was only as an adult that I learned about the mass suicide of Jews in Clifton Tower in York, the expulsion of Jews from England and the terrible history of the Crusades. Rather, I had grown up to identify with Richard the Lionheart as a symbol of goodness, never learning about the brutal part he played in the Crusades. We learned this history as *our* own and it helped to shape our identities and sense of self. There was little room for naming the relationship we had with our history as Jews or thinking about different visions of the nation that could be more inclusive and give recognition to alternative counter-history. Rather, we were anxious to belong and so to accept whatever history we learned as our own.[7]

Often, it was difficult to name the unspoken tensions we carried within us and it was easy to believe that if we felt marginalised or some-how 'outside' of the school communities, then we only had ourselves to blame. A liberal moral culture encouraged us to psychologise any sense of difference, making us feel we just had to make more of an effort to belong. There was little space in which to explore the dialectics of iden-tity and belonging. British culture was quite different from that of the United States, which considered itself to be a 'melting pot' of different immigrant cultures. In England, it was still a matter of disavowing a cul-tural inheritance to claim the dominant culture as one's own. This has changed since the 1980s, within a more diverse and multicultural Britain.[8]

This situation helped to produce inner spaces in which we had to resolve conflicts on our *own* that could not be named publicly. It was part of establishing space for an inner dialogue with ourselves that could sometimes be shared within Jewish youth cultures of the time. Buber was vital in giving us a language of dialogue in which we could learn to *value* diverse Jewish traditions that would otherwise be silenced. His vision of *I And Thou* named the quality of different rela-tionships and the ways in which we can treat others as 'objects' or 'things' without realising. Buber was implicitly questioning a Kantian ethical tradition that focuses upon the moral worth of individual actions and which abstracts from everyday relationships through the distinction it makes between the 'empirical realm' in which we are influ-enced by our emotions, feelings and desires – Kant's 'inclinations' – and the 'intelligible realm' in which we recognise each other as rational moral selves who discern duties of the moral law through an indepen-dent faculty of reason.

Kant gives secular form to a dominant Christian disdain for the body and sexuality which remain identified with an 'animal nature' and thus with the 'sins of the flesh'. Somehow individuals have to *prove* their moral worth through individual moral actions that will win them sal-vation. At some level, everyday life and relationships are disdained through the distinction that Kant sustains between reason and nature. Learning from Kant's injunction that we should not treat others as a means, but as an end in themselves, Buber is able to express, at least partly out of the sources of Judaism, the difficulties Kant has in elucidating what it means to treat others as an end in themselves. This is partly because Kant's rationalism does not allow him to understand the place of emotions and feelings within moral life, and his focus upon individual moral actions leaves him without a sense of the moral significance of relationships.

In the *Religion Of Reason,* Hermann Cohen insists that within his vision of Jewish philosophy it is 'man, and not the people and not Moses, man as a rational being is the correlate of the God of revelation' (p.79). Cohen's line of thinking is close not only to Kant but also to Maimonides, who considers the Torah in *The Guide To The Perplexed* as a foundation of human ethical behaviour. The highest stage is then described by Cohen as transferring Sinai into the human heart (p.84). As Rivka Horwitz recognises, 'Buber and Cohen are in many ways opposites, especially in their understanding of myth', for Buber 'saw the greatness of Judaism in the fact that it was not occidental rationalism, but stories in a mythical way; for the Jew "an event is worth telling only when it has been grasped in its divine significance"' (*On Judaism*, p.105).[9]

Whereas for Cohen the events of Sinai were spiritualised and based on reason, for Buber they were to be understood differently. Buber asks in *Israel And The World*: 'What are we to find in the statement that God came down in fire, to the sound of thunder and the horn, to the mountain that smoked like a furnace, and spoke to His people?' (p.97). As Rivka Horwitz explains: 'He rejects Cohen's type of interpretation that explains the event in "figurative language" which is used to express a "spiritual" process, and he equally rejects an allegorical interpretation that argues that the Bible does not recall actual events. Buber goes in a third direction: he thinks that the event is a verbal record of a natural event that took place in the world of the senses common to all human beings' (p.356). For Buber, as Horwitz seeks to understand him, natural events 'are the carriers of revelation, implying that it is not carried by the supernatural. There is, however, a voice that comes out of the event and communicates to the hearers. Buber thinks that what occurred is an "otherness", the touch of the other' (p.356).

Buber explains revelation, both old and new, by using Nietzsche's phrase: 'You take, you do not ask who it is that gives' (p.98). Buber continues: 'but when we do find the Giver, we find out that revelation exists' (*I And Thou*, p.158). The mystic often wants to remain with God and has no interest in the world so that revelation is often a goal in itself, but as Horwitz explains: 'for Buber revelation is a demand by God that one act in the world and help to bring closer its redemption. All human beings have their own ways by which they fulfil this mission, by which they act in the world with God in their hearts' (p.356). Revelation for Buber is not formal, but is rather the personal address of God to humanity. The biblical verse 'In all thy ways know him' (*Prov.* iii:6) allows for there to be a *multiplicity* of ways in which God can be worshipped and through a multiplicity of cultures and traditions. Buber laid little weight on the divine rules or commandments and insists 'no prescription can lead us to the encounter and none leads from it'.

In *Israel and the World*, Buber explains that the sages insist that the Torah speaks 'in the language of man' (p.99) and that this can conceal an awareness that the unutterable can only be uttered in the language of humans. Buber insists that each person stands alone before God and that the task is to discover *how* to stand in the presence of God. He believed in the personal character of revelation that comes through *listening* to the small voice within, as Hasidic tradition recognised. Though Judaism is often identified with law and commandment, its reality is an ethic of love and the commandments assume their significance through bringing people into closer contact with God.

In a letter to his friend Franz Rosenzweig, Buber makes clear that he sees little value in traditions or customs: 'I do not believe that revelation is ever formulation of law. It is only through man in his self-contradiction that revelation becomes legislation'. (Franz Rosenzweig, On Jewish Learning, p.11. Letter from Buber of 24 June 1924.) At the same time, he also shares in the biblical view of revelation, based on the dialogue between God and humanity. Buber wrote 'Man is addressed by God in his life' and 'God never ceases instructing man'. In this way, Buber rejects any idea of dialogue as 'psychological', as if revelation could be considered as an event in the human soul alone.[10]

Buber concretised a different Jewish ethical tradition through his writings on Hasidism that strengthened his own spirituality. There remain some unresolved tensions between Buber's spiritual and more directly philosophical writings that tend to work from epistemology towards ethics, from knowledge towards an appreciation of goodness. In his own philosophical work, he draws upon Max Scheler's discussions of ethical values.[11] This might have helped shape ways in which some people have been tempted to understand Buber's distinction between an I-it relationship which exists within time and space as part of the rational knowledge of an ordered material world, and an I-thou relationship which somehow takes us beyond the limits of time and space to give us an experience of transcendence.

Relationships

Rather than think about these as separate moments that cannot be prepared for or connected to everyday living, we can recognise *how* these moments might show us possibilities that can remain dormant in our relationships. There may be little continuity, but we can remind ourselves of moments when we fell in love and the kind of meeting which this allowed. This reminder can bring back feelings that might no longer be so present. Buber can also help us to understand how distances are created in relationships through ways that people deny their own emotions, refusing to do the 'emotional work' on their relationships. Here, there is a sense of mutuality within the relationship between a couple in which both parties can recognise a need to discern a distinction between the individual 'emotional baggage' that they bring with them into a relationship and issues within a relationship that need to be addressed.[12]

Buber reflected upon the connection between distance and relationship and he appreciated how lack of emotional dialogue can produce silences that create their own *distances*. He helps to shape an ethical language in which we can recognise the importance of communicating with others, as well as how the ways we learn to talk to ourselves connect to ways we talk to others. This questions a Cartesian philosophy of mind that the later Wittgenstein also questions in his discussions of 'private language', in which the social and cultural nature of language can also be appreciated. Rather than assuming through the Protestant tradition that others cannot really understand 'who' we are and that our 'true selves' somehow remain hidden from view, Buber helps us realise that it is through our relationships with others that we shape our relationships with self and can also can learn about ourselves.

It was Buber's sense of 'inner silences' that helped me recognise in my own experience *how* they were working to block any dialogue through the ways aspects of an inherited Jewish identity were being shamed. This also made it difficult to begin a process of 'coming to terms' with the Shoah because in the 1950s, while I was growing up in north-west London, there was still a widespread belief that Jews had 'gone like lambs to the slaughter'. Not only had communication between generations become disrupted, the inner dialogue with ourselves had also been disrupted through having been *shamed*. We did not know *how to begin* talking about these things because often we learned that our parents 'had suffered more than enough' and we did not want to add to their sufferings.

This understanding of the relationship of shame to silence and the ways dialogue between generations can be *blocked* because the older generations want to protect their children from the effects of the traumatic history they have experienced can resonate with diverse histories of trauma, migration and exile. It can also recall a Hasidic note about prayer, thus proving that psychological awareness can be carried within spiritual tradition. It is an awareness of the *silent cry* of the soul that people often cannot articulate for themselves, one that comes through different spiritual traditions but in the Jewish tradition is expressed through an awareness of dialogue that is a constant presence, particularly within Hasidic writings.

'We do not even know how we are supposed to pray. All we do is call for help because of the need of the moment. But what the soul intends is spiritual need, only we are not able to express what the soul means. This is why we do not merely ask God to hear our call for help, but also beg him who knows what is hidden, to hear the silent cry of the soul' (*Forms Of Prayer*, Daily and Sabbath Meditations before Prayer, p.4).

When we reflect back to childhood often what we miss is a kind of recognition from parents that allows us *to say* what we did not even know we needed to say. But if this dialogue is not possible, as children who can often feel isolated and alone in the midst of family life, we can find ourselves turning to God with the hope of recognition of needs we cannot even name, let alone express for ourselves. I can recall such a spiritual turning point in my childhood when I felt confused and frightened because little explanation had been offered to me about my father's death in New York when I was just five years old. I prayed for his return and like so many children somehow felt responsible for his death and hoped that' if I was 'good', he might somehow return. But this is a 'recognition' goes beyond Kant's vision of people as rational selves that was to shape the 'common sense' of my education. So there was a *split* which I learned to live with between an inner reality that I could not hope to share and the ways in which I learned to present myself to others.

Often, as children growing up within secular cultures, we do not know how 'to hear the silent cry of the soul'. Though a language of soul has remained a feature of African-American traditions of resistance, it has largely disappeared within rationalist modernity. It has become difficult to think about different *levels* of experience, even though this might be a feature of everyday life. We have learned to absorb philosophies of mind that would often ridicule ideas of soul as if this were a superstition that needed to be left behind. This could make it difficult for us to acknowledge *what* we needed to hear, say for example, what I needed to hear from adults as an explanation of my father's death. As children, we grow up with different expectations and I am struck with how I grew up with little sense of the possibilities of recognition from adults. As far as I was concerned, they lived in different worlds and whatever distress we carried as children had to be resolved for ourselves.

At the same time, a Jewish tradition gives due recognition to the importance of *hearing* – both of being listened to but also of hearing validation for our own experience – and this is something we can imagine Freud developing when he thinks about psychoanalysis as a talking cure. Freud recognises the need people have to be listened to, at the same time acknowledging how many people grow up feeling that they have never been really listened to in their lives. Sometimes this involves a painful recognition that they have not been loved in the ways they needed. Their parents might have cared for them but they did not know how to listen as a form of love. As bell hooks has described it, she had the experience of being cared for well but not really of being loved. For years, she had identified love with being cared for, only to learn that love also meant being recognised for who you are as a person.[13]

Both Buber and Levinas could have learned from Rosenzweig's notion of his new thinking as a 'speaking listening'. Rosenzweig makes clear that the 'new thinking needs another person and takes time seriously – actually these things are identical. In the old philosophy, "thinking" means thinking for no one else and speaking to no one else....But "speaking" means speaking to some one and thinking for some one' (Nahum Glatzer, 'The New Thinking' in *Franz Rosenzweig: His Life And Thought*, p.200). This understanding of a need for 'new thinking' challenges the terms of Western philosophy that have been expressed within rationalist traditions and thus brings people to a different understanding of the possibilities of philosophy.[14] Rosenzweig criticises both Plato's dialogues and the Gospels because in those writings 'the thinker knows his thoughts in advance', and in Platonic dialogues the other is only raising the objections the author thought of himself: 'This is why the great majority of philosophical dialogues – including most of Plato's – are so tedious. In actual conversation something happens'. Though Wittgenstein does not talk explicitly about the significance of dialogue, as we have already noted, he expresses his own dissatisfaction with Socratic dialogues.

In conversation, we do not know what we might be drawn into saying, and as Rosenzweig says: 'It does not know in advance just where it will end. It takes its cue from others. In fact, it lives by virtue of another's life...' These are Jewish insights Wittgenstein could also have responded to in his later writings because he was also aware of how thinking has a tendency to abstract itself and disconnect from everyday speech. He wanted people to recognise the ease with which language becomes instrumental so that people can *lose* themselves in speech. He was also concerned with helping people to recover a sense of their own humanity through returning language to its living context of use. He wanted people to be aware of his later philosophical reflections as a form of 'therapy' that helps break with a tradition of philosophical rationalism. This notion is also present in Rosenzweig's *Understanding The Sick And The Healthy*, in which sometimes he is also tempted to think of philosophy itself as a form of 'sickness'.

Dialogue and Ethics

In Levinas's paper entitled 'Dialogue: Self-Consiousness and the Proximity of the Neighbour', which is published in *Of God Who Comes To Mind*, he expresses in his own terms 'that the philosophy of dialogue is oriented toward a concept of the ethical (*Begriff des Ethischen*) that is separated from the tradition that derives the ethical (*das Ethische*) from knowledge and from reason as the faculty of the universal, and sees in the ethical a layer superposed upon being. Ethics would thus be subordinated either to prudence, or the universalisation of the maxim of action (where to be sure is, to be sure, a question of the respect for the human person, but only as a secondary formulation, and deduced from the categorical imperative), or again to the contemplation of a hierarchy of values constructed like a Platonic world of ideas' (p.149–50). In *Kant, Respect And Injustice*, I also showed *how* respect for the person in Kant was really respect for the moral law that could be perceived *through* a person's moral action. I showed the inadequacy of Kant's conception of person and relationship that informed Kantian ethics, partly through its inherited tacit disdain for the personal and the emotional.

As Levinas explains: 'Ethics begins in the I-You of dialogue insofar as the I-You signifies the worth of the other man or, still more precisely, insofar as within the immediacy of the relation to the other man (and without recourse to some generalisation) a meaning such as worth (*valoir*) is sketched out'. This remains a somewhat abstracted formulation, but Levinas goes on to refer to Buber when he clarifies what has been said, again translated in gender-specific terms, saying: 'This is a worth attached to man coming out of the value of the You, or of the man who is other; a value attached to the other man. The description of the "encounter" in Buber never avoids a certain axiological tonality' (p.150).

Levinas goes on to ask whether there is not an '*urgency* in the attitude to take with regard to the other man, a certain urgency about the intervention?' He then goes on to formulate some more specific questions that can help us grasp more of what is involved. Levinas asks: 'Is not the very opening of the dialogue already for the I to uncover itself, to deliver itself, a way for the "I" to place itself at the disposition of the "You"? Who should there be saying it? Would it be because the thinking being has *something* to say? But why should he have *to say* it? Why *would it not suffice* for him to think about this thing which he thinks? Does he not say what he thinks precisely because it goes beyond that which *suffices him* and because *language* carries this deep movement? Beyond insufficiency, in the indiscretion of saying "you" (*tutoiement*) and of the vocative case, a demand for responsibility and an allegiance are signified simultaneously' (p.150).

An example might help to illuminate what seems to be being suggested here, and it might also help to think about issues of responsibility and different ways they might be conceptualised by Buber and Levinas. A friend shared an experience of being together with one of his daughters who was visiting. For some reason he felt it was appropriate to raise something her mother, who he has been separated from for many years, had mentioned at the time of the divorce. She had said that she 'had done something to the eldest daughter while the other children were around'. She had not clarified what she meant and the sentence had puzzled him for years, though he had never really thought of mentioning this to either of his two daughters or his son. But today he felt he wanted to mention it to Harriet who, somewhat surprisingly, said that she was about to mention the very same thing. She said that her mother had hit her eldest sister Jane whenever she wet her bed. Harriet had been forced to sit quietly and watch these beatings with her brother David. She could still recall the fear that she felt and remembered that David used to count the number of blows that were given. She had never felt to mention it to her father, until this moment.

Phil was shocked to hear these stories of abuse in his own family. These were the kinds of stories that he had listened to as a therapist but he did not have the slightest idea that it had been going on in his own family. He felt shocked and responsible for his own silence. He had never consciously suspected anything like this and had never been told about it before. *It shook* his sense of his own family life and wondered what else was going on that he had no idea about. He thought that he had had a close relationship with his wife and that they had talked a great deal about how they were bringing up their three children.

But even though they spoke, they did not share emotionally what was going on. He had no idea that his partner had hit their eldest daughter in this way or even that she wet the bed. He realised that the family had lived with a secret for all these years. His wife probably felt some guilt that she wanted to share, or felt he should know about, but she could not bring herself to speak about it directly. He had lived with the puzzle for years, but somehow it was never the appropriate time to raise it with any of his children. In this way, silence was preserved and distance was created in relationships.

Over the years, Phil had become much closer to his second daughter Harriet. They had learned to talk about their family history and share their feelings with each other. She had told him how she felt that he was often *absent* from the family and that he had left looking after the children to their mother. This was a traditional gender-specific division of labour and, at the time, Phil did not realise the price he would be made to pay in the distance that it created with his children. It was only after the separation that he could begin to develop his own relationships with his children and thus undo some of the distancing. But it took time and effort. He had learned to feel responsible for his absence from their lives and was doing his best to make up for this. He also felt terrible that his daughter had been made to suffer for something that she could not really help. The fear of being hit could only have made the problem worse. He is still amazed that he did not know anything about it and that his partner somehow felt a need to keep all this from him.

Levinas recognises the dangers of presenting Buber's I-Thou relationship too formally, knowing 'To be sure, in Buber, the I-Thou relationship is frequently also described as the pure face-to-face of the encounter, as a harmonious co-presence, as an eye-to-eye' (p.150).

As he knows, 'In this extreme formalisation, the Relation empties itself of its "heteronomy" and of its transcendence of association'. In contrast, Levinas strives to emphasise that 'From the outset, the I-you comprises an obligation in its immediacy, that is, as urgency without recourse to any universal law' (p.150). As Levinas wants to argue, 'There would be an inequality, a dissymmetry, in the Relation, contrary to the "reciprocity" upon which Buber insists, no doubt in error. Without a possible evasion, as though it were elected for this, as though it were thus irreplaceable and unique, the I as I is the servant of the You in Dialogue' (p.150).

In this essay, Levinas places emphasis upon God in order to account for the sense of *inequality* that is part of the dialogue. In a section that is entitled 'From Dialogue to Ethics', he shows how through the dialogue we discern the inequality of the divine. As Levinas explains it: 'An inequality that may appear arbitrary; unless it be – in the word addressed to the other man, in the ethics of the welcome – the first religious service, the first prayer, the first liturgy, the religion out of which God could first have come to mind and the word "God" have made its entry into language and into good philosophy...What counts here is that, from out of the relation to the other, from the depths of the Dialogue, this immeasurable word signifies for thought, and not the reverse' (p.151).

What seems important for Levinas is his understanding of what he identifies as a 'philosophy of dialogue' that according to this essay at least 'attests to a new orientation toward the idea that Western society has had of the essence of the meaningful and the spiritual' (p.137). He thinks that this turn in philosophical thinking 'is perhaps a result of the trials of the twentieth century since the First World War'. Drawing together the work of Martin Buber and Franz Rosenzweig in Germany and Gabriel Marcel in France, he thinks: 'It is thus not out of the question, in our time, to speak of a philosophy of dialogue and oppose it to the philosophical tradition of the unity of the I or the system, and self-sufficiency, and immanence'. But again this tradition is given a particular inflection in Levinas in a way that can make it difficult to appreciate the particular strengths and insights to be found in Rosenzweig and Buber.

Recognition

There is a Hasidic notion that 'One who thinks he can live without others is mistaken. One who thinks others cannot live without him is more mistaken'. This reminds us of the need we have for others at the same time as it teaches a certain humility in relation to others. It warns us against a certain pride, a feeling that we can be indispensable. Somehow, the different poles are held in relation to each other, as they are so often with Buber. This shapes the kind of welcome we need to give to others and the kind of *recognition* we owe to others in their individuality. In this way, Buber calls into question a Kantian tradition that gives recognition to others as human beings *as* rational selves. Often we are encouraged within an Enlightenment rationalism to see people as instantiations of a shared capacity for reason, which implicitly carries a disdain for the physical body and emotional life.

This makes it difficult to give *adequate* recognition to individualities that are shaped as much by emotional histories as they are by reason and thought.

There is a well-known Hasidic question worth reminding ourselves of:

'Question: Our sages say: "And there is not a thing that has not its place". And so man too has his place. Then why do people sometimes feel so crowded?

'Answer: Because each wants to occupy the place of the other' (*Forms Of Prayer*, Study Anthology, p.392).

Possibly this can be helpfully read next to one of the famous sayings of Rabbi Bunam of Pzhysha, who sustained an important sense of Jewish dialectic to do with self-worth and of being created in the image of God, whilst maintaining a sense of humility and human equality when he said: 'Everyone must have two pockets, so that he can reach into the one or the other, according to his needs. In the right pocket are to be the words: "For my sake was the world created" and in his left: "I am dust and ashes"'.

The reminder that we are 'dust and ashes' carries a particular weight living as the second generation in the shadows of the Shoah. But at the same time, it reminds us that 'for my sake was the world created'. Somehow we have to keep both these thoughts in balance. There is the recognition that at different times and possibly in different places we need to be reminded of these different aspects, recognising how hard it can be *to live* sustaining a balance between these different poles of experience. Buber sustains this sense of diversity and thus resists the insistent pressure towards recognising our responsibilities for others. There is often more space in Buber for people to recognise responsibilities that people have for themselves and thus the *limits* of the responsibilities we can have for others. We often have to learn, for example as parents, when to be silent and not interfere so that our children can take more responsibility for themselves. It can be painful but still necessary to watch them make their own mistakes.

As I know from my own experience, sometimes a child can be made to feel responsible for his/her mother, say, when a father has died unexpectedly. Children can often carry a sense of responsibility for the death. The son or daughter might feel responsible for her mother while *not* being able to understand the responsibility she feels and the idealisation of the mother that often goes along with this can be inappropriate. Children might feel unable to express any anger towards their mother, let alone against the father who has died. But this can block a process of mourning. A child can feel that it is wrong to express anger since this just proves that he/she is ungrateful. A rationalist culture can make it difficult for him/her to offer hospitality to her anger that can often be turned inward against itself, sometimes producing physical symptoms of illness. The anger might spill out indirectly, but he/she might never have learned *how* to take responsibility for his/her emotional life. In different ways, Buber and Levinas are suspicious of insights that can be drawn from Freud and psychoanalysis, but Buber is potentially more open to recognising the mutuality involved in post-analytical psychotherapies.[15]

Often it is the youngest child that 'carries' the unresolved emotions in a family. Sometimes a person is able to speak to someone who has been through a similar experience, say of a father dying when they were young. Previously, he/she might have found it difficult to speak about his/her experience and the inner conflicts he/she carries, but talking to someone who has been through a similar experience as a child can sometimes create an 'opening' in which someone feels that their inner experience is being recognised. Sometimes it can be difficult to talk in this way to close friends, so it can feel like a gift when such a dialogue is possible with a therapist. He/she might have almost given up hope that he/she could speak in a way that another person could understand. Here there is a mutuality and reciprocity in a therapeutic encounter that Buber is able to appreciate.

Feminism has also appreciated the importance of women taking time and space to explore their own experience. At some level, there is a *resonance* between feminist critiques of modernity and the potential challenges that Jewish philosophies can make to Western cultures. In consciousness-raising groups women learned to listen to each other, for instance, sharing experiences of a break-up of a relationship. They take *time to listen*. Rather than turn the blame inwards against themselves, they often learned to recognise how 'the personal is political' and thus *how* to connect their inner emotional experiences with gender relations of power. They could learn to take greater responsibility for their emotional lives as they learned to listen to others who were not only willing, but somehow also able, to share a similar level of their own experience.

There was a sharing of experience that marked it off from a rationalisation of experience in which people talked about their experience, but did not really *share* what was going on for them. Again, there was a sense of equality in which women and men could learn to recognise themselves through their refigured individuality. As reasons were connected to emotions, so people learned to accept aspects of their experience which they might otherwise have rejected and excluded. There is a living tension between contemplation and experience and between language and expression, as people find words in which they can share what they have been living through.

Experience/s

Buber helps us recognise what goes on in the space between people so
that he questions notions of relationships as exchanges or contacts. As Buber's thinking about dialogue and relationship is expressed, he moves from knowledge towards ethics, while Levinas draws out the particularity of a Jewish tradition through the priority it gives to ethics as the 'first philosophy'. But if Levinas appreciates how it is through ethics that we come to knowledge, somehow there is less space to explore a relational ethics, partly because of the particular focus he gives to the responsibility we have towards others. A sense of the *relational* can also be a feature of Jewish philosophies in their complex relations with Western cultures.

Nahum Glatzer, who wrote the original introduction to *Understanding The Sick and The Healthy,* records a chance remark by Rosenzweig made shortly after writing the book. Stating that he is just as little an 'expert' on Judaica as is Max Weber, Rosenzweig added: 'The Jewish way (*Das Jüdische*) is not my object but my method' (Franz Rosenzweig, *Briefe*, p.407). According to Glatzer, 'Jewish, in Rosenzweig's estimation, is the insistence on the concrete situation; the importance of the spoken word and the dialogue; the experience of time and its rhythm and, in connection with it, the ability to wait; finally, finally, the profound significance of the name, human and divine' (p.31).[16]

I thought Glatzer's suggestion helpful when he says 'These elements and others contribute towards a *method* of thinking'. Equally, they become for Rosenzweig the means of expressing his thought. He uses the ancient words of classical Judaism, because, as he says, he has received the New Thinking in these ancient words. 'I know that instead of these, New Testament words would have risen to a Christian's lips. But these were the words that came to me. And I really believe that this (*The Star Of Redemption*) is a Jewish book; not merely one that treats of "Jewish matters" ....but a book of which the old Jewish words have formed the expression of whatever it has to say, and especially of what is new in it. Jewish matters are always past, as is matter generally, but Jewish words, however old, partake of the eternal youth of the word' (*Franz Rosenzweig: His Life and Thought*, p.144ff).

Rosenzweig did not feel the same need to translate Hebrew into Greek and was somehow able to acknowledge, in contrast to Levinas, that philosophy could also be expressed *in* Hebrew. If he thought there was a need for translation it was not in the same terms as Levinas. As Glatzer puts it, while for Kafka 'with the expulsion from Paradise, man lost his name (Kafka's heroes go mainly by initials), lost his language (there is no real communication), lost his love (only sex remains)', Rosenzweig admits the biblical idea of Revelation (love). 'Thus man finds his place *next* to his fellow man, *in* the world and *before* God. He speaks and he is spoken to. He is called by his name and he names beings around him. And he has overcome his distrust of time; he had learned to wait (man was driven out of paradise because of impatience, says Kafka) until he "perceives in proper time", until time itself becomes a mirror of eternity' (Introduction, *Understanding The Sick and The Healthy*, p.32).

In the Questions and Answers that Levinas gave in a conversation in March 1975 to mark the occasion of the 400th anniversary of Louvain University, he was asked by J.G. Bonhoff: 'Cannot moral experience be translated as an experience of the other as identical to oneself?' He thought that this corresponded to the biblical imperative to 'Love your neighbour as yourself'. Levinas gave an interesting response which showed that he was trying to avoid the term 'moral experience' because he thought that 'moral experience supposes a subject who is there; who, first of all, *is* and who, at a certain moment, has a moral experience, whereas it is in the way in which he is there, in which he lives, that there is this ethics; or more precisely, the dis-inter-estedness un-does his *esse*. Ethics signifies this' (*Of God Who Comes To Mind*, p.90).

This rehearses a crucial insight that it is the sense of responsibility which someone has to the other that *undoes* the egoism which, within a Cartesian tradition that has been so significant in shaping 'modern philosophy' within Western culture, otherwise controls and shapes their experience. Through responsibility, 'Jewish philosophy', if we can allow such a term to Levinas who so often insists that philosophy has to be 'Greek', questions the terms of Western culture. It is through the challenge of this demand for responsibility that a moral subject can be said to come into being, *through* the sense of responsibility for the other.

Levinas goes on to ask about 'What does "as yourself" signify? Buber and Rosenzweig were very perplexed by the translation. They said to each other, does not "as yourself" mean that one loves oneself most?' (p.90). They translated it, 'love your neighbour, he is like you'. But Levinas wants to separate himself from this reading, saying that 'if one first agrees to separate the last word of the Hebrew verse, *kamokha*, from the beginning of the verse, one can read the whole thing still otherwise. "Love your neighbour; this work is like yourself"; "love your neighbour; he is yourself"; "it is this love of your neighbour which is yourself". Would you say that this is an extremely audacious reading?' (p.90).

Levinas wants to translate this critical passage in this way partly because it is in line with the entirety of the biblical text for him where, as Levinas puts it, so separating himself from Buber and Rosenzweig, 'there is always a priority of the other in relation to me. This is the biblical contribution in its entirety' (p.90). But this notion is not as clear as Levinas presents it and it is a strength of Buber that he keeps open this particular complexity. I do not think that either Buber or Rosenzweig was saying 'as yourself', meaning that one loves oneself most *nor* is self-love to be identified with a form of egotism which means that we are thereby unresponsive to our responsibilities to others and thus exist within the space of an amoral egoism.[17]

Rather, we have to be careful *how* we understand Levinas when he declares so categorically that 'The Bible is the priority of the other (*l'autre*) in relation to me. It is in another (*autrui*) that I always see the widow and the orphan'. It is to particular others that I feel responsibilities in their situation as widows and orphans, but this does not mean, as Levinas puts it, that 'The other (*autrui*) always comes first'. As Levinas explains his own translations: 'This is what I have called in Greek language, the dissymmetry of the interpersonal relationship' (p.91). He then goes on to say that 'If there is not this dissymmetry, then no line of what I have written can hold. And this is vulnerability. Only as vulnerable can I love his neighbour' (p.91). I do not follow the point here about vulnerability, but it suggests a wider issue that deserves examination.

Vulnerability

In an earlier question from the audience, Levinas was asked: 'If I am vulnerable, as you emphasise in your books, how can I be responsible? If one suffers, one can no longer do anything'. His response clarifies the particular meaning he gives to vulnerability: 'By vulnerability, I am attempting to describe the subject as passivity. If there is not vulnerability, if the subject is not always in his patience on the verge of an already senseless pain, then he posits himself *for himself*' (p.83). There is an implied contrast between positing 'himself for himself' which is connected in some way to egotism and a sense of substance as a pre-given identity 'who has experience'. As Levinas says: 'In this case, the moment at which he is substance is not far away; the moment at which his is pride, at which he is imperialist, at which he has the other like an object' (p.83). In contrast, Levinas wants to present my relationship with another 'as the fact of my destitution, of my deposition...It is only then that a veritable abnegation, a substitution for the other, may take on meaning in me' (p.83).

Levinas goes on to respond to the last part of the question, saying 'You say, in suffering one can no longer do anything. But are you sure that suffering stops at itself? When one suffers because of someone, vulnerability is also to suffer for someone' (p.83). This is not how Levinas thinks that we act towards others, but he thinks that cultivating vulnerability *can* be a way of escaping from the world that we usually live in. As he says: 'If one does not posit this, then you are immediately in a world of revenge, of war, of the preferential affirmation of the I'. Here these identifications follow each other and one can realise the dualism that can still inform his thinking, a dualism Buber can sometimes help us question. Levinas explains his own position: 'I do not contest that we are always, in fact, in this world, but this is a world wherein we are altered. Vulnerability is the power to say *adieu* to this world. One says *adieu* to it in growing old. Time endures in the form of this *adieu* and this *à-Dieu* (unto God)' (p.83).

At some level, this links to the absolutism that can be part of the appeal but also part of the difficulty in establishing what Levinas means. Again, this is where Buber can come in to moderate the claims, showing a complexity in matter of relationship, if not so much in matters of emotional life. Levinas makes clear our responsibilities to others: 'If there were only the other facing me, I would say to the very end: I owe him everything. I am for him. And this even holds for the harm he does me: I am not his equal, I am forevermore subject to him' (p.83). But this can make it difficult to reflect upon different kinds of passivity in different forms of relationships.

A young woman might, for example, feel that she has given up too much of herself in her heterosexual relationship, not wanting to abandon her partner who had been abandoned when he was young. But this means that she has allowed herself to tolerate abusive behaviour on his part, somehow taking responsibility for actions he should have been responsible for. He was acting abusively and thus unjustly towards her, showing her a lack of respect. But rather than draw a line for herself and withdraw from the relationship, her sense of self-worth has been undermined and she has given up her own emotional ground.

An example such as this can help us question Levinas's assertion that 'My resistance begins when the harm he does me is done to a third person who is also my neighbour. It is the third party who is the source of justice, and thereby of justified repression; it is the violence suffered by the third party that justifies stopping the violence of the other with violence. The idea that I am responsible for the harm done by the other – an idea rejected, repressed although psychologically possible – brings us to the meaning of subjectivity. It is attested by this sentence of Dostoevsky, which I always quote. It is Alyosha, I believe, who says it, "Each of us is guilty before all, for all and for everything, and I am more than the others".....The I (*moi*) as I (*moi*) is the I (*moi*) who escapes his concept. It is this situation that I have called vulnerability, absolute culpability, or rather, absolute responsibility' (p.84). But this remains a notion I feel uneasy with, especially when expressed so generally.

Levinas acknowledges that the idea of priority is itself a Greek idea so he can feel uneasy about the question of whether the other is at the centre of a Judeo-Christian tradition, as opposed to a pagan tradition in which the 'I' can be said to be at the centre and 'the other' exists in relation to it. As Levinas makes clear: 'This is not at all a situation in which *one* poses the question; it is the question that takes hold of you: there you are brought into question' (p.85). So it is that subjectivity is formed through our sense of responsibility for others. As Levinas puts it: 'All these situations are probably different in the Greek way and in the way that is very deeply inscribed in the biblical tradition. My concern everywhere is precisely to translate this non-Hellenism of the Bible into Hellenic terms and not to repeat the biblical formulas in their obvious sense, isolated from the context that, at the level of such a text, is *all* the Bible. There is nothing to be done: philosophy is spoken in Greek'.

Rosenzweig and Buber, in their different ways, can help us to think otherwise. They can help us to appreciate that philosophy can *also* be spoken in Hebrew and that there is still learning to be gained from appreciating the conflicts that separated Athens from Jerusalem. For Levinas, in his essay entitled 'Dialogue' in *Of God Who Comes To Mind*, 'It is in the dialogue of transcendence that the idea of the good arises, merely by the fact itself that, in the encounter, the *other counts* above all else. The relationship in which the "I" encounters the "You" is the original place and circumstance of the ethical coming (*avènement*). The ethical fact owes nothing to values; it is values that owe everything to the ethical fact. The concreteness of the Good is the worth (*valoir*) of the other man' (p.147). As far as Levinas is concerned, 'Dialogue is not merely a way of speaking. It is transcendence. The saying involved in dialogue would not be one of the possible forms of transcendence but its original mode' (p.147).

Again, this is to look towards a single source of values and thus break with the pluralism and multiplicity that Buber is more easily able to appreciate, if they can come together around Levinas's notion that 'In the worth of the other man, the Good is more ancient than the evil' (p.147). We need to explore *diverse* sources of value as we need to explore ways in which people also learn to relate to themselves as part of relating to others. Otherwise we shall unwittingly reproduce denials of bodies, sexuality and emotional lives that are part of a modernity that has been shaped according to a secularised Christianity. If Levinas can help us uncover some of these silences through his enriched phenomenology, he also sustains particular silences. By making people responsible for others in such an exclusive way, he can help to produce resentment that can be projected on to others.

This is reflected in the unease we can still feel in how the notion of 'love they neighbour' is interpreted by Levinas, since it can sustain an *excessive* responsibility for the other that is out of balance with a vision of self-acceptance. We need to be able to name as I have argued traditions of self-rejection and self-hate as part of a Western inheritance that has fostered the domination of colonised others, including, in their own way, long-resident Jewish communities, who have experienced ambivalent hospitality within Western cultures. Brought up to be suspicious of our 'animal' natures within a secularised Protestant tradition, we can feel divided against ourselves, sometimes feeling unloveable and incapable of loving others.

Learning to blame ourselves for these feelings, on the assumption that they reflect a personal flaw or inadequacy, can be difficult to question within secular Western cultures. One has to appreciate, as Max Weber appreciated, how the 'common sense' of a capitalist ethic continues to be shaped through a Protestant ethic. There are complex legacies within different religious and spiritual traditions and over the centuries they have been shaped in relation to each other. Through opening a dialogue between religious secular transitions we open up possibilities for different ways of living and learning for more just and equal lives on a precarious planet. They provide complex resources that can be helpful, especially as they disturb our own assumptions. As we have shown, there are different, often competing and contrasting, voices that claim to speak in the name of tradition – Jewish, Christian, Islamic – but offer us very different approaches to life.

As Israel Salanter has expressed similar hopes for freedom and justice: 'The Torah demands that we seek what is best for our fellow man: not by repressing our hatred or rejection of him, nor by loving him out of a sense of duty, for this is no genuine love. We should simply love our neighbour as we love ourselves' (*Forms of Prayer,* p.122). Or, as the Hasidic rabbi, Mendel of Kotzk, puts it: 'Take care of your own soul and of another man's body but not of your own body and another man's soul' (*Forms of Prayer*, p.84).

Endnotes

Chapter 1 – Introduction

1. Martin Bernal (1987), *Black Athena*, London: Free Associations Books, has made a significant contribution to the revision of Western culture by disputing the particularly nineteenth-century construction of Greek history and culture that sought to perceive it through a relationship with 'whiteness', and thus through a denial of its Semitic, Egyptian and African sources. This has nothing to do with a search for origins but with a recognition of how 'the West' has been constructed in different historical periods to meet the needs of powerful interests in the present. It has been a strength of post-modern tradition to decentralise Western conceptions of modernity, thus opening up the possibilities of a more equal dialogue between different cultures, religions and spiritual traditions.

2. For a reflection on Freud's sense of the significance of minor differences, see, for instance, Peter Gay *(*1988), *Freud: A Life for our Time,* London: Macmillan.

3. For some helpful philosophical and literary discussion concerning the implications of different constructions of the 'Christian West' in the relationships between Judaism and Islam and the ways in which the notion of 'enemy' has been shaped at different historical periods, see, for instance, Jacques Derrida (2001), *Acts of Religion* (ed. Gil Anidjar), New York and London: Routlege; and Gil Anidjar (2003), *The Jew, the Arab: A History of the Enemy*, Stanford: Stanford University Press.

4. For some discussion of the significance of the seventeenth-century Scientific Revolutions upon shaping a relationship between nature and culture

that has sustained a gender-specific vision of a rationalist modernity and forms of social and political theory within modernity, see Victor J. Seidler (1994), *Unreasonable Men: Masculinity and Social Theory*, London, Routledge.

5. For some helpful historical papers that explore the different forms that antisemitism has taken within different periods, cultures and traditions, see, for instance, Shmuel Almog (ed.) (1988), *Antisemitism Through The Ages*, Oxford: Pergamon Press.

6. For some illuminating discussions on the place of evil within Western philosophical traditions and the difficulties of thinking evil within rationalist modernities, see, for instance, Susan Neiman (2002), *Evil in Modern Thought: An Alternative History of Philosophy*, Princeton: Princeton University Press.

7. For a helpful background to the Spanish Inquisition and its relationship to the Jewish and Islamic communities in Spain, see, for instance, Henry Kamen (1977), *The Spanish Inquisition: a Historical Revision*, London: Orion Publishers. For the classic account of the Spanish Inquisition that still remains an informative text, see Henry Charles Lea (1966), *A History of the Inquisition in Spain*, New York: AMS Press. See also Simon Whitechapel (2003), *Flesh Inferno: Atrocities of Torquemada and the Spanish Inquisition*, London: Creation Books. The book reprints the decree of Expulsion of the Jews of Spain, known as 'The Alhambra Decree' of 31 March 1492, and recognises that 'the symbolism of issuing the decree there was unmistakable. The *reyes catolicos* had triumphed over one enemy of the Church, the Moors, and now they sought to triumph over another, the Jews' (p.145).

8. For an introduction to the different ways of thinking about the changes in Simone Weil's writings, particularly her later affinity for Christianity and what this meant for her relationship with Judaism, see, for instance, Lawrence A. Blum and Victor J. Seidler (1991), *A Truer Liberty: Simone Weil and Marxism*, New York and London: Routledge. For a discussion that focuses more specifically on her relationship to Judaism, see Thomas R. Nevin (1991), *Simone Weil: Portrait of a Self-Exiled Jew*, Chapel Hill: University of North Carolina Press. For biographies that explore her thought in the context of changes in her life, see, for instance, Gabriella Fiori (1989), *Simone Weil: An Intellectual Biography*, Athens: University of Georgia Press; and David McLellan (1990), *Utopian Pessimist: The Life and Thought of Simone Weil*, New York: Simon and Schuster.

9. For some helpful reflections on the Jewish community in Gerona which was the home of Nachmanides, who engaged with Maimonides in his diverse writings and commentaries, and on the gradual decline of the community before its eventual expulsion, see, for example, Eduard Feliu i Mabres (1994), *The Life and Times of Moses ben Nahman: A Symposium to commemorate the 800th Anniversary of His Birth 1194–1994*, Girona: Ajuntament de Girona.

10. For a collection of essays by Leo Baeck that explore in interesting ways the relationships between Christianity and Judaism and the idea of Jesus as the

'son of man', see Le Baeck (1981), *Judaism and Christianity*: *Essays by Leo Baeck*, New York: Atheneum.

11. I was concerned with issues of respect and equality and recognised, partly through the influence of Wittgenstein when I was a post-graduate student in Philosophy at UCL, working with Richard Wollheim, that concepts in social and political life have a history that needs to be *traced*, and cannot simply be explored as if they were timeless and could yield to the conceptual analysis of analytical philosophy. This was also an insight that I gained from attending all the lectures and seminars I could that were given by Isaiah Berlin while I was reading philosophy at Oxford (1964–7). At the time, he presented the 'history of ideas' that he taught as being a break with philosophy, rather than, as Bernard Williams was to recognise much later, as a move towards a different approach *to* philosophy. At the memorial meeting after Berlin's death, Williams notes that because Berlin tended to retain a somewhat positivist vision of philosophy, 'he did not notice that he had discovered or rediscovered a different kind of philosophy, one that makes use of history' (Bernard Williams (1999), *The First and the Last: Isaiah Berlin*, London: Granta (p.122)). At some level this insight shaped my project on respect and inequality which eventually focussed upon Christian conceptions in (1991), *The Moral Limits of Modernity*: *Love, Inequality and Oppression*, Basingstoke: Macmillan; liberal conceptions in (1986), *Kant Respect and Injustice*: *The Limits of Liberal Moral Theory*, London: Routledge; and (1994), Marxist traditions in *Recovering the Self: Morality and Social Theory*, London: Routledge.

12. I came across this quotation from St John Chrysostom, and the virulence of the antisemitism that was to become the received wisdom for a period for so many in the Catholic Church, in Simon Winchester (2002), *Flesh Inferno*: *Atrocities of Torquemada and the Spanish Inquisition*, London: Creation Books. Its general position is fiercely anti-religious but at the same time thought-provoking.

13. For an illuminating discussion of Heine's relationship to his own Jewishness and his relationship to Hellenism and Christianity, see Bluma Goldstein (1992), *Reinscribing Moses: Heine, Kafka, Freud and Schoenberg in a European Wildnerness*, Cambridge, Mass.: Harvard University Press.

14. For a wonderful collection that brings together seminal pieces of Walter Benjamin's work, see (1968), *Illuminations* (Trans. Harry Zohn), New York: Schocken Books. For a helpful introduction to Benjamin's work in relation to the Frankfurt School, see Susan Bucks-Moss (1977), *Origins of the Negative Dialectic*, New York: The Free Press.

15. For an illuminating introduction to Wittgenstein's life and thought, see Ray Monk (1991), *Ludwig Wittgenstein*: *The Duty of Genius*, London: Penguin; and for some personal recollections on his life that include remarks where he talks about the ways in which his later philosophy is Hebraic rather than Greek, see Rush Rhees (ed.) (1981), *Ludwig Wittegenstein*: *Personal Recollections*, Oxford: Blackwell.

16. For an illuminating exploration of the different ways the Jewish people in diverse settings responded to the demands of modernity and the ways this reflects upon the complex antagonisms between identity and difference and ways in which these were to be shaped within modernity, see, for instance, Sander Gilman (1989), *Jewish Self-Hatred*, Baltimore: Johns Hopkins University Press; and Zygmunt Bauman (1988), *Modernity and Ambivalence*, Cambridge: Polity Press.

17. For some helpful reflections that provide a historical background to the philosophical writings of Moses Mendelssohn, a central figure in the Berlin Enlightenment, see, for instance, David Sorkin (1996), *Moses Mendelssohn and the Religious Enlightenment*, London: Peter Halban.

18. Gillian Rose wrote these reflections on her life and philosophical influences towards the end of her life when she was already suffering from cancer and did not have long to live, in Rose, Gillian (1995), *Loves Work*, London: Chatto and Windus. She made an outstanding contribution to opening up a conversation between Jewish philosophies and modernity from within a tradition of 'continental philosophy', both in Rose, Gillian (1992), *The Broken Middle: Out of Our Ancient Society*, Oxford: Blackwell; and in her collection of essays, Rose, Gillian (1993), *Judaism and Modernity*, Oxford: Blackwell.

19. I have explored post-Holocaust Jewish identities and the particular experiences of growing up in post-war Britain within a refugee second generation family, in Victor Jeleniewski Seidler (2000), *Shadows of the Shoah*: *Jewish Identity and Belonging*, Oxford: Berg.

20. In Moses Hess (1958), *Rome and Jerusalem.* New York: Philosophical Library, Hess sets out the shift in his thinking and his break with secular Marxism in ways that recognise a contrast between Athens and Jerusalem that we will also explore: 'The Hellenists conceived the world as an eternal Being; the Jews viewed it as an eternal Becoming. The Greek spirit contemplates space while the Jewish spirit contemplates time. The Greek spirit conceives the world as a completed creation; the Jewish spirit contemplates it as an invisible world of becoming, a creation in which social life began only after nature had already arrived to its Sabbath celebration' (p.46). Hess also insists 'The Jewish religion is not threatened, as is Christianity, by the national and humanitarian aspirations of the time. It is an error rooted in Christianity to believe that a total outlook on life can be incorporated in a fixed dogma. ...That is the reason why Judaism has never excluded or interdicted philosophic thought' (p.50).

Chapter 2 – A Time for Philosophy

1. For some helpful introductions that have aided in keeping alive a notion of philosophy as a love of wisdom, see, for instance, Stanley Cavell (2004), *Cities of Words*, Cambridge Mass.: Harvard University Press; Jacob Needleman (1965), *Sense of the Cosmos: The Encounter of Modern Science & Ancient*

Truth, New York: Dutton; and (1986), *The Heart of Philosophy*, New York: Bantam Books.

2. For a sense of how 'common-sense' in Western cultures are still shaped within largely secular cultures through inherited religious traditions that might have been consciously disavowed, see, for instance, Erich Fromm (1942), *The Fear of Freedom*, London: Routledge and Kegan Paul. See also reflections about the fragmented and historical layers within 'common sense' in Antonio Gramsci (1971), *The Prison Notebooks*, London: Lawrence and Wishart.

3. For some helpful introductions to the life and work of Martin Buber, see, for instance, Grete Schaeder (1973), *The Hebrew Humanism of Martin Buber* (trans. Noah J. Jacobs), Detroit: Wayne State University; Maurice Freedman (1991), *Encounter on the Narrow Ridge: A life of Martin Buber*, New York: Paragon House, 1991; Sidney and Beatrice Rome (eds.) (1964), *Philosophical Interrogations*, New York: Holt, Rinehart and Winston; and Paul Schilpp and M. Friedman (eds.) (1967), *The Philosophy of Martin Buber*, Cambridge: Cambridge University Press.

4. For some reflections upon the changing place of religion and spirituality within secular societies in Western culture, see, for instance, Peter L. Berger and Thomas Luckman (1973), *The Social Construction of Reality: a Treatise in the Sociology of Knowledge*, London: Penguin Books (p.111–30); Louis Dupré (Winter, 1982), 'Spiritual Life in a Secular Age' in *Daedalus 3/1*. In a culture in which 'religious experience is perhaps less available that ever before', as Louis Dupré observes, 'this inward trend' may seem paradoxical. But precisely because the public realm is bereft of the divine, as Dupré astutely explains for modern religious man, 'there is nowhere to turn but inwardly'. This is an insight shared by Paul Mendes-Flohr who writes in 'Law and Sacrament: Ritual Observance in Twentieth-Century Jewish Thought' in Arthur Green (ed.) *Jewish Spirituality: From Sixteenth Century Revival to the Present*, New York: Crossroad Publishing Company.

'Heir to the aggressive humanism of previous generations, twentieth-century Western culture is incontestably secular. God and the religiously sacred have been effectively banished from the most significant areas of public life. Yet this culture that has lost of the presence of the divine has witnessed ever since the turn of the century a markedly renewed interest in spirituality and, correspondingly, a quest for religious experience that is intensely personal, indeed often mystical' (p.317).

5. For an introduction to Max Weber's thinking about the ways in which modernity has been shaped through a Protestant ethic and its relationship to the disenchantment of nature, see Max Weber (1958), *The Protestant Ethic and the Spirit of Capitalism*, New York: Scribners and Hans Gerth; and C. Wright Mills (eds.), *From Max Weber*, New York: Oxford University Press, 1969 and Sam Whimster (2006), *Understanding Weber*, London: Routledge.

6. For some helpful discussion that can illuminate how modernity has been shaped by a vision of progress as the control and domination of nature, see,

for instance, Caroline Merchant (1980), *The Death of Nature: Women, Ecology and The Scientific Revolution*, London: Wildwood House; Brian Easlea (1981), *Science and Sexual Oppression: Patriarchy's Confrontation with Women and Nature*, London: Weidenfeld and Nicholson; and Evelyn Fox-Keller (1985), *Reflections on Gender and Science*, New Haven: Yale University Press, 1985.

7. For some reflections upon the crisis of meaning that is brought about with the disenchantment of nature that defines modernity, see Susan Griffin (1982), *Women and Nature*, London: The Women's Press; (1980) *Pornography and Silence*, London: The Women's Press; Victor J. Seidler (1984), *Unreasonable Men: Masculinity and Social Theory*, London: Routledge; and Maurice Berman (1990), *Coming to our Senses*, London: Harper Collins.

8. For some reflections upon the impact of the Holocaust on the shaping of the experience of the second generation in complex and often unacknowledged ways, see, for instance, Helen Epstein (1988), *Children of the Holocaust*, London: Penguin Books; Anne Karpf (1997), *The War After*, London: Minerva; and Victor Jeleniewski Seidler (2000), *Shadows of the Shoah: Jewish Identity and Belonging*, Oxford: Berg.

9. For these critical early essays by Martin Buber on the renewal of Judaism that help shape his understanding of the relationship of Athens to Jerusalem, see Martin Buber (1967) (ed. Nahum N. Glatzer), *On Judaism*, New York: Schocken Books; *ibid.* (1963), *Israel and the World* New York: Schocken; and *ibid.* (1973), *On Zion: The History of an Idea*, New York: Schocken.

10. For some helpful introductions to Heschel's developing thoughts and spirituality see, for instance, A.J. Heschel (1959), *God in Search of Man*, Philadelphia: Jewish Publication Society; and *ibid.* (1966), *The Insecurity of Freedom*, New York: Farrar, Straus and Giroux. Heschel's last work (1973), *A Passion for Truth*, New York: Farrar, Straus and Giroux, contains glimpses of his feelings towards the end of his life and his reactions to the tragedy of the Holocaust. For a reflection on Heschel's work, see Edward Kaplan 'The Spiritual Radicalism of Abraham Joshua Heschel' in *Conservative Judaism 28* (1973) p.40–49. While emphasising the existential situation of the individual as the locus of faith, Heschel, in the final analysis, affirmed the claim of rabbinic tradition to divine authority. This sets him in contrast to Buber though he insists 'Halakha must not be observed for its own sake, but for the sake of God. The law must not be idolised. It is a part, not all, of the Torah. We live and die for the sake of God rather than for the sake of the law' (p.326), New York: Search Press. He also says here: 'All mizvot are means of evoking in us the awareness of living in the neighborhood of God, of living in the holy dimension.....reminders of the fact that man does not live in a spiritual wilderness, that every act of man is an encounter of the human and the holy' (p.356).

11. For a sense of Victor Frankl's writings and the ways they were shaped through his experience in a Nazi concentration camp, see Viktor Frankl (1963), *Man's Search for Meaning*, New York: Washington Square Press.

12. For some reflections upon the significance of listening, see, for instance, Richard Sennett (2003), *Respect: The Formation of Character in an Age of Inequality*, London: Penguin; and Les Back and Michael Bull (eds.) (2004), *The Auditory Reader*, Oxford: Berg.

13. For some of Martin Buber's reflections upon the importance of learning how to listen within a dialogue, see, *I and Thou* (1970) (trans. Walter Kaufmann), New York: Scribner. It can be helpful to read this together with the first two essays in *The Knowledge of Man* (1965) (trans. and ed. M. Friedman), New York: Harper and Row; and *ibid.* (1958), 'The Way of Man according to the Teachings of Hasidism' in *Hasidism and Modern Man*, New York: Horizon Press (p.126–76).

14. I have explored the complex relationships between diverse aspects of masculinity, the human body and emotional lives in (1986), *Rediscovering Masculinity: Reason, Language and Sexuality*, London: Routledge; (1999), *Man Enough: Embodying Masculinities*, London: Sage; and more recently in (2006), *Transforming Masculinities: Men, Cultures, Bodies, Power, Sex and Love*, London: Routledge.

15. For some helpful introductory discussions about transitions towards post-modern cultures in the West, see, for instance, J-F Lyotard (1994), *The Postmodern Condition: A Report in Knowledge*, Manchester: Manchester University Press; Linda Nicholson (ed.) (1990), *Feminism/Postmodernism*, New York: Routledge; and Linda Nicholson and Steven Seidman (eds.) (1996), *Social Postmodernism: Beyond Identity Politics*, Cambridge: Cambridge University Press.

16. For some helpful introduction to the philosophy of the later Wittgenstein, see, for instance, Stanley Cavell (1969), 'The Availability of Wittgenstein's Later Philosophy' in *Must We Mean What We Say?* New York: Charles Scribner's Sons (p.44–72); and Norman Malcolm (1986), *Nothing is Hidden*, Oxford: Blackwells.

17. This is a helpful insight that tended to be rediscovered in Western cultures through feminism. See, for instance, Sheila Rowbotham (1972), *Woman's Consciousness, Man's World*, Harmondsworth: Penguin; and her collected essays that reflect upon issues of power, trust and conscious-ness (1983), *Dreams and Dilemma*. London: Virago. See also Sara Ruddick (1989), *Maternal Thinking: Towards a Politics of Peace*, London: The Women's Press.

18. For an introduction to the thinking of Shmuel Hugo Bergman who came from Prague to Jerusalem, see S.H. Bergman (1961), *Faith and Reason: An Introduction to Modern Jewish Thought*, New York: Schocken. Bergman par-ticipated with several colleagues at the Hebrew University in a group brought together by a former American Rabbi, Judah L. Magnus, who was later to become the first chancellor of the university, around the question 'Is there any possibility of knowing God's "Face" either by direct communication or (by means of) an authoritative tradition, or by virtue of His deeds?' For some inter-esting reflections upon this group, see Paul Mendes-Flohr (1988), 'Law and

Sacrament: Ritual Observance in Twentieth-Century Jewish Thought' in Arthur Green (ed.) *Jewish Spirituality*. New York: SCM Press (p.317–45).

19. William James' (1902), *Varieties of Religious Experience*, Harmondsworth: Penguin Books, was committed to listening to the experiences that people were willing to share and thus learn from the terms in which they shaped their religious experiences. As a text it had a significant influence on Wittgenstein, partly because of its refusal to categorise too quickly and willingness to listen to what people had to say. For an interesting biography of James, see *http://psychology.about.com/ od/profilesofmajorthinkers/p/james-bio.htm*.

20. For a helpful introduction to Kafka's writings and a sense of his changing relationship to Judaism, see, for instance, Max Brod (1947), *The Biography of Franz Kafka* (trans. G. Humphreys Roberts), London: Secker & Warburg.

21. Daniel Boyarin considers questions of bodies, genders and sexualities within Talmudic Judaism in (1993), *Carnal Israel: Reading Sex in Talmudic Judaism*, Berkeley: University of California Press.

22. For an interesting introduction to the thinking and philosophy of Franz Rosenzweig, see, for instance, Nahum N. Glatzer (1953), *Franz Rosenzweig: His Life and Thought*, New York: Schocken; and Paul Mendes-Flohr (ed.) (1988), *The Philosophy of Franz Rosenzweig*, Hanover and London: Brandeis University Press.

23. For an interesting introduction to Maimonides thinking and practice, see, for instance, David Hartman (1976), *Maimonides: Torah and Philosophic Quest*, Philadephia: Jewish Publication Society.

24. For Erich Fromm's reflections on Judaism and its relationship to Western culture, see, for instance, Erich Fromm (1967), *You Shall Be as Gods: A radical interpretation of the Old Testament and its tradition*, New York, Holt, Rinehart & Winston.

25. For a helpful introduction to the Talmud that brings out some of its central themes and shows its importance in different ways, see Adin Steinsalz (1989), *The Talmud, The Steinsaltz Edition: A Reference Guide*, New York: Random House.

26. For a helpful introduction to the thinking and practice of Rav Kook who was to become the first Chief Rabbi in Palestine, see, for instance, Benjamin Ish-Shalom (1993) (trans. Ora Wiskind Elper), *Avraham Itzhak HaCohen Kook: Between Rationalism and Mysticism*, Albany: SUNY Press.

Chapter 3 – Reading, Texts and the Human Body

1. For some interesting context and reflections on Levinas' 1934 essay 'Reflections on the Philosophy of Hitlerism', see Levinas' (1990), 'Prefactory note' to the translation, in which he says its central thesis is that 'the bloody barbarism of National Socialism lies not in some contingent anomaly within

human reasoning, nor in some accidental ideological misunderstanding. This article expresses the conviction that this source stems from the essential possibility of *elemental Evil* into which we can be led by logic and against which Western philosophy had not sufficiently insured itself', *Critical Inquiry, 17*. Howard Caygill observes that the theological category of evil is absent from the 1934 essay in his illuminating (2002), *Levinas and the Political*, London: Routledge (p.31). See also the interesting discussion in Josh Cohen (2003), *Interrupting Auschwitz: Art, Religion, Philosophy*, London: Continuum. Zygmunt Bauman seeks a different relationship between modernity and the Holocaust through the workings of instrumental reason and technological rationality in (1989), *Modernity and the Holocaust*, Cambridge: Polity Press.

2. For an exploration of relationships of gender to modernity within the seventeenth-century Scientific Revolutions that helped to shape a concept of 'the death of nature', see, for instance, Brian Easlea (1981), *Science and Sexual Oppression: Patriarchy's Confrontation with Women and Nature*, London: Weidenfeld and Nicholson; C. Merchant (1980), *The Death of Nature: Women, Ecology and the Scientific Revolution*, London: Wildwood House; Susan Griffin (1982), *Women and Nature*, London: The Women's Press; and Victor J. Seidler (1994), *Unreasonable Men: Masculinity and Social Theory*, London: Routledge.

3. For some helpful reflections upon historical relationships between gender, bodies, sexualities and health, see, for instance, Barbara Ehrenreich and Deirdre English (1970), *For Her Own Good: Two Centuries of the Experts Advice to Women*, London: Pluto Press.

4. For some reflections upon Greek, Islamic and Jewish discussions to do with bodies and health see for instance, John Corrigan (2004), *Religion and Emotion: Approaches and Interpretations*, Oxford: Oxford University Press.

5. In (1993), *Recovering the Self: Morality and Social Theory*, London and New York: Routledge, I investigate both the strengths of Marx's vision of creative labour as a challenge to an Enlightenment rationalism and as a break with a Cartesian dualism of mind and body. At the same time, I show how this focus upon creative labour can also foster a disregard for other aspects of life and other forms of fulfilment and self-realisation.

6. Joshua Cohen in *Interrupting Auschwitz* (op. cit.) accepts that 'the renewal of thought after Auschwitz is indissoluble from the task of a thorough philosophical and ethico-political anatomy of Nazism's racialised metaphysics. This anatomy, however, is intended not to bring the death-camps into conformity with some determinate historical logic, but to show precisely the conditions under which any such logic is ruined'. He draws support for saying this from Agamben who says 'The aporia of Auschwitz is, indeed, the very aporia of historical knowledge: a coincidence between facts and truth, between verification and comprehension. Some want to understand too much and too quickly; they have explanations for everything. Others refuse to understand; they offer only cheap mystifications. The only way forward lies in investigating the space between these two options'. See Giorgio Agamben (1999), *The*

Remnants Of Auschwitz: The Witness and the Archive (trans. David Heller Roazen), New York: Zone Books (p.12–13). This was written as a sequel to *ibid.* (1998), *Homo Sacer: Sovereign Power and Bare Life*, Stanford, California: Stanford University Press.

7. For some reflections on the nature of Luther's anti-Semitism, see, for instance, Martin Luther (1543), *On the Jews and their Lies (Von den Jüden und iren Lügen)*, Wittenburg.

8. For some helpful reflections on the transitions towards Judaism in the philosophical thinking of Herman Cohen who was deeply indebted to a Kantian tradition, see, for instance, Gillian Rose (1993), *Judaism and Modernity*, Cambridge: Polity Press. Rivka Horwitz in 'Revelation and the Bible according to Twentieth-Century Jewish Philosophy' argues that Herman Cohen, the great rationalist and founder of the Marburg School, considered in his last book, *Religion of Reason out of the Sources of Judaism* (1918), that revelation means God revealing to humanity ethical reason: 'Revelation is the sign of reason, which comes from God and relates humanity to God. For Cohen, God always reveals himself to humanity. Cohen says that the Torah does not contain any mystery, any unveiling. In prayer God is called "*noten ha-Torah*", the "Giver of the Torah", in the present…God gives the Torah as he gives everything else: life, bread, and also death. Hence, revelation is universal, rational, and present; there is nothing supernatural related to it….Cohen quotes a Midrash that calls heaven and earth as witness that the holy spirit may rest "on an Israelite or on a pagan, a man or a woman, a slave or a maidservant"' (p.348). She also affirms later that 'The real conclusion of Cohen is that "man, and not the people and not Moses, man as a rational being is the correlate of the God of revelation". Cohen's line of thinking is close not only to Kant but also to Maimonides who considers the Torah in *The Guide to the Perplexed* as a foundation of human ethical behaviour. The highest stage is then described by Cohen as transferring Sinai into the human heart' (p.355).

9. For some sense of the historical influence of Shleimacher and Rudolf Otto on developing theological writings across the boundaries of different religious traditions, see, for instance, Paul Tillich (2001), *Dynamics of Faith*, New York: Harper; Rudolf Otto (1968), *The Idea of the Holy*, New York: Oxford University Press, Inc.: and Huston Smith (1992), *Essays on World Religion*, M. Darrol Bryant (ed.), New York: Paragon House.

10. For some helpful introductory writing on the development and influence of phenomenology, particularly through the writings of Husserl, see, for instance, Maurice Merleau-Ponty (2002), *Phenomenology of Perception*, London: Routledge; and Robert Sokolowski (1999), *Introduction to Phenomenology*, Cambridge: Cambridge University Press.

11. For some helpful introductory discussion of Adorno's work and its later relationship to issues of anti-Semitism and the Holocaust, see, for instance, Simon Jarvis (1998), *Adorno: A Critical Introduction*, Cambridge: Polity; Martin Jay (1973), *The Dialectical Imagination: A History of the Frankfurt School and the Institute of Social Research, 1923–1950*, Toronto: Little, Brown and

Company; (1984), *Adorno*, Cambridge Mass.: Harvard University Press; Susan Bucks-Morss (1977), *The Origin of Negative Dialectics: Theodor W. Adorno, Walter Benjamin, and the Frankfurt Institute*, NY: Free Press; Gillian Rose (1978), *The Melancholy Science: An Introduction to the Thought of T.W. Adorno*, London: Macmillan; Josh Cohen (2003), *Interrupting Auschwitz*, London: Continuum; and T. Huhn and Z. Zuidevaart (eds.) (1997), *The Semblance of Subjectivity: Adorno's Aesthetic Theory*, Cambridge Mass.: MIT Press.

12. For some introductory explorations of the relationship of Judaism to Hellenistic culture, see, for instance, Victor Tcherikover (1979), *Hellenistic Civilization and the Jews*, New York: Atheneum.

13. For some reflections on the early relationship between Islam and Judaism, see, for instance, Karen Armstrong (1994), *A History of God*, London: Ballantine Books; Zachary Karabell (2007), *Peace Be upon You*, New York: Alfred A. Knopf; and F.E. Peters (2006), *The Children of Abraham* (foreword J.L. Esposito), Princeton: Princeton University Press.

14. For some helpful introductory discussions about the importance of the Kaballah within Jewish traditions, see, for instance, Gershom Scholem (1946), *On The Kabbalah and its Symbolism*, New York: Schocken; (1965), *Major Trends in Jewish Mysticism*, New York: Schocken Books; and (1971), *The Messianic Idea in Judaism*, New York: Schocken Books.

15. For some sensitive and responsive readings of Genesis that are careful not to foreclose or reach too quickly for conclusions, see Avivah Gottlieb Zornberg (1995), *The Beginnings of Desire: Reflections on Genesis*, New York: Doubleday Random House.

Chapter 4 – Preaching, Revelation and Creation

1. For a helpful introduction to the writings and context of Leo Baeck, see, for instance, Albert Friedlander (1968), *Leo Baeck: Teacher of Theresienstadt*, New York: Holt Rinehart Winston. His essay 'Greek and Jewish Preaching' appears in his collection *The Phariseees* that was later absorbed in (1981), *Judaism and Christianity: Essays by Leo Baeck*, New York: Atheneum.

2. For an exploration of different religious movements and how they emerged in different places across the world so transcending boundaries of East and West, see, for instance, Karen Armstrong (2006), *The Great Transformation: The Beginning of Our Religious Traditions*, New York: Knopf Publishing Group.

3. For some interesting reflections upon Socrates that help to place him historically and philosophically, see, for instance, Jacob Needleman (1982), *The Heart of Philosophy*, New York: Tarcher/Penguin.

4. Mary Warnock, sharing her reflections of philosophy in Oxford after the Second World War, in (2000), 'Some Women Philosophers' in *A Memoir: People and Places*, London: Duckworth, explains how the German regard for

Greek philosophy, drama and science travelled across from the continent with refugee scholars who had found a new home in Oxford. Talking of Iris Murdoch, a personal friend, she says: 'Iris's knowledge and love of Greek, her willingness to try to understand what Aeschylus's words actually meant, and had meant at the time they were written, all of which she had learnt from Fraenkel, led later to a deep love of Plato. Those of us who had been taught by some of the most brilliant refugee scholars during the war had learnt, among other things, a respect for Greek authors, poets, historians and philosophers, as they existed on their own, separate, alien and original, not merely as precursors of the European enlightenment, their words having connotations perhaps different from the English words traditionally used to translate them' (p.87).

5. For a helpful introduction to the nature of Midrash and the kind of readings that it encouraged, see, for instance, Reuven Hammer (1995), *The Classic Midrash*, Mahwah, NJ: Paulist Press; Daniel Boyarin (1994), *Intertextuality and the Reading of Midrash*, Bloomington: Indiana University Press: Jacob Neusner (1987), *What is Midrash?*, Minneapolis: Fortress Press; and Geoffrey H. Hartman and Sanford Budick (1988), *Midrash and Literature*, New Haven: Yale University Press.

6. In contemporary Moral Philosophy, it has been Iris Murdoch who has possibly been the most Platonist in inspiration. In (1970), *Sovereignty of Good*, London: Routledge (1977), *The Fire and the Sun*, Oxford: Oxford University Press, and finally in (1992), *Metaphysics as A Guide to Morals*, London: Chatto and Windus, she showed a sympathy for the Idea of the Good, the object both of intellectual contemplation and of ineffable love. No longer able to accept the idea of a personal God, she had also been drawn to Buddhism for a while. It was the intellectual purity of this search for a vision of this idea and the desire to protect this purity that led Plato to attempt to exclude artists, as seducers and false comforters from *The Republic*. As Murdoch was to write at the close of her final philosophical work, with sympathy about Paul Tillich: 'We need a theology which can continue without God. Why not call such a reflection a form of moral philosophy? All right, so long as it treats of those matters of "ultimate concern" (Tillich's expression), our experience of the unconditioned and our continued sense of what is holy'. Such a moral philosophy was what she hoped to find in Plato, but she realised the dangers. Earlier in the same book, as Warnock reminds us, she writes 'In my own case I am aware of the danger of inventing my own Plato and extracting a particular pattern from his many-patterned text to reassure myself that, as I see it, good is really good, and real is real. I have been wanting to see Plato's image as a sort of Ontological Proof of the necessity of Good, or rather...to put his argument into a modern context, as a background to moral philosophy, as a bridge between morals and religion, and as relevant to our new disturbed understanding of religious truth' (p.512).

7. The different implications of what it means to be 'born into sin', and the ways it has helped to define an unease and antagonism towards pleasure

within Western culture with implications for the place of love within moral philosophy, is a theme I have explored further in (1991), *The Moral Limits of Modernity*: *Love, Inequality and Oppression*, Basingstoke: Macmillan.

8. For some helpful introductory discussion into the form and shaping of Hellenistic Judaism, see, for instance, Erich S. Gruen (2002), *Heritage and Hellenism: The Reinvention of Jewish Tradition*, Berkeley: University of California Press; John J. Collins (1982), *Between Athens and Jerusalem*, New York: Crossroads Publishing Co.; Martin Hengel (2003), *Judaism and Hellenism*, Eugene, OR: Wipf and Stock Publishing: and Carol Bakhos (2004), *Ancient Judaism in Its Hellenistic Context*, London: Brill Academic Publishers.

9. Mathew Fox has been part of a movement that has been concerned to imagine a different relationship between Christianity and Judaism, thus finding ways of reclaiming bodies, sexuality and emotional lives that have for so long been disdained within Western culture. Through his vision of a 'Creation Spirituality', Fox has attempted to allow for an embodied conception of love that honours its Jewish sources and thus questions the dualistic vision that has informed a Catholic tradition which has sought to present Judaism as a religion of justice and law, while Christianity is a religion of love, mercy and caring relationships. This has helped sustain a tradition of contempt and made it difficult to acknowledge that justice and love *can* be brought together as we imagine a different relationship between Jewish philosophies and western cultures. Mathew Fox's work that is often pulling in different directions, partly because of his Catholic training and its embedded vision of a superseding of other traditions that can never be granted full equality. He thus still tends to frame a future in relation to a notion of 'Cosmic Christ'. See for instance (1983), *Original Blessing*: *A Primer in Creation Spirituality*, Santa Fe, NM: Bear and Co.; (1990), *A Spirituality Names Compassion*, San Francisco: Harper and Row; and (1991), *Creation Spiritualty*: *Liberating Gifts for the Peoples of the Earth*, San Francisco: Harper Row.

10. For an account that helps place Wittgenstein's late work *On Certainty* within the larger context of his life and work, see, for instance, Ray Monk (1991), *Ludwig Wittgenstein: The Duty of Genius*, London: Penguin Books.

11. Iris Murdoch is also drawn to reflect upon the nature of Platonic love and the different stages through which humans can develop in (1977), *The Fire and the Sun*, Oxford: Oxford University Press. She is also influenced in her reading of Plato through Simone Weil, though there were differences in relation to embodied and sexual love. Weil felt a need to escape from sexual love while Murdoch seemed to explore in Plato a recognition of different forms of love that were suppressed within a dominant Christian tradition that tended to accept that pure love *had* to be a love that was untainted by sexuality. This was the vision that Weil was reaching for, even though it meant forsaking her Jewish sources that could have led her in a different direction. But at the same time Weil's sense of affliction and the workings of relationships of power gave her a different sense of embodied suffering. These are themes I explored in the

chapter on Power in Lawrence Blum and Victor J. Seidler (1991), *A Truer Liberty: Simone Weil and Marxism*, New York: Routledge.

12. Martin Bernal in *Black Athena* (op. cit) helps us understand the place that Greek culture had, particularly in Germany, in shaping the self-conceptions of Western culture in ways that framed an antagonism between Athens and Jerusalem. Bernal investigates the ways antisemitic discourses were implicitly framed in this vision of Western culture through its *exclusions* of semitic influences and the assertion of a 'purity' in Greek culture that failed to appreciate the different strands that were feeding into each other, and ways that Greece was learning both from African sources in Egypt as well as from sources in the East through trade roots to India. Different cultures were communicating and learning from each other as they were developing hybrid forms and shaping their own cultural traditions, rituals and symbolic appropriations.

13. Gershom Scholem explores the interrelation across Jewish, Christian and Islamic traditions in relation to the development of Kabbalah in R.J. Zwi Werblowsky (ed.) (1990), *The Origins of Kabbalah*, Princeton: Princeton University Press.

Chapter 5 – Hellenism, Christianity and Judaism

1. For some helpful introductions to different philosophical steams within the Middle Ages, see, for instance, Anthony Kenny (2007), *Medieval Philosophy*, Oxford: Oxford University Press; Moshe Halbertal (2007), *Concealment and Revelation*, Princeton: Princeton University Press; Tamar M. Rudavsky (2000), *Time Matters: Time, Creation and Cosmology in Medieval Jewish Philosophy*, New York: State University of New York Press. For a sense of the development of Jewish philosophy and its relationship to Christian and Islamic traditions, see, for instance, Mourad Wahba and Mona Abousenna (1996), *Averroes and the Enlightenment*, New York: Prometheus Books; Oliver Leaman (2006), *An Introduction to Classical Islamic Philosophy*, Cambridge: Cambridge University Press; and Lenn E. Goodman (1999), *Jewish and Islamic Philosophy*, New York: Rutgers University Press.

2. For some helpful discussions of the ways in which Judaism was imagined within dominant Christian traditions within the Middle Ages, see, for instance, R.I. Moore (1990), *The Formation of a Persecuting Society: Power and Deviance within Western Europe 950–1250*, Oxford: Blackwell; David Nirenberg (1996), *Communities of Violence: Persecution of Minorities in the Middle Ages*, Princeton: Princeton University Press; J.M. Powell (ed.), *Muslims Under Latin Rule 1100–1300*, Princeton: Princeton University Press; and Joshua Trachtenberg (1983), *The Devil and the Jews: The Medieval Conception of the Jews in relation to Modern Antisemitism*, Philadelphia: Jewish Publication Society.

3. The recognition that Christianity possessed a truth and a revelation that other religions lacked affirmed its supremacy in its own eyes. The fact that

others could not recognise its self-evident truths showed how they were lacking and at fault as religious traditions. See, for instance, John Tolan (ed.) (2000), *Medieval Christian Perceptions of Islam*, London: Routledge; Tomasz Mastnak (2002), *Crusading Peace: Christendom, the Muslim World and Western Political Order*, Berkeley Calif.: University of California Press; Ernst Kantorowicz (1997), *The King's Two Bodies: A Study in Medieval Political Theology*, Princeton: Princeton University Press; and Maurice Olender (1992), *The Language of Paradise: Race, Religion and Philology in the Nineteenth Century*, Cambridge, Mass.: Harvard University Press.

4. For a sense of the development of Kant's political thought providing some historical context for his political philosophy, see, for instance, Hans Sauer (1973), *Kant's Political Thought: Its Origin and Development* (trans. E.B Ashton), Chicago: University of Chicago Press; and Hannah Arendt (1982) (Ronald Breiner, ed.), *Lectures On Kant's Political Philosophy*, Chicago: University of Chicago Press.

5. The way that a Kantian ethical tradition gives secular form to a dominant Protestant tradition and sustains an implicit sense of inadequacy as people are constantly comparing themselves with the demands of the moral law is a theme I have explored in *ibid.* (1986), *Kant, Respect and Injustice: The Limits of Liberal Moral Theory*, London: Routledge.

6. For some suggestive discussions of Plato's *Republic*, see Adi Ophir (1991), *Plato's Invisible Cities: Discourse and Power in the Republic*, London: Routledge; and Leon H. Craig (1994), *The War Lover: A Study of Plato's Republic*, Toronto: University of Toronto Press.

7. For some helpful introductory discussion that helps place Paul within historical and theological context, see, for instance, Karen Armstrong (1983), *The First Christian: St. Paul's Impact on Christianity*, London; Daniel Boyarin (1994), *A Radical Jew: Paul and the Politics of Identity*, Berkeley, Calif.: University of California Press.

8. For some discussion around dream interpretation within Western culture, see, for instance, Sigmund Freud (1911), *The Interpretation of Dreams* (trans. A.A. Brill), London: Penguin Freud Library vol. 2; and Carl Jung (1961), *Memories, Dreams and Reflections*, London: Fontana Paperbacks.

9. For a helpful introductory account to themes within the Talmud that talks about its structure and offers guidance in relation to forms of reading, see Adin Steinsalz (1992), *The Talmud* (op.cit.) For some of Levinas' readings of the Talmud, see Emmanuel Levinas (1990), *Nine Talmudic Readings* (trans. A. Aronowicz), Bloomington, Indiana: Indiana University Press.

10. In this way, Baeck suggests a different relationship between Plato and what was to emerge as certain totalising inclinations within Christianity than Weil wanted to recognise. For a sense of Weil's explorations of the relationship between Plato and Christianity, see, for instance (1957), *Intimations of Christianity Amongst the Ancient Greeks*, London: Routledge and Kegan Paul; and Richard Rees (ed.) (1968), *On Science, Necessity and the Love of God*, London: Oxford University Press.

11. For some reflections upon how notions of 'purity' can inform certain totalitarian impulses, especially when a tradition assumes that it alone is the bearer of a truth that others lack, see discussions in Hannah Arendt (1958), *The Orgins of Totalitarianism*, New York: Meridan Books. See also discussions in Gil Anidjar (2003), *The Jew, The Arab: A History of the Enemy*, Stanford: Stanford University Press.

12. For some discussion of how the power that Christianity held within Western culture allowed it to define its relationships with 'others' without really having to listen to what they had to say for themselves, see, for instance, Norman Daniel (1960), *Islam And The West: The Making of an Image*, Edinburgh: Edinburgh University Press; Allan Harris Cutler and Helen Elmquist Cutler (1991), *The Jew as Ally of the Muslim: Medieval Roots of Anti-Semitism*, Notre Dame: University of Notre Dame Press; and Shelomo Dov Goitein (1974), *Jew and Arabs: Their Contact through the Ages*, New York: Schocken Books.

Chapter 6 – Creation, Ethics and Human Nature

1. For some helpful introductory reading about the historical, cultural and philosophical context for the writings of Moses Mendelssohn that were to have such an influence in thinking about Jewish emancipation see, for instance, Alexander Altman (1973), *Moses Mendelssohn: A Biographical Study*, Tuscaloosa: University of Alabama Press. Mendelssohn devotes the first half of his essay (1969), *Jerusalem*, New York: Schocken Books, to developing a political theory that carefully details a doctrine of Church and State which separates the two powers, forbidding any attempts to coerce religious loyalty. Mendelssohn felt that, with emancipation and temptations to convert and assimilate, Jewish faith would only survive if the nature of Jewish commitment were seriously re-thought.

2. The term 'emancipation' technically applies to the granting of legal and civil rights but, with time, the problem of civil rights shifted to the social and political arenas. Social and political discrimination remained a serious problem, however, until after the Second World War, the war that destroyed most of European Jewry. An age of emancipation refers to the period beginning with the introduction of the Napoleonic Code into French-occupied Germany after the defeat of Prussia in 1806, through to the legal enfranchisement of Jews in Austria and Germany in 1867 and 1871, respectively. See, for example, Jacob Katz (1972), *Emancipation and Assimilation: Studies in Modern Jewish History*, Westmead: Gregg International; Jacob Katz (1973), *Out of the Ghetto: The Social Background of Jewish Emancipation*, New York: Schocken Books; and David Bronson (ed.) (1979), *Jews and Germans from 1860 to 1933: The Problematic Symbiosis*, Heidelberg: Winter.

3. Moses Mendelssohn, writing in the late eighteenth century, distinguished between an eternal, rational truth and a historical truth, Judaism as a revealed

religion being a historical truth. He states that the Torah is binding because of the covenant at Mount Sinai, where God, as an absolute sovereign, made his laws known through Moses. Herman Cohen, writing in the middle of the nineteenth century, no longer considered Judaism as a historical truth. Rosenzweig, who was influenced by Cohen, made clear that his relationship to Judaism did not depend on the fact that 600,000 heard the divine voice at Sinai. Cohen, not relying on the historical gloss, considered Judaism to be eternal. He quotes Deuteronomy v:3: 'The Eternal made this covenant not with our fathers, but with us, even with us, who are all of us here alive today'. As Rivka Horwitz (1988) states in 'Revelation and the Bible according to Twentieth-century Jewish Philosophy' in Green, Arthur (ed.), *Jewish Spirituality*, New York: SCM Press, 'The whole historical threat is rejected with the strongest emphasis, and yet it is not abolished, but rather it is immediately attached to the present, living people. Cohen then goes one step further and thinks that the eternal is removed from historical experience altogether. He concludes that the eternal is the warrant of the spirit of history and precedes it. Reason precedes history; the beginning is the eternal origina-tive principle. In the end, his Judaism, does not depend upon the past, but on reason' (p.352). She recognises that 'Rosenzweig also develops his thought on Judaism in relation to eternity and history, but he gives them a different meaning'. With regard to the same verse, Deuteronomy v:3, he writes: 'Our independence from history or, to put it positively, our eternity gives simultaneity to all moments of our history. Turning back, recapturing what has remained behind, is here a permanent necessity. For we must be able to live in our eternity' (p.352), 'The Builders' in *On Jewish Learning* (ed. Nahum Glatzer) (2002), Madison, Wisconsin: University of Wisconsin Press.

4. Martin Buber writes in 'The Man of Today and the Jewish Bible' in (1973), *Israel and the World*, New York: Schocken Books, 'man of today resists the Scriptures because he cannot endure revelation' (p.95). Buber recog-nises that within a secular, contemporary, Western culture, human beings have difficulty in accepting revelation, so they approach the Bible as a book like other books to be studied in similar ways and not as the Biblia which is 'an encounter between a group of people and the Lord of the world in the course of history'. As Buber said, we lock ourselves away 'in one of the unholy compartments and feel relieved' (p.92). Buber was concerned to awaken contemporary human beings to the realities of revelation and wished to help moderns to regain an openness that they had lost so that they would again *be able* to 'hear the Word.' Hence his descriptions of revelation differ drasti-cally from the description found in classical Judaism in later pre-modern periods.

5. For an illuminating discussion of the nature of altruism and feelings for others in Kantian moral theory, see Lawrence A. Blum (1984), *Friendship, Altruism and Morality*, London: Routledge. See also Blum's essays 'Kant's and Hegel's Moral Rationalism: A Feminist Perspective' (1982), in *Canadian*

Journal of Philosophy 12 (p.286–97); (1994), 'Moral Perception and Particularity' *Ethics 10*: 701–25 collected in Lawrence A. Blum (1994), *Moral Perception and Particularity*, Cambridge: Cambridge University Press.

6. In (1986), *Kant, Respect and Injustice: The Limits of Liberal Moral Theory*, London: Routledge, I attempt to show the power that these dualities assume within Western culture and so adopt a different form of argumentation that brings philosophy, usually set within the rationalist terms of arguments, into conversation with social theory through naming the ways in which Kant recognises the workings of relations of power without really being able to *explore* the disruptions they create within rationalist forms of moral theory.

7. The theme of self-denial and the ways in which it is so often rendered invisible within rationalist forms of moral theory that often refuse to interrogate their own masculinist assumptions, even though it was identified and named through Nietzsche and Max Scheler (1991), is developed in my *Recreating Sexual Politics: Men, Feminism and Politics*, London and New York: Routledge.

8. I have explored some of the issues in relation to fathering, respect and authority as they relate to moral theory in (2000), *Man Enough: Embodying Masculinities*, London: Sage. For a more general discussion of respect within contemporary Western cultures that also relates to issues around work, see Richard Sennett (2004), *Respect: The Formation of Character in an Age of Inequality*, London: Penguin. For some discussions that relate more specifically to issues of gender, see Judith Stacey (9 July 2001), *Family Values Forever*, New York: The Nation; and Judith Stacey (1997), *In the Name of the Family: Rethinking Family Values in the Postmodern Age*, Boston: Beacon Press.

9. For various perspectives on Kant's conception of Judaism, see, for instance, E.L. Fackenheim, 'Kant and Judaism,' *Commentary 36* (1983), p.460–67; N. Rotenstreich (1964), *The Recurring Pattern*, New York: Horizon Press; (1984) *German Philosophy and the Jews*, New York: Schocken; and Y. Yovel (1998), *Dark Riddle: Hegel, Nietzsche and the Jews*, Cambridge: Polity Press.

10. Alasdair MacIntyre provides a helpful introductory text to moral theory within Western culture in (1966), *A Short History of Ethics: A History of Moral Philosophy from the Homeric Age to the Twentieth Century*, New York: Macmillan.

11. For some helpful discussions of the Jewishness of Jesus, see, for instance, Geza Vermes (2003), *Jesus in his Jewish Context*, Minneapolis, Fortress Press; and Leo Baeck (1981), in *Judaism and Christianity: Essays by Leo Baeck*, New York: Atheneum.

12. For an important discussion of the place of bodies, sexuality and the 'sins of the flesh' in the writings of the early Church fathers and their anxieties about defining themselves in opposition to Judaism, see, for instance, Peter Brown (1990), *The Body and Society: Men, Women and Sexual Renunciation*

in Early Christianity, London: Faber. See also Charlotte Klein (1978), *Anti-Judaism in Christian Theology*, London: SPCK.

13. For some helpful introductory reflections on Buddhist ethics, see, for instance, Sogyal Rimpoche (2002), *The Tibetan Book of Living and Dying*, London: Harper Collins; and Karen Armstrong (2001), *Buddha*, London: Penguin.

14. For some helpful reflections upon post-modern ethics, see, for instance, Alasdair MacIntyre (1992), *After Virtue*, London: Duckworth; and Zygmunt Bauman (1993), *Postmodern Ethics*, Cambridge: Polity.

15. Singer's essay on Genesis appears in (1989), *Congregations: Contemporary Writers Read the Jewish Bible* (David Rosenberg ed.), New York: Harcourt, Brace, Jovanovitch.

Chapter 7 – Ethics, Deeds and Love

1. For some helpful discussion that explores the development of Hegel's early philosophical thinking, see, for instance, H.S. Harris (1770–1801) (1972), *Hegel's Development: Toward the Sunlight*, Oxford: The Clarendon Press; Charles Taylor (1979), *Hegel and Modern Society*, Cambridge: Cambridge University Press; and *ibid.* (1978), *Hegel*, Cambridge: Cambridge University Press.

2. Jurgen Habermas (1992), in *The Philosophical Discourse of Modernity*, Cambridge, Mass.: MIT Press, has located 'the fundamental problem of Hegel's philosophy' as 'the problem of modernity's self-reassurance' (p.16). In the face of the destruction of the past that is wrought by modernity, philosophy is called upon to create teleological constructions of history to close off the future as a source of disruption. As Habermas presents it: 'Modernity specific orientation toward the future is shaped precisely to the extent that societal modernisation tears apart the old European experiential space of peasants' and craftsman's lifeworlds, mobilises it, and devalues it into directives guiding expectations. These traditional experiences of previous generations are then replaced by the kind of experience of progress that lends our horizon of expectation (hitherto anchored firmly in the past) a "historically new quality, constantly subject to being overlaid with utopian expectations"' (p.12). The Spirit moves in dialectical ascent through various civilisations, following a westward migration. In tracing this migration, Hegel maps out a hierarchy among cultures. Space comes to be divided between the West and the Orient. Time is divided between Universal History and the 'world of nature' which lies beyond its framework. In the West, 'Spirit descends into the depths of its own being, and recognises the fundamental principle as the Spiritual', while for the East, nature remains as 'the primary and fundamental existence'. Hegel often refers to the East-West split in terms of the superiority of Western monotheism, particularly Christian identifications with Spirit in which nature becomes reduced to the 'creature' of God.

3. For some helpful discussion of the Prophets and their relationship to Ancient Judaism, see, for instance, Martin Buber (1960), *The Prophetic Faith*, New York: Harper and Row. From Rivka Horwitz (1978), *Buber's Way to I and Thou*, Heidelberg: Lambert Schneider, you can learn about Buber's early friendship with Rosenzweig and how, for both of them, dialogue also meant revelation.

4. Julius Guttman's (1964), *Philosophies of Judaism* (trans. David W. Silverman), New York: Holt, Rinehart and Winston, remains an invaluable introduction to Jewish philosophy by a disciple of Hermann Cohen. In engaging critically with some of the silences and assumptions, we are questioning a neo-Kantian inheritance and its influence in the presentation of Jewish philosophy's relationship with Western culture. For primary sources on Cohen's later thinking, in which he turns his attention to Judaism, we have Hermann Cohen (trans. S. Kaplan) (1919), *Religion of Reason: Out of the Sources of Judaism*, Oxford: Oxford University Press. A helpful secondary text is provided by Jehuda Melber (1968), *Herman Cohen's Philosophy of Judaism*, New York: J. David. Apart from the letters that have been edited by Bertha Strauss and Bruno Strauss (1939), *Briefe*, Berlin: Schocken Verlag, there is no Herman Cohen archive. His wife Martha was killed in the Holocaust and his papers were lost.

5. M. O'C Drury recalls in his 'Conversations with Wittgenstein', in *Ludwig Wittgenstein: Personal Recollections*, edited by Rush Rhees, that Wittgenstein said: 'All religions are wonderful, even those of the most primitive tribes. The ways in which people express their religious feelings differ enormously' (p.117). In another conversation, Wittgenstein said: 'If what we do now is to make no difference in the end, then all the seriousness of life is done away with. Your religious ideas have always seemed to me more Greek than Biblical. Whereas my thoughts are one hundred per cent Hebraic' (p.175). Something of what he meant has to do with the place of abstractions in Greek thought and the questioning of them within Hebraic traditions that focus upon deeds. As he says to Drury: 'But remember that Christianity is not a matter of saying a lot of prayers; in fact we are told not to do that. If you and I are to live religious lives, it musn't be that we talk a lot about religion, but that our manner of life is different. It is my belief only if you try to be helpful to other people will you in the end find your way to God' (p.129). At the same time, Wittgenstein acknowledges in his *Vermischte Bermerkunken*: 'In religion it must be that at each level of religious life there is a way of speaking which at a lower level means nothing. For someone now on the lower level this teaching, which means something on the higher level, is null and void: he *cannot* understand it except in some way that is false, and these words don't hold for him. St Paul's doctrine of the election of Grace, for example, is, at my level, *ir*religious, a repulsive absurdity. It is not meant for me, since I could apply only wrongly the picture it suggests to me' (Notes, p.185).

6. Wittgenstein might also be affirming the 'Hebraic' character of his thinking in his acknowledgement of the significance of the idea, drawn from Exodus,

that 'in the beginning was the deed'. This is a reference he alludes to more than once and shows that it is through doing things that we can sometimes change our consciousness and ways of thinking. In *Culture and Value*, which translates some of his *Vermischte Bemerkungen*, Wittgenstein writes in (1937): 'The origin and the primitive form of the language game is a reaction; only from this can more complicated forms develop'. Language – I want to say – is a refinement, 'in the beginning was the deed'. In this translation Peter Winch says the source for 'in the beginning was the deed' is Goethe's *Faust*, Part 1 (In the Study).

7. For some sense of the crossovers between different religious and spiritual traditions and the kind of learning that has helped shape the complexities of Western culture that are so often forgotten within attempts to provide a homogenised vision of 'Christian Europe', see, for instance, Chaim Wirszubski (1989), *Pico Della Mirandola's Encounter with Jewish Mysticism*, The Israeli Academy of Sciences and Humanities Jerusalem.

8. For some reflections upon the nature of romanticism and its diverse sources and forms, see, for instance, Isaiah Berlin (1999), *The Roots of Romanticism*, London: Chatto and Windus; Northrop Frye (1963), *Romanticism Reconsidered: Selected Papers from the English Institute*, New York and London; William Wordsworth (1888), *Lyrical Ballads*, Oxford: Oxford University Press; and G.E. Bentley, Jr. (ed.) (1978), *William Blake's Writings*, Oxford: Oxford University Press.

9. Seamus Heaney and Ted Hughes (1985), *The Rattle Bag*, Faber & Faber. For some reflections on Heaney's background and poetry, see, for instance, John Boly (2000), 'Following Seamus Heaney's "Follower": Toward a Performative Criticism', in *Twentieth Century Literature*.

10. This relationship to the body and thus with nature partly explains why Kant, in *Religion Within the Boundaries of Reason Alone*, not only puts Judaism at the bottom of his scale of different religions, but actually outside it. As Yirmiyahu Yovel (1998) records in *Dark Riddle: Hegel, Nietzsche and the Jews*, Cambridge: Polity Press, 'Judaism is not only the lowest religion; it is not a religion at all, but merely a political constitution. What Spinoza and Mendelssohn held to be a unity of religious and political constitution here becomes merely a political affair, devoid of any religious content and significance'.

Kant means this in a pejorative sense: '"Religion" for him has the connotation of spirituality and human value. In denying Judaism a religious content and reducing it to political law, Kant deprives it of any spiritual value, even of the minimal moral significance...' (p.17). As Yovel understands it, 'Kant was a liberal of reason; his civil treatment of Jews came from a sense of propriety and perhaps of moral duty; yet on a deeper level he never overcame his strong anti-Jewish bias. Rather he let it sometimes burst out into the open, both in disguised "philosophical" form and even in blunt ejaculations' (p.18). While he acknowledged that Jewish friends like Mendelssohn, Marcus Herz and Lazarus Bendavid 'can have a developed – even an intense – moral mind, since they are rational beings, but this applies to them as individuals; as Jews, they possess only a political constitution, devoid of moral and spiritual value' (p.17).

11. For an appreciation of Zadie Smith's writings on literature, see for instance (2004), '*Doodle from the Guardian Hay Festival*' in The New Yorker, 14 June 2004 and her writing (2002), *White Teeth*, Penguin and (2006) *Oh Beauty*, Penguin.

12. Wittgenstein seems to be saying something similar when he acknowledges in *Culture and Value*: 'You cannot write anything about yourself that is more truthful than you yourself are. That is the difference between writing about yourself and writing about external objects. You write about yourself from your own height. You don't stand on stilts or on a ladder but on your bare feet, (p.33).

13. Again Wittgenstein is also exploring the limits of a Kantian rationalism as it shapes modern Western culture, when he investigates importance of feelings and how to understand a connection people can make with feelings when he comments in *Culture and Value*: 'There is a lot to be learned from Tolstoy's bad theorizing about how a work of art conveys "a feeling". You really could call it, not exactly the expression of a feeling, but at least an expression of feeling, or a felt expression. And you could say too that in so far as people understand it, they "resonate" in harmony with it, respond to it. You might say: the work of art does not aim to convey *anything else*, just itself' (p.58).

14. For an illuminating biography of Keats, see, for instance, Robert Gittings (2001), *John Keats*, Harmondsworth: Penguin Books.

Chapter 8 – Pleasures, Sufferings and Transcendence

1. For a helpful introductory discussion that helps place Philo in historical, cultural and philosophical context, see, for instance, Ronald Williamson (1970), *Philo and the Epistle to the Hebrews*, Leiden: Brill.

2. As Genevieve Lloyd helps us appreciate in her paper (1993), 'Maleness, Metaphor and the "Crisis" of Reason' in (Louise M. Antony and Charlotte Witt, eds.) *A Mind of One's Own*, Boulder: Westview, how 'Derrida has shown in *White Mythology* that the metaphors through which we describe thought itself are particularly difficult to think away. But his approach also stresses the contingency of metaphors, even those we cannot shed. The insight into contingency that comes with awareness of the operations of metaphor gives us valuable understanding of our ways of thinking, even when we cannot begin to articulate what it would be like to think otherwise' (p.81).

3. There is a possible resonance here with a remark that Wittgenstein makes in (1980), *Culture and Value*, Oxford: Blackwell (p.35): 'No one *can* speak the truth; if he has still not mastered himself. He *cannot* speak it; – but not because he is not clever enough yet. The truth can only be spoken by someone who is already *at home* in it; not be someone who still lives in falsehood and reaches out from falsehood toward truth on just one occasion' (p.34). Possibly this can

be read along with an earlier remark from 1938: 'Nothing is so difficult as not deceiving oneself'.

4. For an interesting discussion of the nature of pleasure within western culture and the ways it has been shaped through a dominant Christian tradition, see, for instance, Herbert Marcuse 'On Hedonism' in *Negation*, London: Allen Lane; and Iris Murdoch (1970), *The Sovereignty Of Good*, London: Routledge, in which Murdoch classes together as Existentialist moral philosophies that concentrate exclusively on the will, on freedom and on decision-making, including the moral philosophy of Kant and contemporary thinkers such as Hare and Hampshire. She regarded them as narrowing the world of morality to actions stemming from the 'needle-thin' will, so forgetting the inner life of individuals, their emotions and powers of attending to the world and other people in the world so 'really seeing' them. Unlike Plato who shaped her vision of seeking the good, she recognised the pleasure of attending to particular things and people in the world.

5. For an illuminating discussion of different readings of Eve, see, for example, Elaine Pagels (1988), *Adam, Eve and the Serpent*, London: Allan Lane; and Aviva Gottlieb Zornberg (1995), *The Beginnings of Desire: Reflections on Genesis*, New York: Doubleday, Random House.

6. Reflections upon the figure of Mary within diverse Christian traditions and within western culture more generally are provided by Marina Warner (1976), *Alone of all her Sex: The Myth and Cult of the Virgin Mary*, New York: Vintage Books.

7. For Foucault's later reflections upon how contemporary subjectivities still need to be understood in relation to disavowed Christian and Greek traditions, see, for instance, Michel Foucault (1984), *The Uses Of Pleasure*, London: Penguin; and (1989), *Care of the Self*, London: Penguin.

8. For some interesting reflections upon the nature of gender and ways it is tied in with theological discourses, see, for instance, Lisa Lampert (2004), *Gender and Jewish Difference: From Paul to Shakespeare*, Philadelphia: University of Pennsylvania Press; Helena Michie (1987), *The Flesh Made World: Female Figures and Women's Bodies*, New York: Oxford University Press; Rosemary R. Ruether (1974), *Religion and Sexism: Images of Women in the Jewish and Christian Traditions*, New York: Simon and Schuster; and Elizabeth Clarke (1986), 'Devil's Gateway and Bride of Christ: Women in the Early Christian World', in *Ascetic Piety and Women's Faith: Essays in Late Ancient Christianity*, New York: Edwin Mellen Press, in which Clarke attempts to provide reasons for this split in traditional Greek and Hebrew belief systems in accordance with woman's role as a symbol of sexuality.

9. For some helpful reflections upon the ways categories of gender have been deployed within Greek traditions in philosophy, see, for instance, Genevieve Lloyd (1993), 'The Man Of Reason: "Male" and "Female"' in *Western Philosophy*, 2nd ed. Minneapolis: University of Minnesota Press; Marcia Homiak (July 1990), 'Politics as Soul-Making: Aristotle on Becoming Good', *Philosophia* 20, p.1–2, 167–93; Julia Annas (1981), *Introduction to Plato's*

Republic, Oxford: Clarendon Press; and Elizabeth Spellman (1988), *Inessential Women: Problems of Exclusion in Feminist Thought*, Boston: Beacon Press.

10. For some reflections upon the ways feminist theologies have tended to identify Judaism as a source of whatever patriarchal relations exist within Christianity, thus suggesting that Christianity somehow needs to be 'purified' of its Jewish sources if it wants to liberate itself from patriarchal traditions, see, for instance, Judith Plaskow (1990), *Standing Against Zion: Judaism from a Feminist Perspective*, New York: Harper and Row; Ilana Pardes (1992), *Countertraditions in the Bible: A Feminist Approach*, Cambridge, Mass.: Harvard University Press; Susanna Heschel (ed.) (1983), *On Being a Jewish Feminist: A Reader*, New York: Schocken; David Biale (1992), *Eros and the Jews: From Biblical Israel to Contemporary America*, New York: Basic Books; and T.M. Rudavsky (1995), *Gender and Judaism: The Transformation of Tradition*, New York: New York University Press.

11. For some helpful introductions to Greek ethics, see, for instance, Bernard Williams (1993), *Ethics and the Limits of Philosophy*, London: Fontana; *ibid.*, *Shame and Necessity*, Berkeley: University of California Press; and Martha Nussbaum (1986), *The Fragility of Goodness*, Cambridge: Cambridge University Press.

12. For some helpful reflections upon the relationship of Judaism to the body, see, for instance, Howard Eilberg-Schwartz (ed.) (1992), *People of the Body: Jews and Judaism from an Embodied Perspective*, Albany: SUNY Press.

13. Kim Chernin illuminates the ways in which contemporary attitudes to the human body within Western cultures are shaped by attitudes that have inherited the dominant Christian disdain for the human body and sexuality identified, as they are, with 'sins of the flesh' in *Womansize: The Tyranny of Slenderness*, London: The Women's Press. See also the reflections in Susan Bordo (1993), *Unbearable Weight: Feminism, Western Culture and the Body*, Berkeley, CA: University of California Press.

14. For some helpful introductory reflections on Freud that show the development of his thinking over time, see, for instance, Peter Gay (1988), *Freud: A Life for our Time*, London: Macmillan; and Bruno Bettelheim (1983), *Freud and Man's Soul*, London: Fontana, in which Bettelheim alerts us to the difficulties of translation into English, particularly in relation to medical language.

Chapter 9 – Language, Ethics, Culture and Denial

1. For some discussion about how a language of the soul gradually gave way to a discourse of the mind, see, for instance, Bruno Bettelheim (1991), *Freud and Man's Soul*, London: Fontana. See also Keith Thomas (1971), *Religion, Science and Magic*, London: Wedienfeld and Nicolson; and Marshall Berman (1999), *All our Senses*, London: Verso.

2. For some historical reflections on the nature of Jewish emancipation in Germany and Austria, see, for example, Jacob Katz (1973), *Out of the Ghetto: The Social Background of Jewish Emancipation 1770–1870*, New York: Schocken; Peter Gay (1978), *Freud, Jews and Other Germans: Masters and Victims in Modernist Culture*, Oxford: Oxford University Press; Michael Mayer (1967), *The Origins of the Modern Jew: Jewish Identity and European Culture in Germany, 1749–1824*, Detroit: Wayne State University Press; and H.M. Graupe (1978) (trans. John Robinson), *The Rise of Modern Judaism: An Intellectual History of German Jewry*, New York: Krieger.

3. It was only through giving some recognition to the ways that the philosophers I had been working on, Kant, Kiekegaard and Simone Weil, had in different ways been writing out of Christian traditions that I found I could complete (1991), *The Moral Limits of Modernity: Love, Inequality and Oppresssion*, Basingstoke: Macmillan. Acknowledging my own complex relationship with Judaism and Jewishness helped me relate differently to the writing.

4. Hegel's relationship to Judaism is traced through its development in different stages of his philosophy in Yirmiyahu Yovel (1998), *Dark Riddle: Hegel, Nietzsche and the Jews*, Cambridge: Polity.

5. Marx's 'On the Jewish Question' has been explored in its relationship to notions of 'the human' that were framed within an Enlightenment vision of modernity in my *Recovering the Self: Morality and Social Theory*. It has also been investigated in Robert Fine (2001), *Political Investigations: Hegel, Marx and Arendt*, London: Routledge; and Norman Geras (1990), *Discourses of Extremity Radical Ethics and Post-Marxist Extravagances*, London: Verso.

6. For some discussion of the terms of Jewish emancipation within the Enlightenment and the compromises that were being demanded in relation to Jewish religion, history and culture, see, for instance, Arther Hertzberg (1968), *The French Enlightenment and the Jews*, New York: Columbia University Press; Alexander Altmann (1973), *Moses Mendelssohn: A Biographical Study*, Oxford: The Littman Library; and David Sorkin (1996), *Moses Mendelssohn the Religious Enlightenment*, London: Peter Halban.

7. For some helpful introductory discussion to Lessing and his intellectual and cultural context, see, for example, Isaiah Berlin (1999), *The Roots of Romanticism*, London: Chatto and Windus; and Charles Taylor (1989), *Sources of the Self: The Making of Modern Identity*, Cambridge Mass.: Harvard University Press. For his writings and plays, including (1963), *Nathan Der Weise* (Nathan the Wise), see *Lessings Werke*, Weimar: Volksverlag, vol. 2.

8. For some discussion of Moses Mendelssohn that helps to place (1983), *Jerusalem*, or *On Religious Power and Judaism*, Hanover, N.H. in historical and cultural context, see David Sorkin (1996), *Moses Mendelssohn and the Religious Enlightenment*, London: Peter Halban; Alexander Altmann (1973), *Moses Mendelssohn: A Biographical Study*, Oxford: The Littman Library; Michael Mayer (1967), *The Origins of the Modern Jew: Jewish Identity and European Culture in Germany 1749–1824*, Detroit: Wayne State University Press; and Aklan Arkush (1994), *Moses Mendelssohn and the Enlightenment*,

Albany: SUNY. As David Sorkin explains: 'By introducing a new method into philosophy, Kant also altered the focus of concern about Judaism. He criticised Judaism by reviving Spinoza's view of Judaism as a theocracy. He denied Judaism the status of a religion...Whereas Mendelssohn has been concerned to show that Judaism was fully congruent with natural religion, Jewish thinkers after Kant were concerned to establish Judaism's status as a religion of morality and belief, an effort for which Mendelssohn notion of 'divine legislation' and heteronomy were an impediment' (p.153).

9. For some discussion of the political and intellectual context for Jean-Paul Sartre *Anti-Semite and Jew* and his later shift of views, see J.H. Friedlander (1990), *Vilna on the Seine: Jewish Intellectuals in France Since 1968*, New Haven: Yale University Press. I have explored the implications of Sartre's discussion in relation to Jewish identities in *ibid*. (2000), *Shadows Of The Shoah: Jewish Identity and Belonging*, Oxford: Berg.

10. These writings from Wittgenstein are drawn from the Postscript by Rhees in Rush Rhees (ed.) (1981), *Ludwig Wittgenstein: Personal Recollections*, Oxford: Blackwell.

11. For discussions of affinities between Wittgenstein and Freud, see Stanley Cavell (2004), *Cities Of Words: Pedagogical Letters on a Register of the Moral Life*, Cambridge Mass.: Harvard University Press (p.282–300).

12. Otto Weininger (1906), *Sex and Character*, London: Heinemann, was extremely popular in Vienna when it was published and had considerable influence in different ways on Freud and Wittgenstein. For some helpful introductory discussion of Weininger that helps to place him in historical and cultural context, see, for instance, Steven Toulmin and Allan Janik (1973), *Wittgenstein's Vienna*, New York: Simon and Schuster; and Peter Gay (1988), *Freud: A Life For Our Time*, London: Macmillan. Gay confirms that Weininger had come to see Freud who had advised him not to publish, but that the manuscript that he had shown him 'had been very different from the book' (p.155).

13. For some of Derrida's reflections on hospitality, see his essay 'Hospitality' in Gil Anidjar (ed.), *Jacques Derrida: Acts of Religion*, p.358–420.

14. For some of Emmanuel Levinas' discourses on various passages in the Talmud, see (1990) (trans. A. Aronowicz), *Nine Talmudic Readings*, Bloomington, Ind.: Indiana University Press. For some helpful readings of Levinas, see, for instance, Thomas Carl Wall (1999), *Radical Passivity: Levinas, Blanchot and Agamben*, Albany, NY: SUNY Press; Tamra Wright (1999), *The Twilight of Jewish Philosophy: Emmanuel Levinas' Ethical Hermeneutics*, Amsterdam: Harwood Academic; and Robert Gibbs (2001), *Why Ethics?: Signs of Responsibility*, Princeton NJ: Princeton University Press.

15. For the Oliner's account of those who rescued Jews during the Second World War and their reflection on the weakness of traditional rationalist theories to account for their discoveries, see S.P. and P.M. Oliner (1988), *The Altruistic Personality: Rescuers of Jews in Nazi Europe*, New York: Free Press; N. Tec (1986), *When Light Pierced the Darkness: Christian Rescuers of Jews*

in Nazi-Occupied Poland, New York: Oxford University Press; and P. Oliner, S. Oliner, L. Baron and L. Blum (1992), *Embracing the Other: Philosophical, Psychological and Historical Perspectives on Altruism*, New York: New York University Press.

16. For some reflections on the inadequacies of a Kantian tradition in the face of the rise of Hitler in Germany and the Holocaust that followed, see, for instance, Lawrence L. Langer (1998), *Preempting the Holocaust*, New Haven: Yale University Press; and (1999), *Admitting the Holocaust: Collected Essays*. See also the biographical reflections in Emil Fackenheim (1982), *Mending The World*, New York: Schocken Books.

17. For Freud's discussion of the emotional suffering that it wrought within Western culture through the repression of sexuality, see *ibid.* (1988), *Civilisation and its Discontents*, London: Penguin Freud Library. To help place this writing in the context, both of his intellectual development and the broader cultural changes with the emergence of Nazism, see Peter Gay (1988), *Freud: A Life for our Time*, London: Macmillan.

18. Simone Weil's essay 'Human Personality', where she explores different conceptions of justice and draws a distinction between distributive conceptions of justice that have shaped liberal moral theory and what she considers to be a prior notion of justice as violation, in Richard Rees (ed.) (1962), *Selected Essays 1934–43*, Oxford: Oxford University Press. I have explored implications of Weil's thinking about justice and a language of rights in the later chapters of Lawrence Blum and Victor J. Seidler (1991) *A Truer Liberty: Simone Weil and Marxism*. New York: Routledge.

19. For an illuminating discussion of the nature of altruistic emotions within Kantian moral theory, see Lawrence A. Blum (1984), *Friendship, Altruism and Morality*, London: Routledge.

20. For Isaiah Berlin's explorations of thinkers of the counter-Enlightenment, see Isaiah Berlin (1891), *Against the Current*, Oxford: Oxford University Press. For his more extended writing on Vico and Herder, see Isaiah Berlin (1977), *Vico And Herder: Two Studies in the History of Ideas*, New York: Vintage, Random House.

Chapter 10 – Traditions, Bodies and Difference/s

1. Martin Bernal's pioneering study into the invention of 'Western' culture and ways it was framed through a relationship with a vision of Greek culture that radically separated it from its connections with Semitic and Egyptian influences in order to affirm its Aryan vision of 'whiteness' in nineteenth-century Germany is (1987), *Black Athena*, London: Free Associations Press.

2. For considerations in favour of the view that even natural slaves are men and women for Aristotle, see W.W. Fortenbaugh (1977), 'Aristotle on Slaves and Women' in *Articles on Aristotle*, vol. 2, Jonathan Barnes, Malcolm Schofield and Richard Sorabji (eds.), London: Duckworth.

3. For some helpful introductory discussion of Mathew Arnolds *Culture and Anarchy*, see, for instance, Raymond Williams (1958), *Culture and Society*, Harmondsworth: Penguin.

4. For some helpful introductory reading that helps to understand the development of Mathew Arnold's thinking, see, for instance, Nicholas Murray (1997), *A Life of Matthew Arnold*, London: Sceptre.

5. For some helpful readings of Wittgenstein that help show the ways he developed his thinking about language games, see, for instance, Norman Malcolm (1986), *Nothing is Hidden*, Oxford: Blackwell; and Stanley Cavell (1989), *The Claim of Reason*: *Wittgenstein, Skepticism, Morality and Tragedy*, Oxford: The Clarendon Press.

6. For some helpful introductory discussions of the history of antisemitism in the West and the ways it has shaped the relationship between Jewish philosophies and Western cultures, see, for instance, Shmuel Almog (ed.) (1988), *Antisemitism Through the Ages*, Oxford: Pergamon Press.

7. For some illuminating discussion of the ways that Levinas frames the relationship between Athens and Jerusalem and the ways he thinks of philosophy as Greek, see Susan Handelman (1991), *Fragments Of Redemption*: *Jewish Thought and Literacy Theory in Benjamin, Scholem and Levinas*, Bloomington: Indiana University Press; A. Perpazak (ed.) (1995), *Ethics as First Philosophy*, London: Routledge; and Tamra Wright (1999), *The Twilight of Jewish Philosophy*: *Emmanuel Levinas' Ethical Hermeneutics*, Amsterdam: Harwood Academic.

8. For a sense of Gafni's writing, see, for example, Marc Gafni (2001), *Soul Prints*, New York: Simon and Schuster.

9. For some helpful reflections through which Christianity is coming to terms with its own histories of antisemitism, see, for example, Charlotte Klein (1978), *Anti-Judaism in Christian Theology*, London: SPCK; Franklin Little (1975), *The Crucifiction of the Jews*, New York: Harper and Row; and essays collected in Richard Libowitz (ed.) (1987), *Faith and Freedom*: *A Tribute to Franklin H. Little*, Oxford: Pergamon Press.

10. For a helpful introductory text that explores some of the main themes of Philo's philosophy and helps to place him in historical and cultural context, see, for instance, Ronald Williamson (1989), *Jews in the Hellenic World*: *Philo*, Cambridge: Cambridge University Press.

11. For some interesting reflections upon Weil's theology and changing ideas about religion and God, see, for instance, Simone Weil (1959) (trans. Emma Craufurd), *Waiting on God*, London: Fontana; and J.B. Perrin and G. Thibon (1953), *Simone Weil as we Knew Her*, London: Routledge and Kegan Paul.

12. For changing Jewish conceptions of bodies, pleasure and sexualities through time and place, see, for instance, David Biale (1992), *Eros and the Jews*, New York: Basic Books; Howard Eilberg-Schwartz (ed.) (1992), *People of the Body*: *Jews and Judaism from an Embodied Perspective*, Albany: SUNY; and Daniel Boyarin (1993), *Carnal Israel*: *Reading Sex in Talmudic Judaism*, Berkeley: University of California Press.

13. For a view of the development of Hartman's thinking and his reflections upon figures in Jewish philosophy and theology that have had a particular influence upon him, see David Hartman (1985), *A Living Covenant*, New York: Basic Books. In his earlier work which serves a helpful introduction to Maimonides (1976), *Maimonides: Torah and Philosophical Quest*, Philadelphia: Jewish Publications Society, he wants to show how Maimonides synthesised a commitment to philosophy with a commitment to the halakhic life.

Chapter 11 – Love, Friendship and Hospitality

1. Hilary Putnam is sharing what he has learned from his readings of Stanley Cavell (1979), *The Claim of Reason*, Oxford: Clarendon Press, in his introduction to the short text by Franz Rosenzweig (1999), *Understanding the Sick and the Healthy: A View of World, Man, and God*. Cambridge, Mass.: Harvard University Press. This is a significant text that Rosenzweig was not always happy with, but which seems to express in more concise form some of the ideas in his major work *The Star of Redemption*.

2. In (1971), *The Prison Notebooks*, London: Lawrence and Wishart, Gramsci explores how we come to consciousness within particular relationships, thus challenging the distinction that has often framed an Enlightenment rationalism that sees the subject as consciousness or mind, facing an external world. This frames his understanding of the potential development of a critical awareness in which people are ready to explore the different elements that make up an inherited 'common sense'. I have explored this theme in Gramsci's writings in (1994), *Recovering the Self: Morality and Social Theory*, London: Routledge.

3. For a very illuminating collection of Putnam's philosophical papers that help us reflect upon shifts in his own thinking, see Hilary Putnam (1998), *Mind, Value and Reality*, Cambridge, Mass.: Harvard University Press.

4. For some helpful discussion of Kant's writings on sexual relationships and marriage, see, for instance, Barbara Herman 'Could it be worth Thinking about Kant on Sex and Marriage?' in Louise M. Antony and Charlotte Witt (eds.) (1993), *A Mind of One's Own: Feminist Essays on Reason and Objectivity*, Boulder: Westview Press, p.49–67; and Hans Fink (1981), *Social Philosophy*, London: Methuen. For a more general discussion on the place of marriage within liberal political theory, see Carol Pateman (1989), *Sexual Contract*, Stanford: Stanford University Press.

5. This view of Kant's understanding of emotions, feelings and desires and their displacement within moral action was initially defended in (1986), *Kant, Respect and Injustice: The Limits of Liberal Moral Theory*, London: Routledge, where I was also concerned to identify a tendency within liberal moral culture. There have been a number of formative discussions that have sought to defend a different view of Kant that can seem to more easily come to

terms with emotional life. See, for instance, Onora O'Neil (1990), *Constructions of Reason*, Cambridge: Cambridge University Press; Onora O'Neil and Christine M. Korsgaard (1996), *The Sources of Normativity*, Cambridge: Cambridge University Press; Barbara Herman (1996), *The Practice of Moral Judgment*, Cambridge, Mass.: Harvard University Press; and Christine M. Korsgaard (1996), *Creating the Kingdom of Ends*, Cambridge: Cambridge University Press.

6. I have explored the theme of how in a rationalist culture shaped traditionally through a dominant masculinity men and women, particularly within post-feminist cultures, can shape their experience through reason and can only allow themselves emotions they know in advance they can rationally defend, in *ibid.* (1999), *Man Enough*: *Embodying Masculinities*, London: Sage.

7. Some of Hegel's early work including *The Life Of Jesus* is quoted by Walter Kaufmann (1965), *Hegel: Reinterpretation, Texts, and Commentary*, Garden City, NY: Doubleday.

8. For a discussion of Derek Parfit (1987), *Reasons And Persons,* Oxford: Oxford University Press, see, for instance, Jonathan Dancy (1997), *Reading Parfit*, Oxford: Blackwells.

9. Ray Monk, in (1986), *Ludwig Wittgenstein: the Duty Of Genius*, London: Vintage Books, explores in an illuminating way the hesitations that Wittgenstein had about the ways his work would be received, while it was still dominated by a tradition of Enlightenment rationalism. He expresses some of these fears more directly in the introduction he wrote to his (1958), *Philosophical Investigations*, Oxford: Blackwell.

10. Norman Malcolm explores the movements we make towards others and ways they are sometimes interrupted and so the relationship between human actions and language, in 'Wittgenstein: The Relation of Language to Instinctive behaviour' that was originally given as the J.R. Jones Memorial Lecture, University College of Swansea, in May 1981 and published in *Philosophical Investigations*, vol. 5 no. 1 (p.3–22). This includes a reflection on Wittgenstein's remark in *Culture and Value* that, as I have mentioned already, contains the reference of Exodus and to a Hebraic recognition of the priority of the deed in relation to language and consciousness.

'The origin and the primitive form of the language-game is a reaction; only from this can the more complicated forms grow.

'Language – I want to say – is a refinement; "in the beginning was the deed"' (p.31)

11. Questions around abortion and the different ways they might be narrated across genders was a central example for the development of Gilligan's ideas around an ethics of care and concern. See Carol Gilligan (1982), *In a Different Voice*: *Psychological Theory and Women's Development*, Cambridge Mass.: Harvard University Press. See also C. Gilligan, J.V. Ward and J.M. Taylor (eds.) (1982), *Mapping the Moral Domain*, Cambridge, Mass.: Harvard University Press. For the influence of Gilligan's work on moral theory, see Lawrence Blum 'Gilligan and Kholberg: Implications for Moral

Theory', *Ethics* 98,3 (1988), p.472–91; and Eva Fay Kittay and Diana T. Myers (1987), *Women and Moral Theory*, Totowa, NJ: Rowman and Littlefield.

12. For some discussions on the shaping of intimacy within contemporary sexual cultures, see, for instance, L. Jamieson (1998), *Intimacy: Personal Relationships in Modern Societies*, Cambridge: Polity Press; Victor J. Seidler (1991), *Recreating Sexual Politics: Men, Feminism and Politics*, London: Routledge; Jeffrey Weeks (1995), *Invented Moralities: Sexual Values in an Age of Uncertainty*, Cambridge: Polity Press; and (2000), *Making Sexual History*, Cambridge: Polity Press.

13. For some helpful reflections upon the nature of friendship and the space allowed for it within Kant's moral theory, see Lawrence A. Blum (1983), *Friendship, Altruism and Morality*, London: Routledge.

14. For an exploration of the emotional lives of men within contemporary Western cultures, see Victor J. Seidler (1999), *Man Enough: Embodying Masculinities*, London: Sage; and (2006), *Transforming Masculinites: Men, Cultures, Bodies, Power, Sex and Love*, London: Routledge.

15. For some interesting discussions of friendships between men in contemporary Western culture, see, for instance, A. Metcalf and M. Humphries (eds.) (1987), *The Sexuality of Men*, London: Pluto Press; S. Miller (1983), *Men and Friendship*, London: Gateway Books; and Peter Nardi (ed.) (1999), *Men's Friendships*, Thousand Oaks, Calif.: Sage; *Gay Men's Friendship: Invisible Communities*, Chicago, Ill.: University of Chicago Press; and J. Weeks and K. Porter (eds.) (1998), *Between the Acts: Lives of Homosexual Men 1885–1967*, London: Rivers Oram Press.

16. For some helpful introductory discussions of Nietzsche's philosophy that helps to place it the development of his thinking in historical and cultural context, see, for instance, Walter Kaufman (1968), *Nietzsche: Philosopher, Psychologist, Antichrist*, Princeton: Princeton University Press; R.H. Thomas (1983), *Nietzsche in German Politics and Society 1890–1918*, Manchester: Manchester University Press. For Nietzsche thoughts about Judaism and Jews, see, for instance, Jacob Golomb (ed.) (1997), *Nietzsche and Jewish Culture*, London: Routledge; Steven Ascheim (1992), *The Nietzsche Legacy in Germany*, Berkeley, CA: University of California Press; and Yirmiyahu Yovel (1998), *Dark Riddle: Hegel, Nietzsche and the Jews*, Cambridge: Polity.

17. For some of Nietzsche's major writings that can give you some sense of his development and shifts over time, see, for instance (1966), *Beyond Good and Evil* (trans. Walter Kaufman), New York: Vintage (trans. R.J. Hollingdale); (1986) *Human, All Too Human: A Book for Free Spirits*, Cambridge: Cambridge University Press; (1969) (trans. Walter Kaufman), *On The Genealogy of Morals*; *Ecco Homo*, New York: Vintage; and (trans. R.J. Hollingdale) (1961), *Thus Spoke Zarathustra*, Harmondsworth: Penguin.

18. The conference on 'The Ethics of Altruism' was held at Royal Holloway College, University of London, by the Society of Social and Legal Philosophy, April 2003.

19. For some discussion of the nature of a midrash as an ethical story from which different meanings can be learned for everyday moral life, see, for instance, Susan A. Handelman (1982), *The Slayers of Moses: The Emergence of Rabbinic Interpretation in Modern Literary Theory*, Albany: SUNY Press; Geoffrey Hartman and Stanford Budick (eds.) (1986), *Midrash and Literature*, New Haven: Yale University Press; Emil Fackenheim (1980), *Encounters Between Judaism and Modern Philosophy: A Preface to Future Jewish Thought*, New York: Schocken; and Harold Fish (1988), *Poetry With a Purpose: Biblical Poetics and Interpretation*, Bloomington: Indiana University Press.

Chapter 12 – Dialogue, Responsibility and Ethics

1. For some helpful introductory reading and discussion of the formation and shaping of Hassidic movements in Eastern Europe, see, for instance, Martin Buber (1969), *The Legend of the Baal-Shem*, New York: Schocken; (1948), *Tales of the Hasidim: Early Masters and Later Masters* (2 vols.), New York: Schocken; and Nahum N. Glatzer (ed.) (1972), *On Judaism*, New York: Schocken. See also for some later stories within the same current, Martin Buber (1974), *The Tales of Rabbi Nachman*, London: Souvenir Press. For an account of Buber's relationship with Hasidism, see Martin Buber (1988), *Hasidism and Modern Man* and *The Origin and Meaning of Hasidism* (both volumes ed. and trans. by Maurice Friedman), Atlantic Highlands, New Jersey: Humanities Press International. When we are thinking about silent appropriations it can be important to recall that in August 1958, Shmuel Hugo Bergman published in the magazine of the German-speaking-Jews in Israel an article about Paula Buber, in which, according to Maurice Friedman in *Encounter on the Narrow Ridge: A Life of Martin Buber*, 'he spoke of her great influence in helping Buber to escape the overtly aesthetic and uncommitted life on his youth'. He concluded: 'Paula Buber was other than we are. But when she, as she often did in her speech, said, as a matter of course "we Jews", then we felt ourselves confirmed. We did not make it easy for her among us. We did not always learn what we had to learn from her great pure, solid, astringent, critical, but always deeply genuine figure. She walked her separate way unerringly' (quoted on p.375).

2. I have reflected upon the impact of the Holocaust as an event that determined the lives of the second generation without really often being spoken in *Shadows of the Shoah: Jewish Identity and Belonging*, Oxford: Berg, 2000.

3. Through a Jewish tradition of naming a child after a relative that has recently died, a connection is formed between the living and the dead. There is a notion that the soul of the dead would somehow be connected and restored through the birth of a child. This tradition assumed a particular significance in the Second Generation when so many children of refugees and survivors carried the names of members of their families who had been brutally murdered

within Nazi extermination camps. This worked to create an inner connection that could be difficult to come to terms with emotionally because it could potentially feel so overwhelming.

4. A notion of 'double consciousness' was invoked by W.E.B. Du Bois in (1989), *The Souls of Black Folk*, New York: Bantam, a book that made him a leader of Black Americans. There was a sympathy for the sufferings of others that resonates in some way with Hasidic traditions that also find a way of giving voice to oppressed souls. Du Bois recognises a historical transformation that could potentially shift the ways an Enlightenment modernity had understood human equality when he says 'The nineteenth century was the first century of human sympathy, the age when, half-wonderingly, we began to decry in others that which transfigures the spark of divinity which we call Myself; when clodhoppers and peasants, tramps and thieves, millionaires and-sometime-Negroes, become throbbing souls whose warm pulsing life touched us so nearly that we half grasped with surprise, crying, "Thou too! Hast Thou seen Sorrow and the dull waters of hopelessness? Hast Thou known Life?" And then all helplessly we peered into those Other-worlds, and wailed, "O World of Worlds how shall man make you one?"' (p.154). This passage is quoted in Paul Gilroy (1993), *The Black Atlantic: Modernity and Double Consciousness*, Cambridge, Mass.: Harvard University Press (p.113), where Gilroy also recognises 'Du Bois began to retell the narrative of western civilizations in systematic ways that emphasised its African origins and expressed a deeper disengagement with modern forms of thought that were discredited by their association with the continuing practice of white supremacy' (p.113).

5. For some helpful introductory reading to the influences and shaping of Levinas' philosophy, see, for instance, Susan A. Handelman (1991), *Fragments of Redemption: Jewish Thought and Literary Theory in Benjamin, Scholem and Levinas*, Bloomington: Indiana University Press; Richard A. Cohen (ed.) (1986), *Face to Face with Levinas*, Albany: State University of New York Press; Robert Bernasconi and David Wood (eds.) (1988), *The Provocation of Levinas*, London: Routledge; and Richard A. Cohen (1994), *Elevations: The Height of the Good in Levinas and Rosenzweig*, Chicago: University of Chicago Press.

6. For Jaques Derrida's explorations of some of the Christian sources in Kant and the difficulties of thinking in terms of 'religion', see his paper 'Faith and Knowledge: The Two Sources of "Religion" at the Limits of Reason alone', which opens *Acts of Religion*, Gil Anidjar (ed.), London: Routledge (p.42–101).

7. It is still possibly true that most histories of Britain are written with little reference to the Jews, who tend to exist as part of a separated history of the Jews. There are histories that are written of Jews as part of a minority community, but otherwise there is little reference. Simon Schama, possibly out of an awareness of his own Jewish background in London, attempted to take some steps towards transcending these boundaries in his BBC (2000), *A History of Britain*, London: BBC Books.

8. For some interesting reflections on the changing character of immigration into the United States and Britain in the twentieth century and the bearing this has had upon different visions of multiculturalism, see, for instance, Arthur Schlesinger Jr (1998), *The Disuniting of America*: *Reflections on a Multicultural Society*, New York: W. W. Norton & Company; Stephen Macedo (2000), *Diversity and Distrust*: *Civic Education in a Multicultural Democracy*, Cambridge, Mass.: Harvard University Press; and R. Baubock (ed.) (1994), *From Aliens to Citizens*: *Redefining the Status of Immigrants in Europe*, Aldershot: Avebury. For a more generalised discussion around issues of multi-culturalism, see, for instance, Bhikhu Parekh (2000), *Rethinking Multiculturalism*: *Cultural Diversity and Political Theory*, London: Palgrave; and C. Willet (eds.) (1998), *Theorising Multiculturalism*: *A Guide to the Current Debate*, Oxford: Basil Blackwell.

9. Rivka Horwitz makes this point in her 'Revelation and the Bible according to Twentieth-Century Jewish Philosophy' in Arthur Green (ed.) (1988), *Jewish Spirituality*, New York: SCM Press (p.355).

10. For some interesting discussion that helps focus some of the differences that separated Buber and Rosenzweig and their attempts to clarify differences, see, for instance, Franz Rosenzweig (Nahum Glatzer, ed.) (1955), *On Jewish Learning*, New York: Schocken.

11. For some helpful introductory reading on the philosophy and social theory of Max Scheler that had a significant influence on Buber, see, for instance, John R. Staude (1967), *Max Scheler 1874–1928*, New York: The Free Press. For some of Scheler's own writings, see, for instance, Max Scheler (1973), *Formalism In Ethics and Non-Formal Ethics of Values*, Chicago: Northeastern Press; (1972) (trans. William W. Holdheim), *Resentiment*, New York: Schocken; (trans. Hans Meyerhoff) (1965), *Man's Place in Nature*, New York: Noonday Press.

12. For a helpful discussion of Buber's conception of relationships within emotional life, see, for instance, the work collected in (trans. Ronald Gregor Smith) (1985), *Between Man and Man*, New York: Macmillan. The opening essay 'Dialogue' serves as a helpful introduction to Buber's philosophy. Besides essays on 'Dialogue', 'Education of Character', and 'The Question of the Single One' that is a reflection on Kierkegaard, it also contains 'What is Man?' on philosophical anthropology and an important Afterward on 'The History of the Dialogical Principal'. As a whole it could be said to represent the next stage after *I And Thou* in the development of Buber's philosophy of dialogue.

13. bell hooks writes about the differences between love and care in her (2005), *Sisters Of The Yam*: *Black Women and Self-Healing*, Boston: South End Press. She has also written beautifully about the importance of Black churches in her growing up and the significance of their narratives of soul in her trilogy.

14. For some helpful discussions of Rosenzweig's notion of 'new thinking' and the shifts this represents in his own philosophy, see Paul Mendes-Flohr

(1988), *The Philosophy of Franz Rosenzweig*, Brandeis University Press: Hanover, NH and London. As Mendes Flohr notes in his introduction, commenting on the paper by Moshe Idel in the collection, Rosenzweig 'had a profound appreciation of kabbalistic spirituality, as expressed in its intensely personalistic view of the divine and its hyperbolic "anthropomorphism", as containing elements that may possibly revivify a Judaism spiritually desiccated by modern rationalism'.

'In more immediate terms, Rosenzweig sought to adumbrate a strategy for the spiritual renewal of modern man in general through a revaluation of speech – the faculty that man shares with God. "The ways of God are different from the ways of man", as he succinctly put it, "the word of God and the word of man are the same". Speech binds man both to God and his fellow man; it is the bridge that arches between the life of the spirit and the realm of humanity. As such it provides, according to Rosenzweig, the crucial link between theology and philosophy. Indeed, grounded in the concrete, time-bound reality of human discourse, speech – as opposed to abstract, timeless reason – is the central epistemological category in Rosenzweig's "new thinking"' (p.17–18).

15. For some helpful introductory readings of post-analytical psychotherapies, see, for instance, Lucy Goodison and Sheila Ernst (1981), *In Our Own Hands*, London: The Women's Press; Victor J. Seidler (1999), *Man Enough: Embodying Masculinities*, London: Sage; Ken Dytchwald (1977), *Bodymind*, Pantheon Books; and Erich Fromm (1993), *The Art of Being*, London: Constable.

16. For an important introduction to Rosenzweig's thinking that also contains a collection of Rosenzweig's letters and some of his essays, see Nahum Glatzer (ed.) (1961), *Franz Rosenzweig: His Life and Thought*, New York: Schocken.

17. For some of Martin Buber's reflections on the Bible, see, for instance, Martin Buber (Nahum Glatzer, ed.) (1982), *On the Bible*, New York: Schocken; and (1949), *The Prophetic Faith*, New York: Macmillan.

Bibliography

Achar, Gilbert (2002), *The Clash of Barbarisms: September 11 and the Making of the New World Disorder*, New York: Monthly Review Press.

Adam, Barbra (1990), *Time and Social Theory*, Cambridge: Polity Press.

Adorno, Theodor and Horkheimer, Max (1973), *Dialectic of Enlightenment* (trans. J. Cumming), London: Allen Lane.

Adorno, Theodor (1974), *Aspects of Sociology*, London: Heinemann.

Adorno, Theodor (1983), *Prisms* (trans. S. Weber), Cambridge, Mass.: MIT Press.

Agamben, Giorgio (1993), *The Coming Community*, Minneapolis: University of Minnesota Press.

Agamben, Giorgio (1998), *Homo Sacer: Sovereign Power and Bare Life* (trans. Daniel Heller-Roazen), Stanford: Stanford University Press.

Agamben, Giorgio (2000), *Means Without End: Notes on Politics*, Minneapolis: University of Minnesota Press.

Agamben, Giorgio (2005), *State of Exception*, Chicago, Ill.: University of Chicago Press.

Ahmed, Akbar (1988), *Discovering Islam*, London: Routledge.

Al-Azmeh, Aziz (1993), *Islam and Modernities*, London: Verso.

Ali, Tariq (2002), *The Clash of Fundamentalisms: Crusades, Jihads and Modernity*, London: Verso.

Alter, Robert (1981), *The Art of Biblical Narrative*, New York: Basic Books.

Altmann, Alexander (1981), *Essays In Jewish Intellectual History*, Hanover, New Hampshire: Brandeis University Press.

Anderson, Benedict (1991), *Imagined Communities: Reflections on the Origin and Spread of Nationalism*, London: Verso.

Anidjar, Gil (2003), *The Jew, The Arab: A History of the Enemy*, Stanford: Stanford University Press.

An Na'im, Abdullahi Ahmed (ed.) (1992), *Human Rights in Cross-Cultural Perspective: A Quest for Consensus*, Philadelphia: University of Pennsylvania Press.

Appignanesi, Lisa and Maitland, Sara (ed.) (1989), *The Rushdie File*, London: Fourth Estate.

Arendt, Hannah (1958a), *The Origins of Totalitarianism*, New York: Meridian Books.

Arendt, Hannah (1958b), *The Human Condition*, Chicago: University of Chicago Press.

Arendt, Hannah (1977), *Eichmann in Jerusalem: A Report on the Banality of Evil*, New York: Penguin.

Arendt, Hannah (1978), *The Jew as Pariah*, New York: Grove Press.

Arendt, Hannah (1982), *Lectures On Kant's Political Philosophy*, ed. Robert Beiner, Chicago: University of Chicago Press.

Armitage, James (2002), 'State of Emergency: An Introduction', *Theory, Culture and Society*, 19 (4), 27–38. London: Routledge.

Armstrong, Karen (2000), *The Battle for God*, New York: Knopf.

Assiter, Alison (1996), *Enlightenment Women: Modernist Feminism In A Postmodern Age*, London: Routledge.

Badiou, Alain (2002), *St Paul: The Foundation of Universalism*, Stanford: Stanford University Press.

Badiou, Alain (2004), *Infinite Thought: Truth and the Return of Philosophy*, London: Continuum.

Barber, Benjamin (1995), *Jihad vs McWorld*, New York: Random House.

Barr, James (1962), *Biblical Words for Time*, London: SCM Press.

Barr, James (1977), *Fundamentalism*, London: SCM Press.

Barr, James (1984), *Escaping from Fundamentalism*, London: SCM Press.

Bartov, Omer (2000), *Mirrors of Destruction: War, Genocide and Modern Identity*, Oxford: Oxford University Press.

Bass, Gary Jonathan (2000), *Stay the Hand of Vengeance*, Princeton: Princeton University Press.

Bataille, Georges (1985), *Literature and Evil*, London, Marion Boyars.

Battersby, Christine (1998), *The Phenomenal Woman: Feminist Metaphysics and the Patterns of Identity*, Cambridge: Polity Press.

Baubock, Rainer (ed.) (1994), *From Aliens to Citizens: Redefining the Status of Citizens in Europe*, Aldershot: Avebury.

Baudrillard, Jean (1990), *Fatal Strategies*, London: Pluto.

Baudrillard, Jean (1993), *The Transparency of Evil: Essays on Extreme Phenomena*, London: Verso.

Baudrillard, Jean (2002), *The Spirit of Terrorism*, London: Verso.

Bauman, Zygmunt (1991), *Modernity and Ambivalence*, Cambridge: Polity Press.

Bauman, Zygmunt (1997), *Postmodernity And Its Discontents*, Cambridge: Polity Press.

Bauman, Zygmunt (2000a), *Modernity and the Holocaust*, Cambridge: Polity Press.
Bauman, Zygmunt (2000b), *Liquid Modernity,* Cambridge: Polity Press.
Bauman, Zygmunt (2003), *Liquid Love*, Cambridge: Polity Press.
Benhabib, Seyla (1997), *Situating the Self*, Cambridge: Polity Press.
Benjamin, Andrew (1997), *Present Hope*: *Philosophy, Architecture, Judaism,* London: Routledge.
Benjamin, Jessica (1990), *Bonds of Love*, London, Virago.
Benjamin, Jessica (1998), *Shadow of the Other*: *Intersubjectivity and Gender in Psychoanalysis,* New York: Routledge.
Benjamin, Walter (1973), *Illuminations: Essays and Reflections* (trans. H. Zohn), London: Collins/Fontana.
Berger, Peter (1969), *The Sacred Canopy Garden City,* New York: Doubleday.
Bergman, Shmuel Hugo (1961), *Faith and Reason: An Introduction to Modern Jewish Thought* (trans. A. Jospé), New York: Schocken.
Berkowitz, Eliezer (1973), *Faith After Auschwitz,* New York: Ktav.
Berlin, Isaiah (1969), *Four Essays On Liberty*, Oxford: Oxford University Press.
Berlin, Isaiah (1981), *Against The Current*, Oxford: Oxford University Press.
Berman, Marshall (1983), *All That Is Solid Melts Into Air: The Experience of Modernity*, London: Verso.
Bettleheim, Bruno (1991), *Freud and Man's Soul*, London: Fontana Books.
Beyer, Peter (1994), *Religion and Globalisation*, London: Sage.
Bhatt, Chetan (1996), *Liberation and Purity: Race, New Religious Movements and the Ethics of Postmodernity*, London: Routledge.
Blanchot, Maurice (1995), *The Writing Of The Disaster* (trans. A. Smock), Lincoln, Nebraska: Bison Books.
Blum, Lawrence and Seidler, Victor (1991), *A Truer Liberty: Simone Weil and Marxism*, New York: Routledge.
Blum, Lawrence (2004), *I'm Not a Racist But...* Ithaca: Cornell University Press.
Bly, Robert (1990), *Iron John,* New York: Addison-Wesley.
Bock, Gisela and James, Susan (eds.), *Beyond Equality and Difference: Citizenship, Feminist Politics and Female Subjectivity*, London: Routledge.
Bordo, Susan (1993), *Unbearable Weight: Feminism, Western Culture, and the Body,* Berkeley, California: University of California Press.
Borowitz, Eugene (1968), *A New Jewish Theology in the Making*, Philadelphia: Westminster Press.
Borradori, Giovanna (2003), *Philosophy in a Time of Terror: Dialogues with Jurgen Habermas and Jacques Derrida*, Chicago: University of Chicago Press.
Bossy, John (1985), *Christianity and the West, 1400-1700,* Oxford: Oxford University Press.
Bourdieu, Pierre (2001), *Masculine Domination*, Cambridge: Polity Press.
Boyarin, Daniel (1993), *Carnal Israel: Reading Sex in Talmudic Judaism,* Berkeley: University of California Press.

Boyarin, Daniel (1994), *A Radical Jew: Paul and the Politics of Identity*, Berkeley: University of California Press.

Boyarin, Daniel (1997), *Unheroic Conduct: The Rise Of Heterosexuality and The Invention of The Jewish Man*, Berkeley: University of California Press.

Braidotti, Rossi (1991), *Patterns of Dissonance,* Cambridge: Polity Press.

Brittan, Arthur (1989), *Masculinity and Power*, Oxford: Basil Blackwell.

Brown, Peter (1982), *Society and the Holy*, London: Faber & Faber.

Brown, Peter (1990), *The Body and Society: Men, Women and Sexual Renunciation in Early Christianity,* London: Faber & Faber.

Browning, Christopher (1992), *Ordinary Men,* New York: Harper Collins.

Bruce, Steve (2000), *Fundamentalism,* Cambridge: Polity Press.

Buber, Martin (1955), *Between Man and Man*, Boston: Beacon Press.

Buber, Martin (1957), *Tales of the Hasidim*, New York: Schocken.

Buber, Martin (1960), *The Prophetic Faith*, New York: Harper and Row.

Buber, Martin (1963), *Israel and the World*, New York: Schocken.

Buber, Martin (1967), *On Judaism* (ed. Nahum Glatzer), New York: Schocken.

Buber, Martin (1970), *I and Thou* (trans. Walter Kaufman), New York: Scribner.

Buber, Martin (1973), *On Zion: The History of an Idea*, New York: Schocken.

Buber, Martin (1982), *On The Bible*, New York: Schocken.

Buck-Morss, Susan (2000), *Dreamworld and Catastrophe: The Passing of Mass Utopia in East and West Cambridge,* Mass.: MIT Press.

Buhle, Man Joe (1998), *Feminism and its Discontents*, Cambridge, Mass.: Harvard University Press.

Butler, Judith (1990), *Gender Trouble: Feminism and the Subversion of Identity*, New York: Routledge.

Canetti, Elias (1962), *Crowds and Power*, New York: Viking.

Caplan, Lionel (ed.) (1987), *Studies In Religious Fundamentalism*, London: Macmillan.

Cardini, Franco (2001), *Europe and Islam*, Oxford: Blackwell.

Casanova, José (1994), *Public Religions in the Modern World*, Chicago: University of Chicago Press.

Cavell, Stanley (1969), *Must We Mean What We Say?* New York: Charles Scribner's Sons.

Cavell, Stanley (1979), *The Claim of Reason*, Oxford: Oxford University Press.

Cavell, Stanley (2005), *City of Words,* Cambridge, Mass.: Harvard University Press.

Chodorow, Nancy (1994), *Feminities, Masculinities, Sexualities: Freud and Beyond*, London: Free Associations Books.

Clark, R.T. (1969), *Herder: His Life and Thought*, Berkeley: University of California Press.

Cohen, Josh (2003), *Interrupting Auschwitz: Art, Religion, Philosophy*, London: Continuum.

Collins, Patricia Hill (1991), *Black Feminist Thought: Knowledge, Consciousness and the Politics of Empowerment*, New York: Routledge.

Connell, R. W. (1987), *Gender and Power: Society, the Person and Sexual Politics*, Cambridge, Polity Press.

Connell, R. W. (1995), *Masculinities*, Cambridge: Polity Press.

Connolly, William (1991), *Identity/Difference: Democratic Negotiations of Political Paradox*, Ithaca: Cornell University Press.

Cornwall, Andrea and Lindisfarne, Nancy (1994) (eds.), *Dislocating Masculinity: Comparative Ethnographies*, London: Routledge.

Craib, Ian (1989), *Psychoanalysis and Social Theory: The Limits of Sociology*, London: Harvester Wheatsheaf.

Craib, Ian (1994), *The Importance Of Disappointment*, London: Routledge.

Dallmayr, Fred (1998), *Alternative Visions: Paths in the Global Village Lanham*, Maryland: Rowman and Littlefield.

Danby, Herbert (ed.) (1933), *The Mishnah*, London: Oxford University Press.

Danielou, Jean (1956), *The Bible and the Liturgy*, Indianapolis, Indiana: Notre Dame.

D'Costa, G. (1986), *Theology and Religious Pluralism: The Challenge of Other Religions*, Oxford: Blackwell.

Dekmajian, R. Hrair (1985), *Islam in Revolution*, Syracuse: Syracuse University Press.

Deleuze, Gilles (1990), *Expressionism in Philosophy: Spinoza* (trans. M. Joughin), New York: Zone.

Deleuze, Gilles (1993), *Nietzsche and Philosophy* (trans. H. Tomlinson), Minneapolis: University of Minnesota Press.

Deleuze, Gilles (1994), *Difference and Repetition*, London: Athlone.

Deleuze, Gilles and Guattari, Felix (1997), *Anti-Oedipus: Capitalism and Schizophrenia*, Minneapolis: University of Minnesota Press.

Derrida, Jacques (1978), *Writing and Difference*, Chicago: University of Chicago Press.

Derrida, Jacques (1998), *Monolingualism of the Other*, Stanford: Stanford University Press.

Derrida, Jacques (1999), *Adieu: To Emmanuel Levinas*, Stanford: Stanford University Press.

Derrida, Jacques (2002), *Acts of Religion*, New York: Routledge.

De Vries, Hent and Weber, Samuel (eds.) (1997), *Violence, Identity And Self-Determination*, Stanford: Stanford University Press.

Dodds, Eric Robertson (1951), *The Greeks and the Irrational*, Berkeley CA and Los Angeles.

Dollimore, Jonathan (1998), *Death, Desire and Loss in Western Culture*, London: Penguin.

Dorfman, Ariel (1984), *Widows*, New York: Aventura.

Dreyfus, Hubert and Rabinow, Paul (1983), *Michel Foucault: Beyond Structuralism and Hermeneutics*, Chicago, University of Chicago Press.

Elias, Norbert (1982), *The Civilizing Process: State Formation and Civilisation* (trans. E. Jephcott), Oxford: Oxford University Press.

Elshtain, Jean Bethke (1981), *Public Man, Private Woman*, Princeton: Princeton University Press.

Epstein, Isidore (ed.) (1935–48), *The Babylonian Talmud*, London: The Soncino Press.

Fackenheim, Emil Ludwig (1970), *God's Presence In History*, New York: Harper Torchbooks.

Fackenheim, Emil Ludwig (1973), *Encounters Between Judaism And Modern Philosophy*, Philadelphia: Jewish Publication Society.

Fackenheim, Emil Ludwig (1978), *The Jewish Return Into History*, New York: Schocken.

Fackenheim, Emil Ludwig (1994), *To Mend the World: Foundations of Post-Holocaust Jewish Thought*, Indianapolis: Indiana University Press.

Featherstone, Mike, Hepworth, Mike and Turner, Bryan Stanley (1990) (eds.), *The Body: Social Process and Cultural Theory*, London: Sage.

Feitlowitz, Margarite (1998), *A Lexicon of Terror: Argentina and the Legacies of Torture*, New York: Oxford University Press.

Finkelstein, Louis (1946), *The Pharisees: The Sociological Background of their Faith*, Philadelphia: Jewish Publication Society of America.

Fishbane, Michel (1985), *Biblical Interpretation in Ancient Israel*, Oxford: Clarendon.

Flax, Jane (1990), *Thinking Fragments: Psychoanalysis, Feminism and Postmodern in the Contemporary West*, Berkeley: University of California Press.

Flax, Jane (1993), *Disputed Subjects: Essays on Pscyhoanalysis, Politics and Philosophy*, New York and London: Routledge.

Flowers, Ronald Bruce (1984), *Religion in Strange Times*, Mercer University Press.

Foucault, Michel (1975), *Discipline and Punish: The Birth of the Prison*, Harmondsworth: Penguin.

Foucault, Michel (1976), *The History of Sexuality, vol. 1*, London: Penguin.

Foucault, Michel (1980), *Power/Knowledge: Selected Interviews and Other Writings, 1972–1977*, New York: Pantheon.

Frankl, Victor (1984), *Man's Search for Meaning*, New York: Simon and Schuster.

Freud, Sigmund (1930), *Civilisation and its Discontents*, New York: Dover.

Freud, Sigmund (1977), *On Sexuality, Vol. 7*, London: Penguin.

Friedlander, Saul (ed.) (1992), *Probing The Limits Of Representation: Nazism and the 'Final Solution'*, Cambridge, Mass.: Harvard University Press.

Friedlander, Saul (1997), *Nazi Germany and the Jews: The Years of Persecution, 1933–39*, London: Weidenfeld and Nicolson.

Friedman, Maurice (1981–4), *Martin Buber's Life and Work (3 Vol.)*, New York: E.P. Dutton.

Frosh, Stephen (1994), *Sexual Difference: Masculinity and Psychoanalysis*, London and New York: Routledge.

Fullinwider, Robert K. (ed.) (1996), *Public Education in a Multicultural Society: Policy, Theory, Critique*, Cambridge: Cambridge University Press.

Fussell, Paul (1977), *The Great War And Modern Memory*, Oxford: Oxford University Press.

Gager, John G. (1983), *The Origins of Anti-Semitism*, New York: Oxford University Press.

Gallager, Catherine and Laqueur, Thomas (eds.) (1987), *The Making of the Modern Body: Sexuality and Society in the Nineteenth Century*, Berkeley: University of California Press.

Gay, Peter (1978), *Freud, Jews and Other Germans: Masters and Victims in Modernist Culture*, New York: Oxford University Press.

Gay, Peter (1988), *Freud: A Life of our Time*, London: Macmillan.

Geertz, Clifford (1973), *The Interpretation of Culture*, New York: Basic Books.

Giddens, Anthony (1991), *Modernity And Self-Identity: Self and Society in the Late Modern Age*, Cambridge: Polity Press.

Giddens, Anthony (1993), *The Transformation of Intimacy: Sexuality, Love and Eroticism in Modern Societies*, Cambridge: Polity Press.

Gilligan, Carol (1982), *In a Different Voice: Psychological Theory and Women's Development*, Cambridge. Mass.: Harvard University Press.

Gilroy, Paul (1987), *There ain't no Black in the Union Jack*, London: Unwin Hyman.

Gilroy, Paul (1993), *The Black Atlantic: Modernity and Double Consciousness*, Cambridge, Mass.: Harvard University Press.

Gilroy, Paul (1995), *After Empire*, London: Routledge.

Gilroy, Paul (2004), *Between Camps*, London: Allen Lane.

Glatzer, Nahum Norbert (1968), *Martin Buber on the Bible*, New York: Schocken Books.

Glatzer, Nahum Norbert (1997), *We Are All Multiculturalists Now*, Cambridge, Mass.: Harvard University Press.

Goldberg, David Theo (1993), *Racist Culture: Philosophy and the Politics of Meaning*, Oxford: Basil Blackwell.

Goldstein, Bluma (1992), *Reinscribing Moses: Heine, Kafka, Freud and Schoenberg in a European Wilderness*, Cambridge, Mass.: Harvard University Press.

Goldstone, Richard (2000), *For Humanity*, New Haven: Yale University Press.

Gordon, Sarah (1984), *Hitler, Germans The Jewish Question*, Princeton: Princeton University Press.

Gramsci, Antonio (1971), *Selections from the Prison Notebooks*, London: Lawrence and Wishart.

Gray, John (1995), *Enlightenment's Wake: Politics and Culture at the Close of the Modern Age*, London: Routledge.

Greenberg, Moshe (1983), *Biblical Prose Prayer*, Berkeley: University of California Press.

Griffin, Susan (1980), *Pornography and Silence*, London: The Womens' Press.

Griffin, Susan (1982), *Women and Nature*, London: The Women's Press.

Grillo, Ralph David (1998), *Pluralism and the Politics of Difference: State, Culture and Ethnicity in Comparative Perspective*, Oxford: Clarendon Press.

Grossman, Vasily (1980), *Life And Fate*, New York: Harper and Row.

Grosz, Elizabeth (1994), *Volatile Bodies: Towards a Corporeal Feminism*, Bloomington: Indiana University Press.

Guttmann, Julius (1964), *Philosophies of Judaism* (trans. David W. Silverman), New York: Holt, Rinehart and Winston.

Hampshire, Stuart (1983), *Morality and Conflict*, Oxford: Basil Blackwell.

Handelman, Susan (1991), *Fragments of Redemption: Jewish Thought and Literary Theory in Benjamin, Sholem and Levinas*, Bloomington, Indiana: Indiana University Press.

Hartman, Geoffrey and Budick, Sanford (eds.) (1986), *Midrash And Literature*, New Haven: Yale University Press.

Heckman, Susan (1990), *Gender and Knowledge: Elements of a Postmodern Feminism*. New England: Northeastern University Press.

Held, Virginia (1993), *Feminist Morality: Transforming Culture, Society and Politics*, Chicago: University of Chicago Press.

Heelas, Paul (ed.) (1998), *Religion, Modernity and Postmodernity*, Oxford: Blackwell.

Heschel, Abraham Joshua (1951), *Man is Not Alone*, New York: Farrar, Straus & Young.

Heschel, Abraham Joshua (1959), *God in Search of Man*, Philadelphia: Jewish Publication Society.

Heschel, Abraham Joshua (1973), *A Passion For Truth*, New York: Farrar, Straus & Giroux.

Hirsh, David (2003), *Law Against Genocide: Cosmopolitan Trials*, London: GlassHouse Press, Cavendish Publishing.

Honig, Bonnie (1993), *Political Theory and the Displacement of Politics*, Ithaca: Cornell University Press.

hooks, bell (1991), *Yearning: Race, Gender and Cultural Politics*, London: Turnabout.

Horwitz, Rivka (1978), *Buber's Way to I and Thou*, Heidelberg: Lambert Schneider.

Huntington, Samuel (1997), *The Clash of Civilisations and the Remaking of the World Order*, London: Simon and Schuster.

Ignatieff, Michael (1993), *Blood and Belonging: Journey into the New Nationalism*, New York: Farrar, Strauss & Giroux.

Ignatieff, Michael (1997), *The Warrior's Honor*, New York: Henry Holt.

Irigaray, Luce (1985), *Speculum of the Other Woman*, Ithaca, New York: Cornell University Press.

Jabes, Edmond (1991), *The Book of Questions* (trans. R. Waldrop), Hanover, NH: Weslyan University Press.

Jabes, Edmond (1993), *The Book Of Margins*, Chicago, Ill.: University of Chicago Press.

Jameson, Fredric (1972), *The Prison-House of Language: A Critical Account of Structuralism and Russian Formalism*, Princeton: Princeton University Press.

Jones, John (1962), *On Aristotle and Greek Tragedy*, Oxford: Oxford University Press.

Josipovici, Gabriel (1971), *The World and the Book*, London: Macmillan.

Josipovici, Gabriel (1988), *The Book of God: A Response to the Bible*, New Haven and London: Yale University Press.

Kedourie, Elie (1980), *Islam In The Modern World*, London: Mansell.

Kekes, John (1993), *The Morality Of Pluralism*, Princeton: Princeton University Press.

Kermode, Frank and Alter, Robert (ed.) (1987), *The Literary Guide to the Bible*, Cambridge, Mass.: Harvard University Press.

Kugel, James (1981), *The Idea of Biblical Poetry: Parallelism and Its History*, New Haven and London: Yale University Press.

Kymlicka, Will (1989), *Liberalism, Community and Culture*, Oxford: Clarendon Press.

Lang, Berel, *Act And Idea in the Nazi Genocide*, Chicago: University of Chicago Press.

Laqueur, Thomas (1990), *Making Sex: Body and Gender from the Greeks to Freud*, Cambridge, Mass.: Harvard University Press.

Latour, Bruno (1993), *We Have Never Been Modern*, Cambridge, Mass.: Harvard University Press.

Latour, Bruno and Weibel, Peter (eds.) (2002), *Iconoclash: Beyond the image wars in Science, Religion and Art*, Cambridge, Mass: Massachusetts Institute of Technology Press.

Lennon, Kathleen and Whitford, Margaret (1994), *Knowing the Difference: Feminist Perspectives on Epistemology*, London: Routledge.

Levi, Primo (1989), *The Drowned and the Saved*, New York: Vintage International.

Levinas, Emmanuel (1967), *Totality and Infinity* (trans. A. Lingis), Pittsburgh, Pennsylvania: Duquesne University Press.

Levinas, Emmanuel (1990), *Nine Talmudic Readings* (trans. A. Aronowicz), Bloomington, Indiana: Indiana University Press.

Levinas, Emmanuel (1994), *Beyond the Verse: Talmudic Readings and Lectures* (trans. G.B. Mole), London: Athlone Press.

Levinas, Emmanuel (1997), *Difficult Freedom: Essays on Judaism* (trans. S. Hand), Baltimore, Maryland: Johns Hopkins University Press.

Levinas, Emmanuel (1998a), *Of God who Comes to Mind* (trans. B. Bergo), Stanford, California: Stanford University Press.

Levinas, Emmanuel (1998b), *Entre-Nous: On Thinking of the Other* (trans. M.B. Smith), London: Athlone.

Lewis, Bernard (1993), *Islam and the West*, Oxford: Oxford University Press.

Lieberman, Saul (1950), *Hellenism and Jewish Palestine*, New York: Jewish Theological Seminary of America.

Lindqvist, Sven (1992), *Exterminate all the Brute*, New York: The New Press.

Lloyd, Genevieve (1984), *Man of Reason: 'Male' and 'Female' in Western Philosophy*, London: Methuen.

Littell, Franklin (1975), *The Crucifixion Of The Jews*, New York: Harper and Row.

Lyotard, Jean-Francois (1994), *The Postmodern Condition: A Report on Knowledge*, Manchester: Manchester University Press.

Maccoby, Hyam (1986), *The Mythmaker: Paul and the Invention of Christianity*, New York: Barnes & Noble.

MacIntyre, Alasdair (1985), *After Virtue: A Study in Moral Theory*, London: Duckworth.

Magonet, Jonathan (1976), *Form and Meaning: Studies in the Literary Technique of the Book of Jonah*, Michigan: Almond Press.

Mastnak, Tomasz (2002), *Crusading Peace: Christendom, the Muslim World and Western Political Order*, Berkeley: University of California Press.

Mattar, Philip (1998), *Islam in Britain, 1558–1685*, Cambridge: Cambridge University Press.

Mayer, Hans (1982), *Outsiders: A Study in Life and Letters*, Cambridge, Mass.: MIT Press.

Melber, Jehuda (1968), *Herman Cohen's Philosophy of Judaism*, New York: J. David.

Mendus, Susan (1989), *Toleration and the Limits of Liberalism*, Atlantic Highlands: Humanities Press.

Merchant, Carolyn (1982), *The Death of Nature: Women, Ecology and the Scientific Revolution*, London: Wildwood House.

Miller, David (1995), *On Nationality*, Oxford: Oxford University Press.

Minow, Martha (1998), *Between Vengeance and Forgiveness: Facing History After Genocide and Mass Violence*, Boston: Beacon Press.

Modood, Tariq and Werbner, Pnina (eds.) (1997), *The Politics of Multiculturalism In The New Europe: Racism, Identity and Community*, London: Zed Books.

Moghissi, Haideh (1999), *Feminism and Islamic Fundamentalism*, London: Zed Press.

Morgan, Michael (ed.) (1987), *The Jewish Thought of Emil Fackenheim*, Detroit: Wayne State University Press.

Moore, Robert Ian (1990), *The Formation of a Persecuting Society: Power and Deviance in Western Europe, 950–1250*, Oxford: Blackwell.

Nancy, Jean-Luc (1993), *The Experience of Freedom*, Stanford: Stanford University Press.

Nettler, Ronald (1987), *Past Trials and Present Tribulations*, Oxford: Pergamon Press.

Neusner, Jacob (1984), *Judaism In The Beginnings Of Christianity*, London: Augsburg Fortress Publishers.

Nicholson, Linda (ed.) (1990), *Feminism/Postmodernism*, New York: Routledge.

Nicholson, Linda and Seidman, Steven (eds.) (1996), *Social Postmodernism: Beyond Identity Politics*, Cambridge: Cambridge University Press.

Nietzsche, Friedrich (1967), *On the Genealogy of Morals*, New York: Vintage Press.

Nietzsche, Friedrich (1974), *The Gay Science*, New York: Vintage Press.

Nirenberg, David (1996), *Communities of Violence: Persecution of Minorities in the Middle Ages*, Princeton: Princeton University Press.

Parekh, Bhikhu (2000), *Rethinking Multiculturalism: Cultural Diversity and Political Theory*, Basingstoke: Palgrave.

Pateman, Carole (1988), *The Sexual Contract*, Stanford, California: Stanford University Press.

Phillips, Anne (1993), *Democracy and Difference*, University Park: Pennsylvania State University Press.

Philo (1954–5), *The Works of Philo Judaeus* (4 vols.) (trans. C.D. Young), Loeb Classical Library London.

Pieterse, Jan P. Nederveen and Parekh, Bhikhu (eds.) (1995), *The Decolonisation of Imagination: Culture, Knowledge and Power*, London: Zed Press.

Rahman, Fazlur (1982), *Islam and Modernity*, Chicago: University of Chicago Press.

Rajchman, John (ed.) (1995), *The Identity In Question*, London: Routledge.

Rawls, John (1971), *A Theory of Justice*, Cambridge, Mass.: Harvard University Press.

Rawls, John (1993), *Political Liberalism*, New York: Columbia University Press.

Rayner, John Desmond (1998), *A Jewish Understanding of the World*, Providence, RI and Oxford: Berghahn Books.

Raz, Joseph (1986), *The Morality of Freedom*, Oxford: Oxford University Press.

Raz, Joseph (1994), *Ethics in the Public Domain: Essays in the Morality of Law and Politics*, Oxford: Clarendon Press.

Ricoeur, Paul (1980), *Essays on Biblical Interpretation*, Philadelphia: Mudge.

Ricoeur, Paul (1994), *Oneself as Another*, Chicago: Chicago University Press.

Robert, Marthe (1967), *The Old and the New* (trans. C. Cosman), Berkeley: University of California Press.

Rosenstock-Huessy, Eugen (1969), *Judaism Despite Christianity*, Alabama: University of Alabama Press.

Rosenzweig, Franz (1970), *The Star of Redemption* (trans. W. Hallo), New York: Holt, Rinehart and Winston.

Rosenzweig, Franz (1972), *Franz Rosenzweig: His Life and Thought* (ed. Nahum N. Glatzer), New York: Schocken.

Rotenstreich, Nathan (1972), *Tradition and Reality: The Impact of History on Jewish Thought*, New York: Random House.

Rotenstreich, Nathan (1984), *Jews And German Philosophy*, New York: Schocken.

Rowbotham, Sheila (1972), *Woman's Consciousness, Man's World*, Harmondsworth: Penguin.

Rowbotham, Sheila (1973), *Hidden from History*, London: Pluto Press.

Rubinstein, Richard (1992), *After Auschwitz: History, Theology and Contemporary Judaism*, Baltimore, Maryland: Johns Hopkins University Press.

Ruthven, Malise (1984), *Islam in the World*, Harmondsworth: Penguin.

Ruthven, Malise (2000), *Islam: A Very Short Introduction*, Oxford: Oxford University Press.

Sacks, Jonathan (1991), *The Persistence of Faith: Religion, Morality and Society in a Secular Age*, London: Weidenfeld and Nicholson.

Sacks, Jonathan (2002), *The Dignity of Difference: How to Avoid the Clash of Civilisations*, London: Continuum.

Said, Edward (1979), *Orientalism*, New York: Vintage.

Salvatore, Anthony (1999), *Islam and Political Discourse of Modernity*, Reading: Ithaca Press.

Sandeen, Ernest Robert (1970), *The Roots of Fundamentalism*, Chicago: University of Chicago Press.

Sandel, Michael (1982), *Liberalism and the Limits of Justice*, Cambridge: Cambridge University Press.

Sanders, Ed Parish (1977), *Paul and Palestinian Judaism: A Comparison of Patterns of Religion*, London: S.C.M.

Sands, Phillipe (2003), *From Nuremberg to the Hague*, Cambridge: Cambridge University Press.

Sayyid, Bobby S. (1997), *A Fundamental Fear: Eurocentrism and the Emergence of Islam*, London: Zed Books.

Schaeder, Grete (1984), *The Hebrew Humanism of Martin Buber* (trans. Noah J. Jacobs), Detroit: Wayne State University Press.

Schmitt, Carl (1984), *Roman Catholicism And Political Form*, Westport, Conn.: Greenwood Press.

Schneidau, Herbert (1977), *Sacred Discontent: The Bible and Western Tradition*, Berkeley: University of California Press.

Scholem, Gershom (1961), *Major Trends in Jewish Mysticism*, New York: Schocken.

Scholem, Gershom (1965), *The Kabbalah and its Symbolism*, New York: Schocken.

Scholem, Gershom (1971), *The Messianic Idea in Judaism*, New York: Schocken.

Scholem, Gershom (1976), *On Jews and Judaism in Crisis*, New York: Schocken.

Seidler, Victor J.J. (1986), *Kant, Respect and Injustice: The Limits of Liberal Moral Theory*, London: Routledge.

Seidler, Victor J.J. (1989), *Rediscovering Masculinity: Reason, Language and Sexuality*, London and New York: Routledge.

Seidler, Victor J.J. (1991a), *Recreating Sexual Politics: Men, Feminism and Politics*, London and New York: Routledge.

Seidler, Victor J.J. (1991b), *The Moral Limits of Modernity: Love, Inequality and Oppression*, Basingstoke: Macmillan.

Seidler, Victor J.J. (1993), *Unreasonable Men: Masculinity and Social Theory*, London and New York: Routledge.

Seidler, Victor J.J. (1994), *Recovering the Self: Morality and Social Theory*, London and New York: Routledge.

Seidler, Victor J.J. (2000), *Man Enough: Embodying Masculinities*, London: Sage.

Seidler, Victor J.J. (2001), *Shadows Of The Shoah: Jewish Identity and Belonging*. Oxford; Berg.

Seidler, Victor J.J. (2005), *Transforming Masculinities: Men, Cultures, Bodies, Power, Sex and Love*, London and New York: Routledge.

Seidler, Victor J.J. (2006), *Young Men and Masculinities: Global Cultures and Intimate Lives*, London: Zed Press.

Seidman, Steven (1996), *Contested Knowledge: Social Theory in the Postmodern Era*, Cambridge, Mass.: Blackwell.

Sennett, Richard (2004), *Respect: The Formation of Character in an Age of Inequality*, London: Penguin Books.

Shilling, Chris (1983), *The Body and Social Theory*, London: Sage.

Sontag, Susan (2002), *On Photography*, London: Penguin.

Sontag, Susan (2003), *Regarding The Pain of Others*, London: Penguin.

Southern, Richard (1962), *Western Views of Islam in the Middle Ages*, Cambridge, Mass.: Harvard University Press.

Soylinka, Wole (2004), *Climate of Fear*, London: Profile Books.

Spivak, Gayatri Chakravorty (1999), *A Critique of Postcolonial Reason: Towards a History of the Vanishing Present*, Cambridge, Mass.: Harvard University Press.

Squires, Judith (1999), *Gender in Political Theory*, Cambridge: Polity Press.

Steiner, George (1967), *Language and Silence*, London: Faber and Faber.

Sternberg, Meir (1985), *The Poetics of Biblical Narrative*, Bloomington, Ind.: Indiana University Press.

Taylor, Charles (1989), *Sources of The Self*, Cambridge: Cambridge University Press.

Thomas, Mordekhai (1993), *Vessels of Evil: American Slavery and the Holocaust*, Philadelphia: Temple University Press.

Todorov, Tzvetan (1977), *The Poetics of Prose* (trans. Richard Howard), Ithaca, NY: Cornell University Press.

Todorov, Tzvetan (1993), *On Human Diversity: Nationalism, Racism and Exoticism in French Thought*, Cambridge, Mass.: Harvard University Press.

Turner, Bryan (1984), *The Body and Society: Explorations in Social Theory*, Oxford: Basil Blackwell.

Turner, Bryan (1994), *Orientalism, Postmodernism and Globalism*, London: Routledge.

Viorst, Milton (1994), *Sandcastles: The Arabs in Search of the Modern World*, New York: Knopf.

Virilo, Paul (2002), *Ground Zero*, London: Verso.

Vries, Hent de (1999), *Philosophy and the Turn to Religion*, Baltimore: Johns Hopkins Press.

Vries, Hent de (2002), *Religion and Violence: Philosophical Perspectives from Kant to Derrida*, Baltimore: Johns Hopkins Press.

Walzer, Michael (1983), *Spheres of Justice: A Defence of Pluralism and Equality*, New York: Basic Books.

Walzer, Michael (1994), *Thick and Thin: Moral Arguments at Home and Abroad*, Cambridge, Mass.: Harvard University Press.

Wasserstrom, Steven (1995), *Between Muslim and Jew: The Problem of Symbiosis under Early Islam*, Princeton: Princeton University Press.

Weber, Max (1970), *The Protestant Ethic and the Spirit of Capitalism*, London: Allen and Unwin.

Weeks, Jeffery (1995), *Inventing Moralities: Sexual Values in an Age of Uncertainty*, Cambridge: Polity Press.

Werblowsky, Raphael Jehudah Zwi (1976), *Beyond Tradition and Modernity: Changing Religions in a Changing World*, London: Athlone Press.

West, Cornel (1993), *Race Matters*, Boston: Beacon Press.

Williams, Bernard (1985), *Ethics and the Limits of Philosophy*, London: Fontana.

Williamson, Ronald (1970), *Philo and the Epistle to the Hebrews*, Leiden: Brill.

Winch, Peter (1989), *A Just Balance: Reflections on the Philosophy of Simone Weil*, Cambridge: Cambridge University Press.

Winnicott, Donald Woods (1974), *Playing and Reality*, Harmondsworth: Penguin.

Wittgenstein, Ludwig (1958), *Philosophical Investigations*, Oxford: Blackwell.

Wittgenstein, Ludwig (1980), *Culture and Value* (trans. Peter Winch), Oxford: Blackwell.

Woodward, Kath (ed.) (1997), *Identity and Difference*, London: Sage.

Yerushalmi, Yosef Hayim (1982), *Zakhor: Jewish History and Jewish Memory*, Seattle: University of Washington Press.

Young, Iris Marion (1990a), *Justice and the Politics of Difference*, Princeton: Princeton University Press.

Young, Iris Marion (1990b), *Throwing Like A Girl And Other Essays In Feminist Philosophy And Social Theory*, Bloomington: Indiana University Press.

Young, Robert (1990), *White Mythologies*, London: Routledge.

Žižek, Slavoj (1989), *The Sublime Object Of Ideology*, London: Verso.

Žižek, Slavoj (2000), *The Fragile Absolute, or Why Is the Christian Legacy Worth Fighting For?* London: Verso.

Glossary of Jewish Traditions and Biographies

Glossary of Jewish Traditions

An explanatory remark: For our knowledge of the early history of the Jewish liturgy, we are largely dependent on Rabbinic literature. This is the work of the Palestinian Rabbis who lived ca. 200 c.e. and are known as the *Tannaim*. The chief Tannaitic source is the *Mishnah*, a compendium of laws arranged in tractates. The most important tractates are *Berakhot*, on the daily liturgy, *Rosh Hashana*, on the New Year Festival, and *Yoma*, on the Day of Atonement. The Palestinian and Babylonian Rabbis who lived during the subsequent three centuries, known as *Amoraim*, are another important source. The chief Amoraic source is the *Talmud*, a vast work expanding upon the Mishnah and divided into the same tractates. There is a Palestinian version known as the *Jerusalem Talmud* and a Babylonian version, known as the *Babylonian Talmud*. There are also a large number of *Midrashim*, collections of interpretations of the Five Books of Moses, known as the *Torah*.

The centuries after the compilation of the Talmud, until ca. 1000 c.e. are known as the Gaonic Age and during this period and the ensuing Middle Ages, the Jewish liturgy was expanded and enriched with different communities making different contributions. The broadest distinction within the diversity of liturgical traditions is between the *Ashkenazi*, the German–Jewish tradition and the *Sephardi* or Spanish–Jewish tradition. The Middle Ages also marks the appearance of a large of number of codifications of Jewish Law, the most important being the *Mishneh Torah* by Moses ben Maimon, known as Maimonides.

Rabbinic Judaism: This draws directly upon its biblical antecedents to emphasise act over intention where righteousness is chiefly a matter of proper behaviour, not correct belief or appropriate intention. There is no fundamental conflict between Law (*Torah* or the letter) and Spirit (*Ruakh* or grace). In place of the elemental dichotomies of Pauline thought, rabbis saw the kind of unity hinted at in Philo's image of body and soul. The life of Torah could not be redeemed through grace, because the giving of the Torah had already been God's greatest grace.

Hasidism: Movement founded by the Ba'al Shem Tov, (Master of the Good Name, Israel ben Eliezer) (1700–1760) but which really flourished after his death, mainly in Poland, in the nineteenth century. It was a movement of spontaneity and joy that arose as a counterpoint to dry Talmudic scholarship and was bitterly opposed at the outset by Lithuanian Jews, through their leader the Vilna Gaon (Rabbi Elijah ben Solomon Zalman, 1720–1797).The inspiration for the Hasidic movement in Eastern Europe as being the Jewish spiritual 'response' to Spinoza. The movement developed at the same time that the Enlightenment was preparing the way for emancipation and eventual modernisation in the West. The philosopher Martin Buber (1878–1965) tried in his own way to revive Hasidic thought but in a more liberal vein.

Kabbalah: Traditions of Jewish mysticism emerging with the *Zohar* in which psychological and cosmological doctrines are closely interrelated, exploring in spatial idiom, the 'descent' of the soul through cosmic spheres as well as its ecstatic of meditative 'ascent'. The Safed Revival in the sixteenth century, including Moses Cordovero and Solomon Alkabez (best known as the author of the prayer *Lekhah Dodi*) talked of 'raising the *Shekhinah* – the 'feminine' spirit of God – from the dust', that is, contributing to the redemptive union of the *sefirot,* spiritual centres of embodied spiritual awareness.

Middle Ages: The term 'Middle Ages' was invented by Renaissance admirers of classical culture; that which was in between the original Graeco-Roman and the renewed (i.e. Renaissance) 'classical' culture, was 'middle'. This division of history into periods itself reflects assumptions of 'western culture'; the Jewish 'Middle Ages' lasted until the end of the second half of the eighteenth century and in some places even later.

Talmud (Teaching): Name applied to the Mishnah, legal codification of the oral law with its Gemara, later commentaries. An analytical method of *iyyun* which had been developed in the academies of Spain during the final generations before the expulsion in 1492. This method guided students in detailed discussions of the Talmud and it commentaries on the basis of clearly defined principles. This fostered a focus on the *halakhah*, the written laws, rituals and practices as opposed to the *aggadah,* the spoken interpretations. The kabbalists had held philosophy responsible for the weakening of Judaism in Spain with an erosion of observance and piety and the leniency regarding expedient conversions to Christianity of the *marranos* and 'new Christians' while the Rhineland communities during the First Crusade had preferred martyrdom to apostasy.

Biographies

Bachya Ibn Pakuda (c.1050–1120): Religious philosopher who recognises solitude and meditation in his book *Hovot ha-Levavot* (Duties of the Heart) a text influenced by Islamic Sufism. He speaks of trust in God and developing qualities of the heart.

Baeck, Leo (1873–1956): Rabbi and teacher of Midrash and Homiletics in Berlin at the Hochschule fur die Wissenschaft des Judentums and author of *Das Wesen des Judentums* (1905, 6th ed. 1932; Eng. trans., *The Essence of Judaism*, 1948). Head of the *Reichsvertretung,* the Representative Council of the Jews in Germany from 1933, deported to Theresienstadt in 1943. Settled in London in 1945 where he wrote *This People Israel: The Meaning of Jewish Existence* (1955).

Buber, Martin (1878–1965): Viennese philosopher and early Zionist whose liberal ideas nevertheless drew him, early in his career, to study Hasidism and retell some of the Hasidic stories in works such as *Die Geschichten des Rabbi Nachman* (1906) and *Die Legende des Baalschem* (1908). Buber considered that revelation, the dialogue between God and humanity, happens in a moment in time. The present offers the potential for revelation and is not seen as the end of an elapsed time. Buber recognised "what is essential is lived in the present" as the central motive of his work *Ich und Du* (I and Thou) (1923).

Cohen, Hermann (1842–1918): A rationalist and founder of the neo-Kantian Marburg School who turned towards Judaism. In his last book, *Religion Of Reason Out Of The Sources Of Judaism* (1918), he argues that revelation means God revealing ethical reason to humanity. Revelation is the sign of reason and, for Cohen, God always reveals himself to humanity. God gives the Torah as he gives everything else: life, bread and even death.

Fackenheim, Emil (1916–2003): Born in Halle, Germany, imprisoned briefly in Sachsenhausen concentration camp in 1939 but escaped and eventually settled in Toronto. Became increasingly concerned with philosophical and theological responses to the Holocaust and left the rabbinate to teach philosophy at the University of Toronto. His books include *The Religious Dimension in Hegel's Thought* (1968), *Quest for Past and Future: Essays in Jewish Theology* (1968) and *To Mend the World: Foundations of Future Jewish Thought* (1982).

Guttmann, Julius (1880–1950): A follower of Hermann Cohen and teacher at the *Hochschule fur die Wissenchaft des Judentums* in Berlin. Author of *Die Philosophie des Judentums* (Reinhardt, 1933). The English title is *Philosophies of Judaism: The History of Jewish Philosophy from Biblical Times to Franz Rosenzweig* (1964).

Heine, Heinrich (1797–1856): German poet and writer, born Jewish but baptised in 1825. After a serious illness in 1847 he increasingly returned to Jewish themes, particularly Moses and the Bible.

Heschel, Abraham Joshua (1907–1972): In the writings of Kirkegaard, Heschel, like Buber, discovered ideas that confirmed the basis views of life and faith learned from the teachings of Hasidism. He believed that a recovery of religious faith is essential if individuals are to rediscover the roots of authentic being. In contrast to Buber (q.v.), he argues in *Man Is Not Alone* (1951) and *God In Search Of Man* (1955) that traditional forms of rabbinic Judaism are essential to Jewish renewal.

Ibn Gabirol, Solomon (c.1021–1056): Spanish poet and philosopher. His *Keter Malchut* (Crown of Kingship) is read during the Days of Repentence, the period between New Year and the Day of Atonement.

Judah Halevi (c.1075–1141): Spanish Hebrew poet and philosopher, a physician by profession who left Spain in old age and fulfilled his dream of settling in the Holy Land during the period of the second Crusade. His *Kuzari* (The Khazars) is an exposition of Jewish life and thought in the form of a disputation before the kind of the Khazars.

Levinas, Emmanuel (1906–1996): Born in Kovno and educated in France at the University of Strasbourg where he turned to philosophy influenced by the phenomenology of Bergson and Husserl. He was a German prisoner of war and after the war rejoined his family in Paris. His books include *Totalité et infini: essai sur l'extériorité* (Totality and Infinity) (1961) and *Autrement qu'être ou au-delà de l'essence* (Otherwise than Being or Beyond Essence) (1974). Though he acknowledged 'all philosophy must pass through' Heidegger's *Sein und Zeit* (Being and Time) (1927), he was also critical of it. Though philosophy remained 'Greek' for him, he also wrote texts on Jewish themes including *Nine Talmudic Readings* (1994) and *Difficult Freedom: Essays on Judaism* (1963 and 1976).

Kook, Abraham I. (1865–1935): Religious and mystical thinker, an orthodox rabbi who was nevertheless in sympathy with secular Zionism and its claim that forced exile had created an imbalance between the material and the spiritual in an exaggerated spirituality. As Chief Rabbi, he helped to shape the 'earthly' tendency of the first generation of native Israelis while committed to traditional halakhah.

Maimonides, Moses (Moses ben Maimon, Rambam) (1135–1204): Philosopher and medical writer, born in Cordoba but eventually settled in Cairo where he became the spiritual head of the community. Wrote the *Mishneh Torah* (1170–1180), a code covering all halakhic subjects of the Talmud and the *Moreh Nevokhim* (Guide To The Perplexed) (1180?), an exposition of Judaism's teachings influenced by Aristotelian thought.

Mendelssohn, Moses (1729–1786): Born in Dessau and studies in Berlin who wrote *Jerusalem* (1783; English translations 1838 and 1852) to affirm that Judaism was a rational religion that could be defended through reason and became a central figure in the Berlin Enlightenment. Translated the Jewish Bible into German. Friend of Lessing who based his play *Nathan der Weise* (Nathan the Wise) (1779) on him.

Nachman of Bratzlav (1772–1811): A Chassidic Rabbi whose parables and stories exalt the spiritual qualities of the *tzaddik*, the righteous person.

Nahmanides (Moses ben Nahman, Ramban) (1194–1270): Spanish Rabbi who lived in Gerona, mystic philosopher and physician. Author of Biblical commentaries into which he introduced mystical interpretations. Defended Judaism in a famous disputation before the King of Aragon in Barcelona, 1263.

Philo of Alexandria (20 b.c.e–50 c.e.): Deeply committed to Plato's philosophy he developed a Jewish Hellenistic tradition that was concerned to effect reconciliation between Judaism and Hellenism thus allowing him to harmonize his ancestral faith with philosophy. The suitability of the *Logos* for Philo's exposition of God's creative aspect lies in the ease with which it could be assimilated to the 'word of God'.

Rosenzweig, Franz (1886–1929): German philosopher who during World War I wrote *Hegel and the State* (1920) and then broke with that inheritance. Born into an assimilated Jewish family he came close to converting to Christianity but then rediscovered Judaism and spent the rest of his life in Jewish education. Rosenzweig came to recognise the significance of human life as lived in the here and now. His *Star of Redemption* (translated1985) already contains the idea of revelation as present. 'Revelation is of the present, indeed it is being present in itself' was a central notion in his philosophy and life.

Scholem, Gershom (1897–1982): The great historian of Jewish mysticism who demonstrated its centrality to Judaism. Born and educated in Germany, he was originally close to the anarchism of Gustav Landauer and was a friend of Walter Benjamin. He emigrated to Palestine in 1923. Scholem recognised that "the demand to sanctify the profane...by the fulfilment of the Torah as the divine commandment, a demand anchored in the purely religious concept of holiness, is diametrically opposed to true secularisation..." Scholem sees a need for a decisive change in both the status and form of Jewish law, the *halakhah* (pathway).

Soloveitchik, Joseph Dov (1903–1998): Born in Poland but lived in the United States where he was a Talmudic scholar and philosopher who wrote *Halakhic Man* (1944, tr. 1983) and *The Lonely Man of Faith* (1965) that show a resonance between Judaism and existentialism in his emphasis on freedom, creativity, self-actualisation and this-worldliness. He talks of the Holocaust and so of 'The God who was hiding...suddenly appeared and began to knock at the entrance of the tent of the bedraggled and bereaved companion, twisting and turning on her bed in....the torment of hell'.

Index

59, 69, 81
120, 60

vs Kantian duty + reason
| 107-8, 158
vs emotion